REPRODUCING *the* FRENCH RACE

REPRODUCING *the* FRENCH RACE

*Immigration, Intimacy,
and Embodiment in the
Early Twentieth Century*

ELISA CAMISCIOLI

Duke University Press
Durham and London
2009

© 2009 Duke University Press

All rights reserved.

Designed by Heather Hensley

Typeset in Monotype Fournier by Tseng Information
Systems, Inc.

Library of Congress Cataloging-in-Publication Data appear
on the last printed page of this book.

For my parents, ELIZABETH AND THEODORE CAMISCIOLI

CONTENTS

ACKNOWLEDGMENTS

So many wonderful and generous people helped me to prepare this book. I owe a special debt of gratitude to Leora Auslander, who taught me to find my voice, express it with care and conviction, and remain fascinated by the work I do. Jennifer Heuer read every word of this book, and thanks to her it is much improved. Moreover, she and Brian Ogilvie provided me with expertly cooked dinners, warm conversation, and easy access to yoga classes in Northampton. Alexis Jahiel and Michael Buckley have been with me almost as long as I have been working on this project, and I cherish how much my experience of Chicago and Paris is intertwined with theirs. They taught me much of what I know about friendship, politics, and the value of living an examined life. Thanks also to my ladies of the archives — Carolyn Comiskey, Daniella Sarnoff, and Kristen Stromberg Childers — whose company was so precious to me during those halcyon years in Paris, and on whose shoulders I continue to lean. Paul Schor, French ambassador to American oddballs, was always available to help with translations, demystify Parisian life, and encourage me to refine my command of Gallic slang. For two decades Anne-Marie Chapron and her family have opened their doors with unbelievably gracious hospitality, and in many ways I came to love France through them. I am also indebted to Catherine Peyroux, whose intellectual engagement has never ceased to inspire me, and whose fire in the belly has sustained and entertained me while providing a much-needed sense of perspective. And of course, my life would have been so much less vibrant without Gary Wilder in it. I would have laughed a lot less, suffered more fools gladly, and only scratched the surface of my thinking about race.

A number of other colleagues, friends, teachers, institutions, and family members have supported me in various ways. I am grateful to Fabienne Bock, Antoinette Burton, Herrick Chapman, Laura Lee Downs, Rachel Fuchs, Laura Frader, Tom Holt, Leslie Page Moch, Gérard Noiriel, Karen Offen, Jean Pederson, the late Jack E. Reece, Bill Sewell, and Tyler Stovall for their kind assistance over the years. Moreover, I have been incredibly fortunate to work in the history department at Binghamton University, where I have been intellectually challenged while also having an enormous amount of fun. Thanks especially to Nancy Appelbaum, Bonnie Effros, and David Hacker, the ultimate friends-and-colleagues. I am also grateful to John Chaffee for encouraging my work outside of European history; to Tom Dublin and Kitty Sklar for making me feel profoundly at home from the moment I arrived in New York; and to Don and Jean Quataert for the endless laughter and passionate conversation their company inevitably brings. Outside of the history department I have been equally lucky. Benita Roth showed me the ropes with wry humor. Joe Keith intervened at a critical moment and offered guidance and insightful suggestions. Aruna D'Souza, Pamela Smart, and Nancy Um have intelligently commented on various portions of this book, and have been my partners in crime and the sweetest of friends through icy winters and verdant summers.

Namaste to the yoga kula in Chicago, upstate New York, and western Massachusetts; from them I learned things I could not find in any book, for I only had to look within. I am especially grateful to Karen Haberman, Ana Forrest, Seane Corn, and Desirée Rumbaugh, and to all of my students in this practice. Thanks also to my research assistants Jaime Wadowiec and Emory Davis, whose attention to detail and joyful company could even make indexing a blast. Students from my graduate seminars at Binghamton University have pushed me to think hard about gender, race, and sexuality. I am particularly indebted to Jaime Wadowiec, Denise Lynn, Melissa Madera, and Luis Sierra, whose energy and intellectual curiosity have made me a better teacher. And of course, I could not have completed this book without the funding graciously provided by the Bourse Chateaubriand, the Social Science Research Council, the National Endowment for the Humanities, the National Italian-American Foundation, and Binghamton University.

I cannot begin to express the debt of gratitude I owe my family. Thanks to my cousin Jon Nemeth and his wife Shari Matras, my experience of Chicago was exciting, inviting, and warm. Riccardo Losito and Giuseppina Minisini have welcomed me into the Italian branch of my family since my very first trip to Europe, and their home has been a haven during those extended bouts of research overseas. My brother Christopher has long been the person to whom I turn for advice and support, and his wisdom frequently astonishes me. My father Ted urged me to study the French language, spend a year of university in Paris, and immerse myself in a culture which has since become my second home. I would not have come to write this book without him. Finally, my mother Elizabeth's generosity of spirit and understated grace has always been an inspiration. She gave me the space to become the person I wished to become, and she unfailingly respected my choices. This book is therefore dedicated to my parents.

Earlier versions of some chapters have been published previously. Chapter 1 appeared as "Producing Citizens, Reproducing the 'French Race': Immigration, Demography, and Pronatalism in Early Twentieth-Century France" in *Gender and History* 13, no. 3 (fall 2001), 593–621. Chapter 5 appeared as "Intermarriage, Independent Nationality, and the Individual Rights of French Women: The Law of 10 August 1927" in *French Politics, Culture, and Society* 17, nos. 3–4 (summer–fall 1999), 52–74.

EMBODIMENT AND THE NATION

M ass international migrations dramatically recon-
figured the early-twentieth-century world. Much
of this story is familiar: nations supplemented their labor power by employing foreign workers, and in particular instances buttressed their populations
by incorporating foreigners who were deemed assimilable. The movement
of human populations across national borders promoted new hybridities,
drew increasingly stark distinctions between self and other, and aided in the
formulation of ever more nuanced racial hierarchies. Immigration therefore
generated an intense debate on the embodied nature of the national citizenry.

We tend to think of immigration as the founding narrative of new nations
like the United States, or as a "problem" located in multicultural Europe.
However, the case of early-twentieth-century France provides an alternative
example, as it was neither a new nation, nor did its discussion of immigration begin with decolonization. But France was squarely at the center of the
demographic transformations that characterized the early twentieth century.
After the American quota system was implemented in 1921 and revised in
1924, France was second only to the United States in receiving immigrants
across its borders. By the mid-1920s France had become the most important
destination for immigrants in the entire industrialized world.[1] In 1930 three
million foreigners resided in France, composing 7 percent of its total population.[2] The issue of immigration was particularly salient in France, where
concern for declining population rates had been a central feature of public
and political discourse at least since the 1870s. We will see that a wide range

of public preoccupations and political debates were refracted through the problem of immigration, and that immigration policies and politics were crucial and constitutive features of the French Third Republic (1870–1940).

This book examines how French anxieties about demographic decline, labor productivity, interracial sex, race-mixing (*métissage*), and women's nationality and citizenship were deliberated with reference to both European and colonial migrations to the metropole. The immigration of white and nonwhite foreigners — two unstable categories that I will reconstruct and complicate in the course of this book — generated a multifaceted racial discourse, as well as immigration policies which differentially targeted European and colonial migrants. By reading parliamentary debates, nationality laws, police and army records on prostitution, feminist newspapers, legal journals, propaganda from the social hygiene crusade, and published works in demography, anthropology, and medicine, I investigate how social critics, in this period of immense human mobility, imagined the parameters of a racialized and gendered national identity.

In these texts politicians, practitioners of "work science" (*science du travail*), reformers, racial theorists, jurists, and feminists insisted that the integration of foreign populations depended not only on their productivity as industrial or agricultural workers but also on their capacity to mix with the native population, and to insure the reproduction of generations to come. This is because the Republican national narrative underscored the imperatives of production and procreation, and was never uniquely concerned with individual rights, universal humanism, and assimilationism. I therefore recast the question of immigration and citizenship in France to highlight the salience of racial hierarchies and the reproductive practices which sustained them, as well as the predominance of a necessarily hybrid Republican form which facilitated the proliferation of racialized embodiments. By investigating the interrelated realms of pronatalism, prostitution, the marriage contract, racial mixing, and the rationalization of labor and the laboring body, I show how race and reproduction were critical to the construction of French national identity, and how gender intervened in fabricating racial hierarchies which cast white Europeans alone as assimilable.

I suggest that "the intimate" is an analytical category at the core of the study of immigration. In the anthropologist Ann Laura Stoler's account, the intimate encompasses affective ties, moral sentiments, sexual relations, and a nation's demographic calculus; it is a vital facet of the "management of life" described by Foucauldian biopolitics.[3] To explore the intimate requires us to confront the corporality of historical subjects, the degree to which their bodies mattered, and why. It also requires that we interrogate the meanings attributed to desire, whether ordinary or transgressive, and evaluate the perceived relationship between desire and the stability of family, nation, and race. Such an analysis necessarily highlights the mechanisms of the domestic sphere, which is the heart of "private," quotidian life and the site of so many intimate acts and expressions.[4] Yet as this book will show, the impact of intimacy transcends the ostensibly private world of the household and its members, engaging either directly or more furtively with a macropolitics of power. That is, public discourse on immigration depended on a number of private practices and behaviors. Just as immigration complicated notions of inside and out, of citizenship and subjecthood, national boundaries and imperial frontiers, so too did it problematize the divide between public and private, and between self and other, at the most rudimentary level.

In my analysis the intimate is a product of modernity and its disciplinary technologies, a seemingly private realm which has been subjected to the intruding gaze of social reformers, the police, practitioners of the human sciences, and other liaisons to the state.[5] As Nancy Cott succinctly argues, "No modern nation ignores the intimate domain, because the population is composed and reproduced there."[6] My study affirms this observation. In early-twentieth-century France a variety of political actors, social movements, and specialized forms of knowledge engaged the question of how immigration could either enhance or deter the social reproduction of the citizenry. As a result, they interrogated the private life and intimate practices of French citizens, colonial subjects, and European migrants.

By investigating the terrain of the intimate, I wish to highlight a series of critical juxtapositions: the relationship between household and polity, the resonance of familial and national metaphors, and the many parallels between the bonds of citizenship and other affective ties. The intimate is critical to the study of immigration because it was an essential site upon which ideas about assimilability and belonging were elaborated. For example, the "cultural competencies" of Frenchness were learned at least as frequently in the home as in the public world.[7] Likewise marriage, fertility, and conjugal sexuality were considered central to the rebuilding of an underpopulated

France, which was now dependent on successful mixings between foreigners and the native-born, as well as their capacity to produce assimilable children. French social critics were well aware of the importance of intimate matters to the so-called immigrant question, and therefore turned their attention to the racial composition and reproductive value of foreigners and French people alike. In turn, political, demographic, scientific, juridical, and feminist discourses invested the bodies of subjects and citizens with the power to either revivify or degrade the "French race."

Distinguishing citizens from subjects was a critical facet of both imperial and immigration discourses. Subjects included colonized people and non-naturalized European migrants, but these groups' intertwined trajectories ultimately diverged once refracted through the Republican racial taxonomy. While the citizenry was composed of both men and women, each sex was attributed with deeply gendered roles of national service and unequal access to citizenship rights. French women were subject to the legal restrictions of the Civil Code of 1804 and were denied voting rights and other modes of formal political participation until 1944.

As a consequence, immigration discourse reaffirmed a hierarchical social taxonomy in which race and gender differences were explicitly linked to a history of political economy and national identity. This book therefore contributes to the growing body of work on race and nation in the French context,[8] and it interrogates the curious interplay of universalism and particularism in French Republicanism, a theme to which I repeatedly return.[9] However, I wish to move beyond existing scholarship by insisting that as the stakes of immigration were increasingly expressed in terms of racial hygiene, intimate matters of marriage, sexuality, and reproduction became particularly vital to constructing French national identity. The canonical works of scholars such as Gérard Noiriel, Rogers Brubaker, and Yves Lequin, which have richly contributed to our understanding of immigration to France, have not systematically investigated the relationship to this historical and historiographic question of family, reproduction, and gender roles — or the ideologically productive oppositions of masculinity/femininity, maternity/paternity, and husband/wife.[10] And if themes of gender and reproduction were virtually absent from earlier histories of immigration to France,[11] a second wave of scholarship has only recently begun to explore the critical impact of these categories.[12]

By underscoring the salience of reproduction, I am able to bring into focus the role of French and foreign women in reconstituting the nation and its citizen body. This interpretive labor is critical because, in the words of the feminist theorist Anne McClintock, even though women function as "symbolic bearers of the nation," they are typically "denied any direct relation to national agency."[13] As a result, female citizenship is often linked to a woman's reproductive capital, while a woman's desire to control that capital — either by limiting births or by refusing to heed population restrictions — may be construed as treasonous acts of selfish disregard for the nation.[14] For example, in early-twentieth-century France motherhood and warfare functioned as differently gendered versions of the "blood tribute" (*impôt du sang*) to the state, as both were expressions of physical and moral suffering on behalf of the beleaguered nation.[15] To more thoroughly explore these gendered modes of national service, I have relied in particular upon three engagements suggested by the feminist scholars Nira Yuval Davis and Floya Anthias in their groundbreaking work on the gender of nationalism: women as biological reproducers of the members of national collectivities; women as reproducers of the boundaries of national groups (because of restrictions on sexual or marital relations); and women as active transmitters and producers of the national culture.[16]

Attention to the problem of reproduction — including its symbolic representation, its regulation, and the resistance of historical subjects to the disciplinary mechanisms which invest reproduction with ideological value — inevitably returns us to the problem of race, for reproduction is necessarily a racializing force.[17] The literary theorist Alys Eve Weinbaum makes explicit the connections between race and reproduction, as well as their role in generating and sustaining various strategies of exclusion, when she writes that "the interconnected ideologies of racism, nationalism, and imperialism rest on the notion that race can be reproduced, and on attendant beliefs in the reproducibility of racial formations (including nations) and of social systems hierarchically organized according to notions of inherent racial superiority, inferiority, and degeneration."[18] Throughout this book I follow Weinbaum's strategy of illuminating the vital relationship between race and reproduction, tracing its ideological resonance both within and beyond domestic space, and charting how it was deployed in the formation of social hierarchies. I do not argue simply that the domestic sphere was steadfastly political (although

I believe this to be true), but that the intimate acts, identities, and sentiments associated with this realm — among them fertility, childbearing, parenting, sexual practices, and ideologies such as "Republican motherhood" — were deeply implicated with the processes of race making, nation building, and imperial rule.

This book therefore reveals how discussions of the nation and its citizenry persistently returned to the body: its color and gender, its expenditure of labor power, its reproductive capacity, and its experience of desire. Of paramount importance was the question of what kinds of bodies could assimilate into the greater national body; as we will see, this was contingent upon which forms of métissage were thought to benefit the "French race." I argue throughout that to understand national belonging and fitness for citizenship in France at this time, one must account for these marked bodies and their place in an order of desire, signification, and power.[19] Thus I show how French social critics sought to categorize and hierarchize immigrant populations by intervening in debates on production and reproduction, marriage and sexuality, and degeneration and regeneration.

National Narratives and Bodily Practices

This book takes as its starting point the notion that in early-twentieth-century France the concepts of race and race mixing were elaborated and concretized with reference to economic production and procreation. This was due to a widespread concern about demographic decline across a broad political spectrum, a fear that the perceived shortage of French citizens was a symptom of France's degeneration and evidence of national decline. The question of labor power assumed paramount importance for politicians and industrialists confronted with depopulation and the upward social mobility of the French working class; they were forced to concede that only by importing foreign labor could economic growth be sustained. In time, the tremendous needs of the wartime economy heightened the demand for workers from Europe and the colonies, and after 1919 immigrant labor played an integral role in reconstructing postwar France.

I will show how the labor power provided by immigrants was evaluated and hierarchized with persistent reference to racial origins. That is, according to industrialists, government officials, "work scientists," and others, white labor was always preferable to that of Africans and Asians, who were deemed suitable only for unskilled work. However, we will see that the racial taxonomy sketched out in these texts did not simply distinguish between whiteness and color. Instead, the same commentators assigned unequal value to work performed by diverse European populations in France; as a result, they formulated an internal hierarchy within the category of white labor, and fragmented whiteness itself.

For the various social commentators described in this book, depopulation was never construed as a problem of production alone. Instead, it was a total social phenomenon which had decimated the citizenry as well as the indigenous labor force. Thus to replenish the population, immigrant workers would also have to be assimilable, and able to produce children who could reliably become French. Immigrants were therefore evaluated according to their productive and reproductive value, and both of these components determined their place in a racial taxonomy which spanned the metropole and its colonies. In my analysis French population politics was one facet of a wider development in the early decades of the twentieth century, when European nations came to view international competition in terms of demographic strength rather than productive capacity alone. State interest in population reframed reproduction as a public concern, and hence a legitimate object of social inquiry.[20] In time, the nationalist aim of improving the quality and quantity of the French population was extended to racially compatible foreigners as well, for by the interwar years immigrants were largely responsible for demographic growth in metropolitan France.

The association of production and reproduction is especially salient to this story because it signals the confluence of biopolitical strategies of governance and mass international migrations. Productive and reproductive exigencies converged as the consequence of a historically situated political economy subject to the multiple influences of depopulation, rationalization, Republicanism, and empire. For this reason, Thomas C. Holt has suggested that modern debates on immigration may have foregrounded intimate matters of the household and its reproduction in response to the requirements of a capitalist economy: "The iconic power of [family narratives] may well reflect the fact that actual, biological reproduction is perceived to be essential to the reproduction of the nation. Mature capitalist economies generate cultures and values inimical to large families and high levels of reproduction. Immigrants augment the national workforce, but at a cost to its racial and/or cultural homogeneity; fissures therefore emerge between the perceived needs of the nation and those of capital. The timing of these difficulties may be instructive. They arose in the late nineteenth and early twentieth centuries, as capitalism matured and extended its global reach, pressing heavily upon the destinies of nations."[21]

An important aim of this book is to explain how the contradictions invoked by Holt were debated within the specialized forms of knowledge which claimed jurisdiction over the immigrant question. I begin by exploring how the needs of capital were reconciled with the perceived necessity for demographic growth in France, and how this productivist and populationist discussion shaped the development of a historically contingent racial regime. Each chapter considers in detail how the stakes of migration and its projected effects on the national body engendered a proliferation of family narratives, sexual metaphors, and allegorical uses of gender to express these most intimate facets of power and knowledge. For example, we will see how the early-twentieth-century French state defined maternity and paternity as obligations of citizenship, and therefore subjected the bodies of mothers and fathers to a wide array of disciplinary technologies. But the state was so thoroughly invested in reproductive practices that it also concerned itself with men and women who shirked their civic duty to procreate: namely bachelors, "New Women," and prostitutes, along with the "Malthusian couple" described in detail by Foucault.[22]

Because Republicanism envisioned the family as a microcosm of the state, parents and especially mothers were assigned much of the responsibility for nurturing in children the cultural competencies of Frenchness. It follows that for foreigners, assimilability was measured in terms of their ability to execute these gestures with some degree of verisimilitude, as well as the desire and the capacity to impart them to one's offspring. But an aptitude for performing Frenchness in either public or domestic space depended on a complex interplay of innate affinity and acquired behavior, and not simply a willingness to enter into the social contract and thereby affiliate with the nation. For this reason, a merely universalist and assimilationist model of Republicanism masks the racial exclusions upon which the polity was based: as this book will show, biocultural sameness presupposed the possibility for assimilating into the French nation.

This book traces the genealogy of several mutually constitutive racial projects salient to the immigrant question, along with their relationship to the reproductive agenda of pronatalist politics and the Third Republic. The state's desire to safeguard the quality and quantity of its population justified its intervention in the private life of citizens.[23] Reproductive practices and proclivities became subject to the scrutiny of the state, and a variety of experts, institutions, and technologies proliferated, with the aim of assessing the biopower of the population.[24] I therefore insist that histories of immigration, like national and imperial histories, must be understood in an overtly biopolitical framework.[25] As we will see, the Foucauldian touchstones of demography, eugenic science, prostitution, disease, and procreative duties to the body politic surfaced again and again in the immigration debate, while the foreigner's intimate life, bodily constitution, and quotidian deeds heavily influenced the state's perception of his or her assimilability.

By focusing on what I have termed the *embodiment* of the "French race," I am engaging two interrelated strains of analysis. First, I call attention to the intimate bodily practices which came to signify national and racial membership: the sexual acts of citizens and subjects, eugenically sound modes of heterosexual coupling, the affective labor of the domestic sphere, and a national narrative, formulated by reproduction, which envisioned France's past as well as its future. In this regard, embodiment may be defined as a "process of making and doing the work of bodies," as well as an exploration of how bodies are sites of inscription and intervention subject to the influence of language.[26]

But "embodiment" is also a useful analytical category because it is the antithesis of the *abstract individualism* upon which modern French political theory is based. By abstracting individuals from their differentiated social statuses, abstract individualism posited an "essence of human commonality," which, taken to its logical conclusion, dictated that all people were equal and therefore entitled to natural rights.[27] But such a radically inclusive universalism had never existed for either women or colonial subjects. Thus embodiment becomes a way to investigate the exclusions necessary to and created by Republican citizenship, exclusions which at the outset were neither "accidental nor . . . inconsistent with the ideal of universal citizenship" as it was understood by its original theorists.[28]

By definition, the embodied person cannot function as the abstract individual of Republican universalism, because that person is infused with her or his particularist identity — whether gender, race, class, religion, or ethnicity — and is therefore informed by the distinctive experiences said to emanate from these subject-positions. For this reason, Nancy Leys Stepan has argued that the "history of embodiment must be seen as part of the story of citizenship and its limits."[29] She writes: "The historical counterpart to the disembodiment of the individual citizen of modernity — an individual imagined stripped of all substantiation — was the ontologizing via embodiment of sex and racial difference, a rendering of groups as distinct in their biology and differentiated from an implicitly, white male norm."[30]

The notion of embodiment therefore highlights what Joan Wallach Scott has called the "paradox" of French Republicanism, which posited a universal, rights-bearing individual who was simultaneously coded as male. This tension in Republican discourse between the purported universality of citizenship and the particularity of the female body structured modern French feminist interventions on behalf of women's equality. Scott contends that because feminists have argued from within the framework of Republicanism, they have variously affirmed and denied the significance of sexual difference, thereby frustrating their efforts to achieve formal equality.[31] In a similar vein, Gary Wilder has described the "antimony" of universalism and particularism within French Republican discourse. His work underscores how Republican sovereignty *simultaneously* universalizes and particularizes, and is therefore compelled to both include and exclude those over whom it reigns:[32] "A more integrated treatment of universality and particularity as interrelated dimensions of republican, national, and colonial politics would address the way universalizing practices have had particularizing effects and particularizing practices have served republican objectives over the long term history of modern France."[33] Taken together, Scott's and Wilder's accounts draw our attention to two perturbing categories generated by the hybrid logic of French Republicanism: the female citizen who lacked voting rights, and the colonial subject who possessed French nationality but without access to citizenship status. Thus a primary concern of this book is the elaboration of gendered and racialized subjectivities within the Republican narrative, as well as their relationship to national identity, social circulation, and the reproduction of the citizenry.

In theory, Republican universalism professed a hostility to particularism, or those interests which contradict the general will and mediate the relationship between citizen and state. But in practice universalism generated difference and facilitated exclusion without ever abandoning its contractarian and assimilationist logic. This tension is rooted in the simultaneous grounding of rights in one's humanity (a universalist category) and one's nationality (a particularist category).[34] French women, colonial subjects, and foreign immigrants were all subject to the paradoxical play of universalism and particularism. In the case of immigration, the uneasy incorporation of the Enlightenment concept of Man into a national and hence particularist system necessitated a distinction between citizens and foreigners which was, strictly speaking, antithetical to its universalizing project. Because the nation—a bounded entity composed of like people—required citizens and laborers from outside its realm, their particular nature had to be transformed into one which was unitary, homogenous, and French. In imagining the transition from foreigner to potential citizen, the immigrant's proximity to a biocultural and essentialized notion of Frenchness became the standard by which assimilability was measured.

Faith in this universalist vision has propagated the myth of a "colorblind France" which enthusiastically welcomed foreigners from any nation. Instead, this book challenges the universalist claims of French national belonging, as well as some French national histories, by demonstrating how social critics employed racial hierarchies to judge the quality of foreign labor, and its prospects for citizenship. The predominance of white European immigrants to France in the period before the Second World War—namely Italians, Belgians, Spaniards, and Poles—has led scholars and popular commentators to assume that race played no role in constructing French national identity at this time.[35] On the contrary, I suggest that in the late nineteenth century and the early twentieth, racial discourses were elaborated and deployed with reference to both immigration and colonization.

Of course, racial hierarchy did play a prominent role in the early French empire in the Caribbean and the Indian Ocean.[36] But by turning instead to modern examples, I will show how race articulated with class, nation, culture, and color in a mutually constitutive and discursively productive manner. For example, before the mid-nineteenth century the concept of race was primarily used to differentiate populations *within* France itself. Since about the sixteenth century, race had functioned as a marker for class, assigning members of the aristocracy to the Germanic, Teutonic, and Nordic races, and those of the Third Estate to the Gallo-Roman.[37] In the second half of the nineteenth century, however, the doctrines of racism and nationalism fused, and an understanding of race as nation became increasingly prevalent all across Europe.[38] Individual nation-states fabricated discourses of origin to explain the transmission of national essences from one generation to the next; this served to concretize the boundaries between European nations while simultaneously distinguishing the metropole from its colonies. In France the elaboration of the "French race" was the product of a particular historical moment, coinciding with the onset of mass immigration, preparation for revenge against Germany, and the expansion of the colonial empire.[39]

Imperial politics in particular generated a supranational European identity which, without displacing distinct national identities, was made coherent and intelligible through its reference to white authority, civilized culture, and superior military might. Despite the potency of modern nationalisms, the social theorist Étienne Balibar explains, "the colonial castes of the various nationalities . . . *worked together* to forge the idea of 'White' superiority, of civilization as an interest that has to be defended against savages."[40] Mass immigration, like colonialism, generated a variety of discourses distinguishing white Europeans from their colonial subjects. According to these discourses, European immigration upheld the purity of the white race while assuring the homogeneity of the French national body.

In this period the attempt to create or maintain a white polity through immigration was not a French project alone. Similar efforts occurred in the United States, Latin America, Australia, and elsewhere. For example, David Roediger has argued that the entire legal and social history of immigration in the United States has been framed by the question "Who is white?"[41] The Naturalization Law of 1792 defined Americans as "free *white* citizens," thus permitting the massive European migrations of the nineteenth century. More than a century later, restrictive legislation passed in the early 1920s, informed by eugenic nativism, overwhelmingly favored the entry of Anglo-Saxons.[42] Meanwhile, in Latin American nations such as Brazil, Argentina, and Cuba, social critics argued that European immigrants could "whiten" the nation by mixing with indigenous and mestizo people. Brazilian proponents of immigration favored the settlement of European workers in the hope of creating a white citizen body.[43] Similarly, Argentine racial theorists claimed that European immigration could whiten a population already "degraded" by a long history of crossings between Spanish colonizers and indigenous people. In Cuba the Immigration Laws of 1902 and 1906 prohibited Chinese immigration, restricted the entry of other nonwhite people, and yet encouraged the settlement of European families, especially Spaniards and Canary Islanders.[44] Finally, in Australia the Immigration Restriction Act of 1901 was essentially a literacy test which required immigrants to write out a dictation in a specified *European* language.[45]

Despite the ideal of whiteness that inspired these immigration policies, the "white race" that they invoked was only sometimes viewed as a monolithic grouping of individuals with a common identity distinct from people of color. At other junctures of the immigration debate the various members of the Latin, Slavic, Nordic, and Germanic races, to use the parlance of the time, were considered relationally, with each group assigned a particular capacity for assimilation. In France all participants in the immigration debate agreed that the integration of Italians and Spaniards, fellow members of the "Latin race," would occur by the second generation. According to Georges Mauco, one of the foremost authorities on immigration to France in this period, although these "Mediterranean elements" were products of a "less evolved civilization," their assimilation was seen as ultimately possible. This is because Italians and Spaniards belonged to the same race as the French, and thus had a similar language, culture, and mores.[46]

This racial hierarchy also included an intermediate category of more distant white populations: Slavs, Eastern European Jews, non-Arab residents of North Africa (i.e. Berbers, also referred to as Kabyles), and Levantines. In the French context, the last may have referred to the inhabitants of present-day Syria and Lebanon, or Western European minorities, usually of French or Italian origin, who had migrated to the Ottoman lands and could not be classified as either Turks or Arabs. Although racial theorists described these populations as fundamentally white, they were said to differ physically, intellectually, and morally from other whites, and to have less aptitude for productive labor. While they would require several generations to assimilate, the goal was nevertheless considered attainable. This middle group demonstrates what Matthew Frye Jacobson has called the "untidiness of the contest over whiteness." According to his analysis, phenotypical whiteness and European origin do not always guarantee a place within that category, and the "rules can be rewritten" at any historical moment to allow full membership within it to "borderline Europeans."[47]

Categories such as "Latin race," "Nordic race," and "Slavic race" occur freely in French writings on immigration; they express a notion of cultural *and* biological sameness which did not necessarily overlap with the boundaries of the nation-state. But these categories did not denote "ethnicity" as it is employed in contemporary America, where it signifies differences among whites. On the whole, French immigration discourse rarely employed the language of ethnicity, and words such as *ethnicité* and *ethnique* were not consistently applied to indicate cultural rather than biological difference.[48] The political scientist Pierre Birnbaum goes as far as to argue that the equivalent of the word "ethnic" does not exist in the French political vocabulary, and furthermore that the rhetoric of ethnicity is "alien to the French political tradition."[49]

In this light, critiques of the "ethnicity paradigm" which have been put forth by historians and sociologists of the United States can help us to analyze the French case, as well as call into question our desire to project ethnicity onto these deeply contextual categories.[50] To begin, we must ask why whites are marked by ethnicity when nonwhites are coded through race. Moreover, we need to think through our resistance to viewing white populations as racialized, and thus our unwillingness to refuse to whiteness the status of the unmarked category from which other groups supposedly differ. And finally, we must ask whether it is possible that in early-twentieth-century France there existed a system of difference in which one was both white and racially distinct from other whites.

I have made eclectic use of immigration studies from the United States and elsewhere because of ample evidence that racial ideologies were constructed and concretized in a world-system rather than confined to the boundaries of one nation. For this reason, the American experience of race need not be cordoned off as somehow exceptional, and the use of non-French methodologies to elucidate a study of immigration to France is not necessarily ahistorical or decontextualized.[51] Instead, I would argue that a more complete understanding of the way racial ideologies passed *between* Europe and the Americas is essential, echoing Tyler Stovall's conviction that "if the Empire provided [France with] one model of race relations, the United States furnished another."[52] For example, the eugenics movement was international in scope, linking like-minded thinkers in Europe, Latin America, and the United States.[53] And French observers were keenly aware of the American experience of immigration, its restrictive legislation and quota system, and the trials of a post-Emancipation society.[54] Thus in a study in 1930 of race and immigration in France, Jean Pluyette resoundingly praised American immigration laws, which he claimed were "founded on the basis of the fundamental inequality of the human races."[55]

By assigning race to white foreigners, I am not equating their experience in France with that of immigrants of color. A pervasive discourse of hierarchy clearly favored white Europeans while situating Africans and Asians in the least desirable position. Nevertheless, European immigrants were also the victims of discrimination, and their integration into the national body was an uneven and often turbulent process. This must be underscored because even though contemporary rhetoric on immigration has cynically juxtaposed the easy assimilation of white foreigners with the supposed recalcitrance of immigrants of color, many themes invoked by the "New Racism" in France, including the impossibility of assimilation, were previously applied to European immigrants whose racialization has since been effaced.[56] However, while Jews, colonized people, and white immigrants were all racialized in early-twentieth-century France, the weight assigned to this racialization was far from the same. We will see that in the decades which preceded the Vichy state, it was a color-based racism which commanded the most authority.

International Migrations, Racial Hierarchies,
and Gender Complementarity

The experience of mass immigration provided politicians, jurists, industrialists, racial theorists, feminists, and others with ample opportunity to explore the question of French racial belonging, its relationship to the colonial empire and the rest of Europe, and the means by which race articulated with national anxieties of depopulation and degeneration. Rather than provide a linear narrative, I link a series of interconnected stories about the movement of bodies between nations — and between metropole and colony — accompanied by forms of knowledge which also circulated transnationally. To explore the gendered and intimate politics of these racialized bodies, I focus upon five especially rich moments in the immigration debate: those pertaining to pronatalist politics, industrial production, *métissage*, white slavery, and independent nationality for married women. Namely, I consider the construction of racial categories which situate bodies in the social taxonomy, the unanticipated malleability of these identities, and the various technological discourses — such as demography, work science, eugenics, social hygienic reform, and nationality law — which aided in their propagation.

My starting point is the problem of social reproduction as articulated by pronatalist politics. In early-twentieth-century France, a coalition of politicians, industrialists, social scientists, and Catholics put forth a program for national renewal that included immigration as a remedy for French depopulation. Because pronatalist ideology focused on the body's reproductive potential and the family's obligation to the state, it highlighted the nation's need for new citizens as much as fresh labor power. An immigration policy which reconciled production and assimilation was offered as the solution, ranking immigrants according to their imagined capacity to adapt to both the workplace and family life in France. Pronatalists argued that if immigration were to be a temporary palliative to the demographic crisis, only foreigners with high birthrates should be actively selected. However, the surplus population of Africa and Asia — and the potential labor source of the colonies — first had to be dismissed as a possible solution to demographic decline in the metropole. Pronatalists therefore employed the language of contemporary demography to imagine buffer populations of white Europeans untouched by both the benefits and the dangers of civilization. The Italians, Spaniards, and Poles formed a pool of potential immigrants with "traditional" values that promoted high birthrates, but whose whiteness did not threaten the racial integrity of the French household.

From reproduction I turn to industrial production, since both are essential categories to any permanent migration. I show how the language of labor made use of racialized categories to grapple with concerns about skill, deskilling, and industrial output. With the growing rationalization of the labor process, work scientists, employers, and government agencies began calculating optimum output for racialized bodies. For example, in the 1900s

Jules Amar, an important theoretician of pre-Taylorist *science du travail*, compared levels of energy and fatigue among Italian, North African, and French workers. This new productivist idiom reflected contemporary concerns such as the quantification of output, the physical constitution of the worker's body, and the discrete gestures of which the rationalized labor process was composed. Hence studies performed in the 1920s and 1930s rated foreigners according to categories like physical fitness, discipline, regularity, and output on timework and piecework. While employers argued that these experiments shed light on the physical, technical, and moral value of immigrant workers, in reality they constructed and affirmed a preordained racial hierarchy, and deflected it onto an increasingly rationalized labor process.

Only immigrants who established families in France could contribute to the nation's demographic capital. Critics generally agreed that to combat depopulation, marriages between French women and foreigners were necessary. As a consequence, racial theorists carefully explored the civic and biological fitness of the métis, and how métissage with Europeans and colonial subjects could either revivify or debase the "French race." Métissage was explained in political, medical, and juridical circles in terms of two overlapping and mutually dependent ideologies of the nation. The first was assimilationist and universalist, and therefore summoned the power of the French language, the Republican school system, the soil, and French women to render immigrants culturally similar to the French. The second was a blood-based and particularist model espoused primarily by physicians and anthropologists, many of whom were also affiliated with the eugenics movement in France. Through a close reading of medico-hygienic texts on métissage, I show how both progressive and conservative Republicans combined assimilationist and organicist examples. As a result, they imagined a white polity regenerated by "métissage between whites," yet resolutely incapable of integrating its colonial subjects.

I then situate scientific and popular discussions of métissage in the context of commercial sex, analyzing the crusade against state-regulated prostitution in France, along with the related campaign to abolish "white slavery," or the alleged entrapment of (white) women, and their sale into prostitution abroad. Feminists relied on racialized metaphors of dependency to argue that regulated prostitution deprived women of key universal rights. However, the only alternative that feminists offered to the medico-hygienic and police surveillance of women in brothels was the repatriation of wayward female migrants, and their safe return to French husbands or fathers. By relocating women in domestic space and reestablishing paternalistic control, opponents of prostitution enabled a gendered notion of dependency which undermined feminist demands for equality. In addition, social reformers were deeply troubled by the traffic in European women to the colonies, for this particular migration fueled French anxieties about sexual respectability and the nation's fitness for imperial rule. According to both army officials and opponents of sex trafficking, the availability of French prostitutes to colonial subjects undermined France's prestige and tarnished its "civilizing mission." For this reason, the army actively discouraged interracial relationships with French women, whether or not they were prostitutes, and sought to provide prostitutes of color to colonial soldiers.

Finally, I link pronatalism, hybridity, and national identity by exploring the debate on the Law on French Nationality of 1927. Before its promulgation, French women who married foreigners were automatically divested of their nationality and forced to assume that of their husbands. While feminists had called for an independent nationality for married women as early as 1869, only with the death of nearly 1.5 million French men in the trenches of the First World War did the debate gain momentum in parliament. Employing universalistic language and laying claim to a capacious human identity, feminists argued that because women were endowed with duties and rights equal to those of men, they too should be permitted to choose their nationality. This line of reasoning privileged the individual rights of women above the collective interests of the family and the nation. Thus when pronatalist jurists and Radical politicians came to the defense of independent nationality, they framed it as a populationist measure designed to increase the number of French nationals. Insisting that it was illogical to surrender French women and their future children during a demographic crisis, they argued that French women should be permitted to keep their nationality, raise children who were legally French, and employ their particularly feminine influence to assimilate foreign husbands. That is, the overtly populationist concerns of the law of 1927 privileged the reproductive capital of French women over the radically egalitarian promise of individual rights. It thereby affirmed gender complementarity and women's particularism within a universalist vision of the nation.

The conspicuous linking of race and reproduction in immigration discourse was carried out in a national and imperial framework. As a consequence, this book focuses on fields of contact shared by European migrants, French citizens, and colonized subjects, contacts which occurred in both public and intimate space. Moreover, it underscores the importance of hierarchy to the social taxonomy of early-twentieth-century France, the potential hybridities created by immigration, emigration, and colonization, and the compound identities of historical subjects fragmented by gender, race, and nation. The synergism of this approach corresponds well with the French case for a number of important reasons. First, a language of hierarchy permeated the immigration debate, in which each foreign group was tirelessly evaluated according to its economic and reproductive utility. The context of demographic decline both enabled and sustained a discussion of hybridity and its limits, along with the related questions of race mixing, intermarriage, and the French woman's role in generating national identity. Finally, the idea of "Greater France," or a nation affiliated with its empire, must serve as our frame of reference because of how explicitly the assimilability of white foreigners was defined in opposition to immigrants from the colonies.

The vicissitudes of the immigration debate were galvanized by problems particular to this moment in modernity, such as the movement of embodied subjects across national and imperial borders; the question of how freely workers, goods, and other forms of capital should circulate in an increasingly global economy; depopulation; rationalization; a perceived crisis in the gender system; and finally, the patterns of domination characteristic of a society ordered by the social fiction of race. The Third Republic's impulse to hierarchize immigrants with reference to their economic and procreative value would provide the ideological and practical foundations for the Vichy regime, whose policies also heralded the rationalizing of production and reproduction as the path to national regeneration.

Chapter One

IMMIGRATION, DEMOGRAPHY, AND PRONATALISM

In December 1915 the deputy, demographer, and future minister Adolphe Landry (Gauche Radical, Corsica) submitted a bill to the Chamber of Deputies that encapsulated what he believed to be the most significant dilemma posed by mass immigration to France:

> Every nation has the very legitimate concern of protecting itself as much as possible from foreign infiltrations that may alter its composition. Such a desire is especially understandable for those nations that rightly consider themselves to hold an elevated place in the order of civilization. For these nations (and we are proud to count the French nation among them), certain mixings can only lead to its degradation . . . If foreign workers must mix with the French population, if their arrival in France is to introduce new elements into our race, it is necessary that these elements not be of the kind that will profoundly alter or debase the race. Thus we must endeavor to only introduce into France workers from countries whose civilization is related to ours, or those whose origin can elevate our civilization.[1]

Landry's bill is representative of the dominant discourse on immigration in early-twentieth-century France. In the context of what contemporaries described as a "demographic crisis," Landry held that citizens as well as workers were desperately needed by the underpopulated French nation. He therefore formulated the immigrant question with reference to both the labor power and the reproductive value of potential foreigners. Along with a wide array of politicians, industrialists, social scientists, jurists, and racial theorists whom we will examine in the course of this book, Landry agreed that because of demographic decline, immigrants who came to work in France must be assimilable and able to produce French offspring. However, as Landry warned in his proposal, foreigners could contribute either positively or negatively to the "French race," depending upon their origin. If the cultural patrimony and ontological quality of some immigrants were akin to those of the French, he cautioned that the profound difference of other foreigners rendered them inassimilable.

The growing importance of assimilability in this discourse reflected the widespread panic created by depopulation, as social critics with pronatalist convictions lamented the steady drop in French births and the "individualistic" nature of French men and women, which in their view had encouraged the trend toward smaller families.[2] They argued that depopulation had social as well as economic consequences, such as shortages of husbands for French women, young men for the army, and children for the future labor force. Despite the deeply nationalistic character of the pronatalist movement, its leaders conceded that to mitigate the effects of the demographic crisis on the labor market and the French family, the importation of foreign workers was a necessary, though temporary, solution.[3]

This chapter will show how the immigrant question of the early twentieth century intersected with the overtly populationist agenda of Republican France. The modern state's obsession with a "political knowledge" centered on population and its regulation is a primary thesis of the social theorist Michel Foucault.[4] His definition of "biopolitics" explicitly referred to the state's efforts to monitor the birthrate of its citizens,[5] while in the first volume of *The History of Sexuality*, the less than fecund "Malthusian couple" is an integral category of analysis.[6] This calls our attention to the biopolitical state's newfound investment in the various "checks" on population outlined by the political economist Thomas Malthus in the late eighteenth century, and especially to the "neo-Malthusian" practice of birth control as a means to limit population growth. Throughout this chapter I draw upon Foucault's description of the state's populationist imperative to show how the immigrant question was consistently framed with reference to neo-Malthusianism and fecundity, birthrate and potential human capital, and corporeal and national vigor.

By the late nineteenth century the state's power and international influence were no longer measured with reference to its productivity alone. In Europe populationist discourse equating demographic strength with international prominence had become increasingly common,[7] and as a consequence the female sphere of reproduction and the intimate life of domestic space assumed a more conspicuous role in national and imperial politics.[8] An expanding corps of social hygiene reformers turned its attention to the health and well-being of the general population, and specifically to the nation's children and mothers.[9] In accordance with the populationist imperative described by Foucault, these "experts" evaluated the reproductive capital of the citizenry with an eye to ameliorating the quality and quantity of the population. This biopolitical climate was intensified by the prevalence of degeneration theory in several European nations, which pathologized depopulation, high infant mortality rates, venereal disease, and alcoholism.[10] We will see that in France, where the rhetoric of demographic decline was particularly strident, a wide range of social commentators contributed to an explicitly racialized discussion of how to rebuild the citizen body.

No European nation experienced demographic decline more acutely than France, and the casualties of the First World War, added to an already low birthrate, exacerbated French anxieties. By the end of the nineteenth century the French population was reproducing itself at the lowest rate in the world.[11] From 1911 to 1938 it had increased by only two million inhabitants, despite the addition of 1.7 million people through the annexation of Alsace and Lorraine.[12] On the eve of the Great War the average French family was composed of two children, and in 1926, only three families out of ten could claim three or more offspring.[13] French demographic growth in this period was largely due to immigration. The census of 1931 counted 808,000 Italians, 508,000 Poles, and 352,000 Spaniards, to name the most numerous groups.[14] In the interwar period nearly three million foreigners resided in France, and three-fourths of all demographic growth could be attributed to immigration.[15]

Specifically, this chapter explores how pronatalist critics, in their attempt to combat depopulation, debated the possible consequences of foreign immigration to France. Because the "demographic crisis" provided a unique opportunity to remake the citizen body, pronatalist discourse implicated French citizens, European immigrants, and colonial subjects in a biopolitical logic which glorified fecundity, racial hygiene, and a traditional vision of the family. The movement's belief that reproduction was an obligation of citizenship determined its support for immigration from "demographically prolific" nations such as Italy, Spain, and Poland. Its members claimed that in less modernized states "preindustrial" values promoted high birthrates among selfless parents who, unlike their French counterparts, honored their national obligation to procreate. Thus the culturally conservative rhetoric of pronatalism, which heralded patriarchal authority, maternal virtue, fecundity, and traditionalism, was employed to assess the assimilability of potential foreigners. That is, the very values that pronatalists wished to revive among the French were projected onto foreign populations as well.

The debate on fecundity and assimilability focused on reproductive practices within the institution of marriage, and subject to the hierarchies of a historically contingent racial order. Although family migration also occurred in this period, foreigners who came to France in the early twentieth century were overwhelmingly young, unmarried men. Of course male foreigners were especially welcome, particularly in the interwar years: the catastrophic loss of French men in the Great War had created a shortage of husbands for French women while exacerbating the effects of depopulation, a theme we will explore in detail in chapter 5.[16] The demographic crisis had therefore forced hybridity upon the nation. For the various social critics we will examine throughout this book — whether pronatalists, work scientists, social hygienic reformers, racial theorists, politicians, or feminists — the key was to identify when hybridity would benefit the "French race," rather than facilitating further degeneration. In chapter 3 I will discuss how hybridity was conceived in both mainstream racial theory and medico-hygienic discourse on immigration. For now, I will introduce the question of how the French state sought to reconcile production with reproduction, national-imperial borders with international migration, and human difference with universalist social theory by examining pronatalist arguments in favor of white European migration to an underpopulated France.

But first, the surplus population of Africa and Asia, and specifically, the potential labor source of the French colonies, had to be dismissed as a possible remedy for depopulation in the metropole. Although Africans and Asians had immigrated to France before, during, and after the First World War, the pressing need to reconstitute French families in the interwar years reframed the immigrant question. As assimilability and the ability to reproduce French offspring became the most salient criteria by which foreigners were to be judged, the evaluation of simple labor power no longer sufficed. Pronatalists therefore cautioned against importing nonwhite workers, arguing instead that the Italians, Poles, and Spaniards were the most viable candidates for naturalization. Having equated the French race with whiteness, pronatalist critics reaffirmed a primary tenet of Republican imperialism: while colonial subjects were included in the nation in accordance with the doctrine of "Greater France," a nation affiliated with its empire, they were excluded from the polity and denied citizenship rights.[17]

Finally, by examining the relationship between fecundity and civilization in demographic discourse, we see how the perceived consequences of modernity, expressed most starkly by the decline in fertility rates, were conceived in racialized and gendered terms. In their discussion of foreign immigration, various members of the pronatalist movement invoked race, gender, and reproduction in their effort to imagine the ideal citizen body. I focus in particular on three significant contributors to the debate on immigration and repopulation in order to explore the various manifestations of these categories: the Alliance Nationale pour l'Accroissement de la Population Française, France's largest and most influential pronatalist movement, which by 1939 could claim 25,335 members; the journalist Ludovic Naudeau's popular account of French depopulation, which first appeared in the newspaper L'Illustration; and the Conseil Supérieur de la Natalité (CSN), an official ministerial commission created in 1920 by the Bloc National government from within the Ministry of Hygiene, Social Assistance, and Prevention to research measures and recommend legislation to fight depopulation and raise the birthrate.

Fecundity and Civilization: The Search for Compromise

In several important demographic studies of the late nineteenth century and the early twentieth, depopulation was theorized in terms of the relationship between civilization and birthrate.[18] For example, the liberal economist Paul Leroy-Beaulieu of the Collège de France juxtaposed the depopulation of

Northern Europe and North America with escalating birthrates in the African and Asian world, and argued that as a nation modernized, achieving a higher standard of living and increased industrial production, its birthrate necessarily fell.[19] This was of course a dramatic refutation of Malthusian doctrine, which prophesied an exponential increase in human populations and thus a depletion of global resources. After approximately 1860 Malthusianism fell out of favor, and demographers focused instead on the trend toward fertility decline, which Leroy-Beaulieu described as the "true law of population among civilized people."[20] Hoping to attain a greater level of material comfort, even the "humblest of citizens" began to postpone marriage, limit births, and opt for an "individualistic" existence which, according to the pronatalist position, flagrantly ignored the collective concerns of the nation.[21]

According to this formula, a society's birthrate could be expressed as inversely proportional to its level of "civilization." In Leroy-Beaulieu's view, civilization was an urbanized society with a democratic government and a developed middle class, in which education, affluence, and leisure had been extended to the majority of the population.[22] Despite the virtues of the civilized state, depopulation was the necessary outcome: "In recent and present times, the diminution of fecundity among the civilized nations . . . can be considered a general, if not universal fact."[23] Demographers explained that while the state of civilization facilitated global predominance and justified European expansion overseas, it was a double-edged sword, bringing with it degeneration and depopulation. Ironically, the march of progress ultimately compromised the power of "civilized" nations, now confronted with the demographic superiority of less developed societies.

In Africa and Asia, where the colonial project was to transport civilization to "savage" and "barbarous" lands, birthrates remained high despite substantial mortality rates. As the demographer and physician Jacques Bertillon succinctly explained, "the most ignorant countries are also the most fecund ones."[24] The anticlerical and socialist-leaning demographer Arsène Dumont echoed the conservative Bertillon's position: "Those who absorb no part of civilization, like the poor in France and barbarians worldwide, conserve their high birthrates, while those who absorb much of civilization ultimately die as a result."[25] Philippa Levine has noted that "sex was one of the most widely remarked upon mechanisms for measuring distance from civilization."[26] In accordance with this logic, Europeans attributed an unbridled sexuality to colonized people, evidenced by robust population growth in Africa and Asia, as well as polygamy, sexual violence, and an unquenchable need for access to prostitution.[27] Colonial fecundity thereby confirmed the backwardness of Africans and Asians, and justified the European impulse to civilize and contain them.

Demographers hypothesized that as African and Asian societies modernized, embracing industrialization, hygienic practices, and democratic values, they too would begin to limit their births. But in the meantime, with African and Asian populations growing unchecked while birthrates in most European nations dwindled, the fertility of nonwhite people was perceived as a threat to white hegemony worldwide.[28] Opponents of nonwhite immigration therefore insisted that it was the duty of the entire Occidental world to form a united front against immigrants of color.[29] According to this view, Malthusianism among Europeans was nothing short of race suicide, a myopic practice that amounted to abdicating the white mission to civilize the globe. If strength was in numbers, as pronatalists argued, Europeans and North Americans must not remain passive while nonwhites propagated at their expense. In the words of Auguste Isaac, the Catholic deputy named minister of commerce in 1919, father of eleven children and founder in 1915 of an offshoot of the Alliance, the pro-family lobbying group La Plus Grande Famille: "If the white race restrains [its births], who will guarantee us that the yellow race will follow its example? Who will assure us that the black race will sacrifice the fecundity which, to cite but one example, is a cause of anxiety for whites in the United States?"[30]

Depopulation was thus characterized as a "general phenomenon . . . which one could note among all people of the white race," now menaced by the fecundity of the Asian and African world.[31] Around the turn of the century, high Asian birthrates in addition to several important examples of Asians asserting themselves against white nations—as with the Boxer Rebellion, the Russo-Japanese War, and the founding of the Congress Party in India—aided in the construction of the fantasmic "yellow peril."[32] The possibility of Chinese or Japanese expansion heightened Europe's wariness with regard to population increases outside the western world. Social reformers warned of the "passive invasion" of depopulated white nations by "Asiatic people."[33] For example, the prominent pronatalist Fernand Boverat explained: "Among the colored races, and the yellow race in particular, birthrates remain formidable. Japan will see its population rise by one million people per year. For a country like France, which has a great colonial empire . . . this demographic disequilibrium is particularly serious."[34]

Pronatalists, colonialists, and economists viewed the "péril jaune" in terms of the possible economic threat that a densely populated Japan or China would pose to the West.[35] Because they believed that demographic strength correlated with the desire for territorial expansion, they feared that the fecundity of East Asians would reverse the accustomed relationship between colonizer and colonized, endangering western markets and challenging European imperial hegemony.[36] Leroy-Beaulieu argued that western surplus population was essential to the construction of empire, as it provided the human capital necessary for white settlement overseas. So too did Paul Haury, a history professor and future president of the Alliance, whose plan for teaching demography and hence depopulation in primary and secondary schools was sanctioned by the minister of public instruction in 1929.[37] By reversing normative population dynamics, demographic decline in the metropole endangered the colonial legacy and threatened to "destroy the equilibrium of the human races."[38] Thus if empire was one manifestation of the vitality of the nation-state, an inability to populate the colonies was evidence of its frailty.

French depopulation was commonly invoked to explain the nation's defeat in the Franco-Prussian War, and for revanchistes demanding retribution against Germany, repopulation was the first important step in reestablishing military power. For this reason one might assume that pronatalist concerns were galvanized by German demographic strength alone, when in fact a vision of colonial imperialism and a "Europe submerged" by nonwhites was also a critical part of French anxiety.[39] Only white immigration could provide assimilable labor power while offsetting the robust birthrates of Africans and Asians. European immigration permitted members of a transnational white polity to secure themselves against the fertility of the nonwestern world. Thus foreign labor would have to be recruited among European countries with surplus populations, such as the partially modernized and demographically prolific nations of southern and central Europe (figures 1 and 2).[40]

Because the economic development of nations like Italy, Spain, and Poland could not accommodate the size of their populations, many workers opted to emigrate to depopulated and industrialized states. But if the Italians,

1. "From the Basque Region: Destitute and Prolific Type of Spanish Family." In Georges Mauco, *Les étrangers en France: étude géographique sur leur rôle dans l'activité économique* (Paris: Armand Colin, 1932).

Spaniards, and Poles were largely motivated by the promise of economic opportunity, for pronatalist critics European foreigners were potential agents in a racialized vision of France's regenerated future. Not only could white European immigrants fill shortages in the fields and factories; they could also reproduce with native women without substantially changing the "racial composition" of the French people. According to the demographer Arsène Dumont, it was best to seek out immigrants like the Italians who had not yet "broken their ties with their native land," as they retained high fertility rates and the values that promoted large families.[41] For the jurist René Le Comte, Italian fecundity was a means to combat the "yellow peril" by providing white, assimilable labor power to industrialized and depopulated nations: "The rapid growth of Italian emigration in the past twenty years is one of the most fortunate occurrences from the point of view of the future of the white races. As the yellow races have started to breach European hegemony, it is high time to reinforce the white element in both Americas, the North of Asia, Australia, South Africa, and the Mediterranean basin."[42]

But a gendered reading of the debate on fecundity and civilization is equally revealing. As Karen Offen's seminal article has shown, one cannot separate arguments regarding fertility decline from a greater discussion of the role of women in French society.[43] Demographers agreed that the state

2. "A Handsome Italian Family, Immigrated to the Isère Region: Northern Italian Type, Robust and Hardworking." In Georges Mauco, *Les étrangers en France: étude géographique sur leur rôle dans l'activité économique* (Paris: Armand Colin, 1932).

of civilization had many consequences, and that nations like Italy, Spain, and Poland had retained the best of the preindustrial world: prolific birth-rates, a commitment to hard work, a strong sense of family, and a more pious Catholicism (a value praised by some but not all pronatalists). In turn, these traits were reinforced by a traditional view of masculinity and femininity, which, by preserving gender difference, promoted fertility and a devotion to family life. In contrast, social critics like Leroy-Beaulieu noted that in modernized nations like France the boundaries between women and men had been blurred, and the feminist movement, which sought to make women identical to men, was largely responsible for depopulation: "The masculinization of women is, from all points of view, one of the grave dangers facing contemporary civilization. It is a desiccating and sterilizing factor [*facteur desséchant et stérilisant*]."[44]

By the turn of the century the connection between depopulation and feminism had been firmly established within demographic discourse. As one further manifestation of the "individualist virus," feminism ostensibly encouraged French women to abandon their prescribed role as mothers and homemakers, and thereby encouraged fertility decline. But normative visions of masculinity were also at stake. Pronatalists issued a sweeping critique of the entire gender order: they called into question the nation's virility, along with that of its male citizenry. Conflating the frailty of a depopulated France with the effeminacy of French men, Fernand Boverat, the most prominent figure in the French pronatalist movement, warned that for the nation and its male inhabitants to be "afflicted with a pernicious anemia" rendered France vulnerable to outside attack.[45] As Kristen Stromberg Childers has demonstrated, paternity and maternity were both integral components of pronatalist discourse from the postwar period through Vichy, and pronatalist critics scrutinized the reproductive practices of French men and women alike. While feminists and other "modern women" were criticized for their dismissal of maternity, domestic life, and other traditional aspects of femininity, pronatalist texts portrayed the bachelor (*célibataire*) as a "social misfit," whether oversexed, homosexual, or both.[46]

Immigration was to reinvigorate the national body by introducing young and robust male elements from Europe into a flagging population further debilitated by the casualties of the Great War. For example, in 1918 Senator Emile Goy (Radical, Radical-Socialist, Haute-Savoie) called for the "addition of foreign, ethnic elements" that would "infuse" France with "new blood."[47] In chapter 3 we will analyze these organicist national metaphors in great detail. For now I wish to emphasize how depopulation was framed with reference to a biological understanding of degeneration and revivification, in which foreigners served as a "blood transfusion" which would curtail or even reverse the effects of national decline. Thus Albert Troullier of the Alliance argued that the nation should select its immigrants like a physician preparing for a transfusion, choosing "an individual without physiological flaws, with blood *compatible* to that of the person requiring the transfusion ... There exist actual blood types and one cannot, without great danger, mix the blood of different and *incompatible* groups."[48]

But unmarried men, even from desirable groups, were considered promiscuous, dissolute, and unstable.[49] Social commentators claimed that foreign bachelors were more prone to alcoholism, criminality, and venereal disease. Without wives to persuade them to settle in one place, they wandered France in search of work, or returned to their native land, thus mitigating their contribution to the national economy. The "excess virility" of male immigrants was therefore to be tempered by marriage, their sexuality channeled through the conjugal union in the interests of repopulating the French nation. For this reason, pronatalists encouraged both family immigration and the marriage of male immigrant workers shortly after their arrival in France. That is, in their effort to remake the domestic life of the nation, pronatalists highlighted the importance of marriage, procreative sex, and traditional gender roles for both French and immigrant families.

Reconciling Labor Power and Race: A Politics of Production Meets a Politics of Assimilation

We have seen that pronatalist critics understood depopulation in explicitly racialized terms: the "French race" had become degenerate, only foreign "blood" could revive it, and declining birthrates among the "white race" contrasted with the fecundity of people of color. Pronatalists also demanded that both the labor power and the reproductive value of potential foreigners be evaluated in order to square productivity with assimilability. Again and again, they insisted that white Europeans were superior workers to Africans and Asians. Specifically, they held that the immigration of Latin and Slavic elements could supply qualified labor without recourse to Chinese and colonial workers. According to the Alliance's monthly journal: "After having been flooded during the war with Kabyle street sweepers, Annamite stokers, Negro stevedores, and Chinese laborers, whom we had to import because it was the best we could get, we were forced to send the majority of these worthless immigrants back to their faraway homelands. They were more disposed to pillage and thievery than serious labor. The re-establishment of the peace has permitted us to replace these 'undesirables' with our usual immigrants, the Italians and the Spaniards."[50]

Pronatalists did not believe that immigration was the ideal means to combat depopulation: they feared that foreigners would form unassimilated pockets within the nation, and that without careful mixing the racial integrity of the French people would be compromised. They agreed that to raise the native birthrate, the utmost priority was to encourage a change in French values; nevertheless, they conceded that immigration could revivify French demographics in the meantime. According to the Alliance member Albert Troullier: "It is indispensable that, starting now, we replace all the dead and the sick by assimilation and naturalization, while waiting for the normal creation of future households. Let it suffice to say that immigration cannot be the primary means of fighting the national danger of depopulation. It is only a temporary remedy, and a perilous one at that. Immigration should only allow us to wait for the re-establishment of French demographic power, without modifying the special characteristics of the race."[51]

The Alliance's presence in the depopulation debate was enduring, determined, and obstreperous. Founded in May 1896 by the demographer Jacques Bertillon, Drs. Charles Richet and Emile Javal, the civil servant Auguste Honnorat, and the Catholic statistician Emile Cheysson, the Alliance initially comprised secular and socially conservative patriots, most of them bourgeois businessmen, industrialists, doctors, and lawyers. However, its blend of anti-individualism, anti-feminism, and nationalism permitted ties with Catholics as well as with those sympathetic to the populationist policies of Nazi Germany and fascist Italy.[52] The Alliance's cultural conservatism is reflected in its ambivalent stance on progress, modernity, and civilization. Its members held that if industrialization were left unchecked, depopulation and degeneration would necessarily ensue. Following Le Play's sociology, many claimed that the transition from an agricultural to an industrial society had weakened the organic bonds of society, while the declining birthrate could be traced to the undermining of patriarchal society which had begun with the Revolution.[53] Nostalgia for the more simple and upright life of the French countryside compelled pronatalists to extol the "pre-industrial" values that they identified with particular immigrant groups.

The Alliance led a widespread propaganda campaign that included the publication of pronatalist brochures, periodicals, films, demographic statistics, and proposals for legislative action, and its lobbying efforts had a direct effect on postwar laws such as one in 1920 repressing propaganda for contraceptives and another in 1923 aimed at increasing prosecutions for abortions, as well as on a provision granting family allowances for dependent children. Members of the Alliance held that depopulation was largely the fault of the Third Republic's institutions and policies, which promoted individual rights at the expense of collective duties. According to Susan Pederson, Alliance members viewed depopulation as the result of a "liberal and individualistic political and economic order that disproportionately awarded the childless." Demographic decline, they claimed, could only be reversed if liberal institutions like the tax system, the military, the civil service, and perhaps even the wage system were reworked to favor prolific fathers.[54]

At annual congresses and in its journal, members of the Alliance frequently debated questions of assimilation and naturalization. In their view, the stability of the family was the key to social peace, but paradoxically, some of the best examples of strong and unified households were to be found among foreigners rather than French citizens. For Boverat, father of four, veteran of the Great War, and president of the Alliance in the interwar period, measures to fulfill the twin demands of labor power and repopulation went hand in hand: "It is not a question of importing any workers to France, but good workers, and assimilable workers."[55] The government, Boverat explained, must implement a tripartite plan to increase native births while encouraging immigration and naturalization.[56] First, depopulation had to be rectified internally, by French men and women, with the support of the state. In the meantime, immigration would serve as a stopgap to replenish the waning French population. While the Alliance claimed that unassimilated, non-naturalized foreigners were a potential danger to the "French race," its members had little sympathy for the harshest French critics of immigration. Auguste Isaac explained: "Those who complain the most about the intrusion of foreigners are generally not those who make the most personal efforts or sacrifices to change the state of affairs. The same pens warning of social ills are often used to propagate the very ideas that foster them: the love of material well-being, the right to happiness, the glorification of pleasure, and distaste for the family."[57]

Naturalization was of course the bona fide emblem of citizenship, and because the Alliance wished to see a clear increase in French population statistics, it demanded that assimilable foreigners be naturalized quickly, without complications or delays. It also called for simplifying naturalization procedures and substantially reducing its cost. Because "those families with the most mouths to feed will have the least disposable income," Boverat argued that extraneous taxes like the *droit de sceau* and the *droit de chancellerie* be eliminated.[58] Moreover, he claimed that the naturalization fee of 1,000 francs was too high for "Belgian, Swiss, Italian, and Polish workers, who account for the majority of those suitable for naturalization."[59] Albert Troullier went further still, insisting that because immigrants from Belgium, Italy, Poland, and Spain were the most likely to assimilate, and in the shortest amount of time, the French state should actively facilitate their naturalization.[60]

Like the authors of the demographic treatises examined earlier, the Alliance framed the problem of immigration and depopulation in terms of white demographic panic. In its official publications, references to the "yellow peril" were abundant, depopulation was repeatedly described as the "plague of the white race," and low European birthrates were explained through recourse to the rhetoric of degeneration. In numerous articles and speeches, President Fernand Boverat hierarchized foreigners according to their assimilability and potential for citizenship. He explained that although Belgium and Switzerland had furnished assimilable workers in the nineteenth century, shrinking birthrates in those nations made it necessary to evaluate other sources. Boverat insisted that the only countries able to supply France with both labor power and assimilable immigrants were Italy, Spain, Czechoslovakia, Poland, and Romania. As for the Greeks, "Levantines," and Kabyles of North Africa, these populations were "with some exceptions . . . second-rate immigrants that no country is actively seeking out, and which we have no interest attracting to France."[61] While these groups were not classified among the assimilable, and in all likelihood not recognized as fully white, their foreignness was less weighted than that of Asians and other Africans who, according to Boverat, should under no circumstances be permitted to enter France in large numbers:[62] "Despite the dangers of depopulation we must carefully avoid the mass immigration of men of color, at the risk of witnessing the development of racial conflicts on French soil, the disastrous consequences of which we have already seen in the United States."[63]

A demographic study of foreigners in the departments proposed by the Commissions Départementales de la Natalité, a federation of local pronatalist associations reporting directly to the CSN, reaffirmed Boverat's position. It concluded that after the Italians, the Spaniards assimilated most rapidly; as for the Poles, although the cohesiveness of their communities slowed their insertion into French society, they nevertheless had the potential to assimilate. In contrast, for the Armenians, Levantines, and Jews of Central Europe, who were said to possess a "mentality very different from that of the French population," assimilation was considerably more difficult, usually requiring the passage of several generations. Finally, the inquiry stated that the assimilation of North Africans was "nearly impossible." Linking them with disease and degeneration in a tendentious social logic, researchers documented a high incidence of syphilis and tuberculosis among North African immigrants, in addition to a crime rate exceeding that of any other group. The study then reaffirmed that French vitality was dependent on its status as a white nation, concluding that the "introduction or maintenance of North African workers on our metropolitan territory, and of all other workers who do not belong to the white race, or who have a mentality different from our own, appears detrimental to both the physical and moral health of our race."[64]

Similarly, the Social Catholic Louis Duval-Arnould, a law professor, disciple of Le Play, and Alliance member who would also become vice-president of the CSN and president of La Plus Grande Famille, agreed that only European immigrants could provide France with both labor power and reproductive value.[65] He explained that because foreign blood would eventually mix with that of the French, "it would not suffice to import good workers": it was also necessary for immigrants to be assimilable. Small additions of Latin and Slavic blood, he claimed, would not substantially modify the "essential characteristics" of the French people.[66] His stance on colonial immigration, however, was far more censorious. Duval-Arnould recycled the racialized and gendered idioms particular to the labor process, a theme to which we will return in chapter 2. Echoing the observations of work scientists, heads of industry, and envoys of the Labor Ministry, he concluded that colonial workers, owing to their "docility" and lack of physical strength, constituted a "feminized" labor force whose productivity was compromised: "The recruitment of European workers is more valuable than that of colonials, which was attempted at the end of the war, and now seems to have been abandoned. The quality of [colonial] labor was revealed to be feminine, no doubt the result of profound differences of mores and climate. Here we have nothing to regret from the ethnographic [*ethnique*] point of view."[67]

Duval-Arnould's fellow Social Catholic, Monsignor Gaston Vanneufville, also affirmed that importing colonial labor in the context of the demographic crisis had far-reaching consequences. He claimed that to advocate the employment of Asian and African immigrants was to view them as nothing more than "human material," or to neglect the obvious fact that male foreigners, "when bringing us their labor, also bring us their personalities." He wrote: "They are or will become heads of households [in France], and just as they were members of civil society in their native country, they will constitute an integral part of ours." Vanneufville therefore called upon Social Catholics and other members of the pro-family lobby to consider both the public and private life of foreigners when gauging their assimilability, as a concern for labor power alone reduced the worker to little more than "human material." But for Vanneufville, once male workers had been envisioned as "heads of household," their difference was automatically reaffirmed. In his words, the vast majority of Africans and Asians were "pagans" who possessed "tastes, sentiments, and passions" which contradicted those of French civilization; as a consequence, their assimilation was impossible.[68]

For Social Catholics and other Catholic-identified members of the crusade against depopulation, the common Catholicism of Spanish, Italian, and Polish immigrants heightened their prospects for assimilation. However, members of the Alliance were overwhelmingly secular Republicans, and as a consequence they rarely employed religious discourse to justify particular exclusions. Although the French public sphere still bore the imprint of pre-Revolutionary Catholic culture, the vehemently anticlerical Third Republic had transformed it, at least in theory, into a secular and universalist space.[69] Indeed, diehard Republicans feared that the piety of Poles and Italians would prevent them from properly assimilating, and noted with relief that these populations generally dechristianized shortly after their arrival in France. Thus Republican pronatalists did not claim that Italians and Spaniards were more assimilable because they were Catholic, but rather because they were Latin and white.

While the Alliance conducted a parliamentary and legislative assault in behalf of the pronatalist cause, one of its most successful popularizers was author Ludovic Naudeau. As an international correspondent for the Paris newspaper Le Temps, Naudeau had earned his journalistic reputation with eyewitness accounts of the Russo-Japanese War and the Bolshevik Revolution. On returning to Paris after the First World War, he was employed by the popular weekly review L'Illustration,[70] in which he published acclaimed exposés of the rise of fascism and Nazism, and reports on modern Japan and Russia which were awarded prizes by the French Academy. Naudeau also turned his flair for travel writing infused with political analysis upon his native France. After a two-year journey through twenty French departments to document the gravity of depopulation, his findings were printed as a serial in L'Illustration in 1929 and 1930. This dense, meticulous, and highly subjective work is indicative of the shift in the 1930s toward an increased public awareness of the populationist platform: its publication generated passionate responses from readers, including a barrage of letters to the author, debates in provincial newspapers, and the undertaking of several local monographs further investigating the depopulation problem.[71] In 1931 Naudeau's study was reprinted as a best-selling book entitled *La France se regarde: le problème de la natalité*.[72]

Like the pronatalist politicians examined previously, Naudeau held that despite the potential dangers of immigration, it was a necessary first step in combating depopulation. Following the demographic arguments of Bertillon, Leroy-Beaulieu, and Dumont closely, he concurred that French depopulation was a reflection of the relationship between fertility and civilization.[73] He agreed that the pernicious "individualism" of the French had produced a population more interested in pursuing pleasure than fulfilling its collective duties to the nation. French women in particular were guilty of this charge, as Naudeau claimed that the female gender was most easily seduced by the desire for luxury and material comfort.[74] Even before the First World War, it was widely accepted by Republicans, Catholics, and Socialists alike that French women, in their quest for economic independence and sexual freedom, had abandoned the obligations of motherhood and care of the domestic sphere.[75] By the interwar years the charge that "female individualism" engendered depopulation and other social ills had become a ubiquitous critique of the perceived gender order.[76]

Naudeau began his study with the uncompromising stance that France had always been, and must remain, a white nation. Despite the magnitude of French demographic decline, he explained, the "integrity of the white race" was a value that must be upheld. Naudeau disdainfully employed assimilationist metaphors which invoked the unity of metropolitan France and its colonial empire, dismissing those who envisioned a "greater France" composed of "one hundred million Frenchmen."[77] In his view the presence of colonial migrants in the metropole destabilized imperial power relations, compromised the safety of French overseas possessions, and promoted hazardous forms of racial mixing: "I affirm that we will not sustain our place in the world if we do not remain what we have always been: a white nation. Our colonial empire is guaranteed by the strength of the metropole."[78]

Naudeau therefore called for encouraging the transition populations of Europe to immigrate. At the end of his long tour of the French departments, he concluded without hesitation that the best candidates for assimilation were the Italians, whom he described as diligent, fertile, and simple people who flourished in the countryside and maintained a strong commitment to family life. Because the Italians had not yet fallen victim to the potential ills of modernity, Naudeau portrayed their immigrant communities as idyllic havens brimming with the most wholesome of pre-industrial values. In contrast, the French family, which had once possessed the same admirable traits, was currently falling into a state of degeneration. When describing his visit to the Lot-et-Garonne, Naudeau praised the Italians as passionately as he excoriated the French. He began his cautionary tale by explaining that throughout this department, there were numerous impoverished Italian families arriving with no money but many children. While sons were hired out as agricultural laborers and daughters worked as maids in neighboring villages, the family labored as a unit to cultivate its land. Because all members of the Italian family were "hardworking, frugal, and humble in their desires," the plot they had farmed together was paid for in the course of a few years. Meanwhile, the former French proprietor of the land, whom Naudeau described as an "old, solitary, hunched-up Malthusian," had retired to the city, where he "sadly vegetated" while paying an enormous rent. Naudeau concluded: "The simple power of fecundity and labor produced the buying power sufficient for [the Frenchman] to be evicted and effaced. Having all his life sought out too many material pleasures, too many egotistical satisfactions, this Frenchman, at the end of his life, is nothing but a lugubrious island, a *déraciné*, and . . . a vanquished man."[79]

Naudeau's trenchant observations illustrate how strongly he believed that civilization was paradoxical: while ushering in progress, it had also undermined paternal authority, work discipline, and a sense of civic duty. Because the French placed material comfort and a higher standard of living before the good of the national community, the birthrate was rapidly declining, the countryside had been left fallow, and society was becoming dangerously atomized. Although Naudeau echoed the familiar conviction that the state of "primitive life" conformed best to high fertility rates, he too called for a reconciliation of fecundity and civilization. Because all societies would eventually undergo the shift to modernity, the state must correct the social ills that this transition had engendered: "When, through the inevitable workings of civilization, [the state of primitive life] is dispelled, it is necessary to substitute powerful social and sanitary organizations, as we must not leave uprooted proletarians to fend for themselves. In short, civilization must remedy the ills that it causes."[80] Thus like other pronatalists, Naudeau called for government-sponsored social reform to counteract the dangers of too much civilization.

Meanwhile, because the Italians lived "close to nature" and subordinated all else to their desire to acquire property to cultivate, they reminded Naudeau of a France that had disappeared several decades ago. He repeatedly called for the French to imitate the Italians' diligence, their sobriety, and the simplicity of their lives. Naudeau was also forced to look abroad for examples of feminine virtue. He contrasted the probity of Italian women with the selfish and pleasure-seeking "New Woman" in France, who refused to procreate for the nation. Reflecting on the high fertility rates of Italian families, he asked: "Is it not because [Italian women], known for the simplicity of their attire . . . and paying little mind to fashion, content themselves with being mothers, as did our French women, one-hundred years ago."[81]

Naudeau saw in the Italians those rooted, conservative, family-oriented values that the French once possessed. However, he understood all too well that if the French had something to learn from the Italians, this greatly complicated the assimilation process. If the pronatalist crusade was primarily about changing the mores and values of the degenerate French, it follows that little was to be gained in making the Italians resemble the French too closely. His greatest fear was one that was echoed in a number of pronatalist circles: what if the Italians, as they assimilated, adopted the neo-Malthusian practices so dear to the French? How could social critics argue for the need to turn immigrants into French men and women if at the same time they were insisting that French mores had to change? Could the fecundity of less "civilized" people be harnessed without their constituting dangerous, unassimilated pockets of foreigners in the midst of French territory? It was possible, Naudeau hypothesized, that first-generation Italians would remain prolific because they brought with them a strong work ethic, a commitment to family life, a disdain for luxuries, and a disposition that allowed them to be content with little. However, the need to assimilate the Italians, while simultaneously benefiting from their particular national character, led him to fear the worst: "Will they remain fecund once they have assimilated our mores? Will the second and third generation be even more prolific, or will they conform to the milieu that surrounds them? If we are to assimilate them, is that not because we want to make them resemble us?"[82]

Several demographic investigations evaluating the fertility of marriages with one or two spouses of foreign origin confirmed Naudeau's worst fears. According to the CSN, while the birthrates of immigrant households were higher than those of the French, they were highest, by a considerable margin, in marriages between foreigners rather than those with one French partner. Moreover, Boverat claimed that a number of statistical studies demonstrated the ease with which foreign women adopted the insidious French habit of limiting births. His colleague M. Beth corroborated this point, maintaining that in one Polish household, after six years of marriage and the birth of only one child, the wife had already undergone six abortions.[83] These findings were also confirmed by a study of foreigners in the departments proposed by the Commissions Départementales de la Natalité. It found that fertility rates for mixed marriages were substantially lower than for immigrant couples, especially when the wife was French. Franco-Italian households had hardly more children than French ones, and beginning with the second generation, the birthrates of foreigners were almost as feeble as those of their French neighbors.[84] Auguste Isaac had reported the same pattern to the Congrès National de la Natalité nearly a decade earlier: "By the second generation, foreign elements from prolific countries frequently assume the habit of voluntary sterility which prevails [in France]."[85]

More evidence was provided by the demographer Georges Mauco's monumental study of immigration to France, the authoritative work on foreign labor in this period, combining fieldwork, statistical analysis, and geography.[86] Mauco also found that the number of children in foreign households was substantially higher than those of the native-born French (figures 3 and 4). For example, while the average French family had only 1.9 children per household, Spanish immigrants topped the list with 2.6, followed by the Poles with 2.5 and the Italians with 2.3. Nevertheless, Mauco claimed that because neo-Malthusian ideas regarding contraception spread rapidly among immigrants, high fertility rates would begin to drop as the length of the immigrants' stay in France increased. While the newly arrived retained the high birthrates of their native lands, they rapidly yielded to French influence, consciously limiting births and striving for small families. Then, in a language common to the most sensationalist of pronatalist texts, Mauco

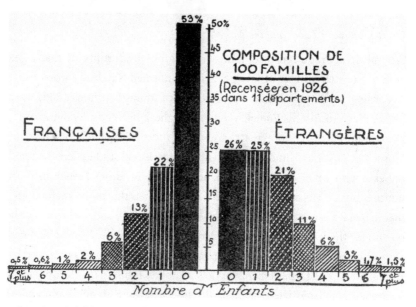

3. "Number of Children in French and Foreign Households, According to the 1926 Census." In Georges Mauco, *Les étrangers en France: étude géographique sur leur rôle dans l'activité économique* (Paris: Armand Colin, 1932).

claimed that among some immigrant groups, women had abortions in a "casual manner that verged on recklessness," while the Poles and Spaniards, the "most uncultivated and simple" of all, even resorted to infanticide.[87]

The notion that mixed households were less fertile than those composed of two foreign spouses was a completely logical corollary of Republican assimilationist theory, according to which immigrants could be rendered culturally similar to the French by the power of the soil, the French language and school system, and French women. All participants in the immigration debate conceded that the best way to assimilate male foreigners was through marriage to French women, who would introduce to their husbands and children the cultural competencies of Frenchness and thereby facilitate their integration. We will return to this theme in chapters 3 and 4, which examine how domestic life and native women were thought to influence a racialized national identity. This intimate labor was an extension of the gendered duties of social citizenship dating from the Revolutionary era, according to which French women, as "guardians of tradition," executed their civic role within the confines of domestic space.[88]

It was "common knowledge," the popular newspaper *L'Amitié Française*

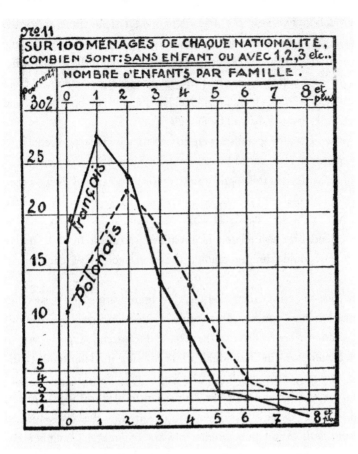

4. "For One-Hundred French and One-Hundred Polish Households, the Number of Children per Family." In Georges Mauco, *Les étrangers en France: étude géographique sur leur rôle dans l'activité économique* (Paris: Armand Colin, 1932).

reported, that foreign men who married French women assimilated very quickly. This tendency was attributed to the "dominant influence of women in the domestic life of the household," a trait that the article claimed was especially pronounced in France.[89] This theme was echoed by Maurice Ajam in the newspaper *La Dépêche*: "An Italian who establishes a household in France is already halfway conquered . . . because French women have always been the best means to assimilate foreigners."[90] Mauco went so far as to argue that intermarriage was more effective than naturalization in integrating foreigners.[91] And even Ludovic Naudeau, whose distaste for the individualism of French women was critical to his critique of French society, recognized their assimilative powers: "The woman is the great protector of the native language, mores, traditions, and even of national prejudices. It is the woman who transmits them to future generations. And it is the woman who, in a few years, assimilates to her race the heterogeneous elements. A child born in France of a French woman will feel French, nothing but French, and besides, according to law, he will be French."[92]

As a consequence, pronatalists were forced to acknowledge the incompatibility of their dual image of French women as corrupters and saviors of the nation. According to this logic, if native-born women had the power to assimilate foreign men, they could also corrupt them with neo-Malthusian practices. And if the soil, capitalist work discipline, and secondary education were to render the second generation indistinguishable from the native population, how could immigrant families be models for their French neighbors?

For this reason, pronatalists insisted that immigration could serve as nothing more than a "temporary palliative" to the demographic crisis.[93] If the French nation were to survive, the state had to extend its protection to the family rather than the individual, while revising its definition of citizenship to encourage reproduction.[94] This vision culminated in government sponsorship of pronatalist reforms by decree-law in 1938 and 1939, and was enshrined in the Code de la Famille of 1939 drafted by the newly formed Haut Comité de la Population. Predictably, the committee's members included Boverat; the demographer, deputy, and Alliance member Adolphe Landry; and Georges Pernot, president of the Fédération des Associations de Familles Nombreuses de France. The Family Code extended the existing family allowance system, which although funded by private initiatives like the *caisses de compensation* (welfare funds), had been regulated by the state since 1932. It also established a "birth premium" to be paid upon the arrival of a first-born child within the first two years of marriage, the mandatory teaching of demography in schools, and intensified repressive measures to combat abortion. The family allowance system mandated equal assistance to households regardless of their social class, favoring those with three or more children. Rather than redistribute income to poorer families, the allowances privileged "fecund" French citizens over those who remained childless.

Thus pronatalism, immigration, and assimilation were inseparable components of the early twentieth century's demographic calculus, with the integration of appropriate foreigners serving as part of a broader project to remake the French family and hence the nation. Meanwhile, because countless French men and women had ignored their civic obligation to procreate, assimilable foreigners could gain access to the citizenry by displaying qualities that pronatalists believed had once been intrinsically French: a love for the countryside, a commitment to family, and a collectivist vision of civic life.

The position of the CSN on foreign fathers of large families provides an important example of the generosity that pronatalists lavished upon white European migrants with high fertility rates. The CSN — an official commission within the Ministry of Hygiene, Social Assistance, and Prevention — met regularly to discuss problems related to depopulation, prenatal and infant care, and the protection of children and mothers. Its thirty members, who included leaders of the Alliance and pro-family groups, along with the indefatigable Boverat as its vice-president, were charged with drafting bills, decrees, and circulars on issues pertaining to the well-being of the French family.[95] Because the government had assigned to the CSN the task of researching methods to combat depopulation, the immigrant question was one of several topics under consideration at its meetings. Most importantly, the organization enthusiastically recommended the naturalization of "assimilable" and prolific foreigners. While pronatalists had long advocated that large French families be rewarded with family suffrage, monetary allocations, a reduction in military service, and the like, their willingness to extend similar privileges to foreign families reveals their support of white European immigration.

In its governmental reports, the CSN called for naturalizing members of the "assimilable races": primarily Latins and to a lesser degree Slavs. The CSN identified Italians and Spaniards as elements of first choice, although it also supported the recruitment of Portuguese and Swiss workers in smaller numbers.[96] It also advised that immigrant populations be selected according to their fertility, for contributing to the French birthrate was one of several "services" that immigrants could offer to the French nation. Boverat wrote: "Of course, [a foreigner's] professional skills must, in most cases, be taken into consideration. But in our opinion, the ability to found on our soil a line of descendants able to become French must prevail over all other considerations."[97]

At the onset of the Depression, the CSN unexpectedly defended the right of select immigrants to continue working in France, dismissing as a "simplistic solution" the widespread call to halt all immigration and send foreigners back to their native countries. While the CSN agreed that French workers should be shielded from unemployment as much as possible, its members insisted that it was a "vital necessity" to retain immigrants who had given birth to "assimilable children" on French soil, as well as those who were likely to do so in the future. But according to Boverat, the nation's efforts must not end there. Because the dangers of depopulation far outweighed those stemming from an economic depression, for the foreseeable future France must continue to attract an assimilable labor force, rather than close its doors to immigration: "A nation does not die from an unemployment crisis, even one that lasts twelve or eighteen months. However, if a nation resigns itself to a feeble birthrate, it is fatally condemned to disappear."[98]

If immigrants were to be expelled from France, the CSN claimed that those who were unmarried, married but childless, or over the age of forty should be the first to leave. In contrast, every effort should be made to retain immigrants who had brought large families with them to France, or who had given birth to several children since their arrival. Foreign fathers of large families were to be protected from unemployment to avoid their repatriating, along with their children, whom the CSN viewed as crucial elements in its strategy for repopulation. Specifically, Boverat called for accommodating the "young people of the prolific races": the Italians, Spaniards, and Poles. He maintained that men from these nations, whether their wives were French or of their own nationality, had the greatest potential for assimilation. Boverat even argued that instead of repatriating immigrants to alleviate unemployment, the circumstances of the Depression should be exploited to French advantage: "Let us make use of the unemployment problem in other countries to attract to France foreigners who are easily assimilable, and who already have young children . . . In order to make room for them, do not hesitate to get rid of those without children. Right now we have an unusual opportunity to select our immigrants. In a few years, this moment will have passed, as the majority of European countries will be too conscious of the value of human capital to allow us to take their young children from them."[99]

The CSN also urged individual industrialists and employers to refrain from firing foreign fathers of large families, and called upon the government, through the Ministries of Labor and Agriculture, to take an active interest in the problem. Because reproduction was construed as a civic duty worthy of compensation from the state, the CSN asked that work inspectors representing the Ministry of Labor compel employers to retain both French fathers and foreign fathers with children living in France. Finally, the CSN demanded that foreign men heading large families should be treated "as Frenchmen" for as long as their applications for naturalization were pending, and more generally, that the Ministries of Labor and Agriculture should refrain from adopting any measures with regard to foreigners that might have a deleterious effect on the French birthrate.[100] Keep in mind that the naturalization of foreign fathers was of critical importance before the passage in 1927 of the Law on French Nationality, a subject to which we will return in chapter 5. Before that time, French women who married foreigners automatically received their husband's nationality, as did any children born of that union. For this reason, pronatalist organizations were well aware of the importance of naturalizing foreign men and thereby linking their destinies to that of the French nation.[101]

Conclusions: Parenting, Politics, and Procreative Obligations to the Republic

According to pronatalist discourse, large families were the cornerstone of an economically productive and internationally recognized nation-state. But as we have seen, both race and gender were critical sites of contestation in the pronatalist effort to reinvent the French family and redefine the practice of citizenship. Pronatalists explicitly defined France as a white nation whose future depended on the immigration and assimilation of European foreigners alone. Insofar as members of this nationalist movement promoted hybridity and race mixture, it was to be achieved through unions with fellow whites, such as Italians, Spaniards, and Poles. That is, in accordance with the universalist and contractarian strain of Republicanism's antinomous logic, white Europeans who were willing to assume the French cultural patrimony were granted access to the citizen body. However, that same logic dictated that immigrants of color, whose biocultural difference both signaled and sanctioned their incapacity for citizenship, were to be excluded from the national community.[102] Rather than embrace a radical vision of hybridity in which all immigrants, regardless of race, could contribute their labor power and reproductive potential to the nation, pronatalist critics reinforced the ontological divide between metropole and colony, in contradistinction to assimilationist rhetoric which envisioned the oneness of France and its colonies.

In this process, pronatalist discourse made explicit reference to the bodies of French citizens, colonial subjects, and European immigrants, bodies which were profoundly marked by gender as well as race. In particular, pronatalism highlighted the sexual and reproductive practices of the female body and the procreative obligations of the conjugal couple, thus allowing very public debates on demography, depopulation, and national health to permeate the intimacy of domestic space. These debates blurred the boundaries of private and public, family and nation, and recreational and procreative sex, a confusion which was also reflected in the nation's conflicting imperatives of production and reproduction. According to this vexed logic, France required productive migrant labor to sustain economic vitality, but at the same time that labor had to be racially and culturally assimilable so as to reproduce future generations of citizens. As a consequence, the pronatalist lobby identified the Italians, Spaniards, and Poles as prime candidates for immigration, assimilation, and citizenship. In contrast, it cast colonial migrants as an unskilled and temporary workforce whose assimilation was neither possible nor desirable.

The language in which pronatalist critics discussed degeneration and national renewal would be echoed in the political and social hygienic discourse of the Vichy state, as the impulse to regulate reproduction, marriage, and domestic life was already present in the populationist politics of the Third Republic.[103] Under Pétain, prominent pronatalists like Fernand Boverat, Paul Haury, Louis Duval-Arnould, and Georges Mauco continued their efforts to revive the traditional family, along with its high birthrates, cultural conservatism, and sharply differentiated gender roles. With the Occupation serving as further evidence of the wounded virility of French men, the selfishness of French women, and the perils of depopulation, the Vichy state would both amplify and more formally institutionalize the pronatalist familialism of the interwar years.

Thus under the Republic, and not after its demise, the politicizing of intimate space began.[104] Vichy's conservative obsession with embodiment—

whether as race, gender, family, or reproduction — had previously been articulated in the Republican debate on depopulation and national regeneration. As we have seen, the immigrant question had been explicitly racialized, reproduction equated with civic responsibility, and women associated with the duties of patriotic motherhood and the intimate labor of the domestic sphere. Thus in contrast to claims that the Vichy state was a radical departure from the Third Republic, I emphasize the continuities between these political forms: both were racial regimes based on gender complementarity, and both demanded the rationalization of production and reproduction in accordance with national-familial values.

In the following chapters I continue to explore how the Republic's immigration policy shaped and was shaped by an embodied politics which required gendered and racialized subjects. We have seen that pronatalist discourse identified assimilability and productivity as the most salient factors in determining which foreigners should settle permanently in France. I turn now to the discipline of work science, which addressed similar questions with reference to immigrant labor from Europe, the colonies, and China.

Chapter Two

LABOR POWER AND
THE RACIAL ECONOMY

I n an article in the *Revue politique et parlementaire* in 1924, Paul Guériot contrasted the two primary positions of the debate on labor and immigration to France. The first, which called for unrestricted migration, viewed workers as an abstract form of "human capital," suggesting a certain interchangeability among them, or the possibility of a uniform potential inherent in all laboring bodies. Since the generic term "human capital" implied that any healthy body could do a given job, in theory a virtually endless supply of foreigners could be mobilized in response to the demands of the labor market. For a nation like France, plagued by depopulation and an especially acute labor shortage, it could easily be argued that a colorblind, liberal immigration policy was the most logical course of action. However, critics of the liberal economic position warned of the potential consequences of reducing the foreigner to an "element of brute strength." They explained that this logic was only valid if "humanity could be likened to livestock, and thus each head would represent what you call capital, that is meat, leather, and labor."[1] In their view, what distinguished men and women from animals was not simply their capacity to engage in purposive labor but also the mark of culture, which could not be understood as universal: "In man there is a moral element composed of his traditions and beliefs, his race, and his attachment to his country. The foreigner brings us a mentality different from our own, which cannot be fused with ours."[2]

Guériot's intervention returns us once again to the intertwined fates of universalism and particularism in the French immigration debate, as it powerfully demonstrates the clash of a universalist social theory and a racialized labor force. Of course the abstract, universal capacity to labor that he describes was never given much credence in France, or anywhere else for that matter. Skill, productivity, and even brute strength have always been ideologically inflected categories, subject to the perceived influences of gender, race, and nation. As a consequence, a mythology of suitable work for differentiated bodies prevailed in both the artisanal and the industrial eras.[3] Nevertheless, in the early twentieth century the metaphor of human capital was endowed with enormous rhetorical value. Protectionists, organized labor, and eventually even many industrialists invoked it to express their fear of mass immigration unaccompanied by a coherent immigration policy. In their view, only those in favor of an untrammeled, radical economic liberalism could argue that any foreigner was capable of performing any task in the French national economy, and to take this position was to show little respect for the integrity of national and racial boundaries.[4] At stake was both the livelihood of French workers, facing competition from foreigners, and the viability of a racialized national identity, now threatened by "undesirable" immigrant populations. In the context of depopulation, the growing internationalism of the labor market, and the productivist impulses of large-scale industry, we will see that a variety of social critics refuted this abstract form of human capital by situating it within a racial hierarchy.

As demonstrated in chapter 1, in pronatalist accounts of immigration both the productive and reproductive value of foreigners had bearing on their assimilability. Pronatalists ranked the fecundity of various foreign populations, advocating the recruitment and eventual integration of prolific whites like the Italians, Spaniards, and Poles. However, while pronatalists insisted that labor productivity was a critical part of an immigrant's desirability, their arguments necessarily focused on the issue of high birthrates and the foreigner's potential to found a family. Pronatalist critics had far less to say about which workers were most productive. Instead, this question was part of the domain of *science du travail*, or work science. This chapter therefore moves from the specialized knowledge form of demography to this pre-Taylorist discourse on rationalization. I examine in detail the debate on mechanization, deskilling, and optimum efficiency in the context of mass immigration to France. Most importantly, I show how industrialists and work scientists, in their quest for maximum productivity, racialized the various components of an increasingly fragmented labor process.

Rationalized methods of work discipline were first implemented in France toward the end of the nineteenth century. Before that time, in both the popular imagination and written accounts of the foreign workforce in France, particular kinds of skilled labor were associated with the European migrants most likely to practice those trades in France. However, with the introduction of work science and even Taylorist methods in the early twentieth century, a number of ostensibly scientific inquiries drew upon productivity theory to demonstrate the uneven performance at labor of various immigrant groups. This chapter therefore examines the efficiency studies conducted by employer cartels, work scientists, and envoys of the French government's Labor Ministry to demonstrate how an increasingly diverse workforce was evaluated and hierarchized in the context of mass international migrations. I begin with a number of queries about abstract universalist categories and their relationship to the nation-state and the global economy, and then consider how racialized workers were constructed and deployed in these universalist accounts of the laboring body—for example, the productivity studies of the work scientist Jules Amar, as well as studies performed in the factories of the First World War. I conclude with some thoughts about the relationship between abstract human capital and the proliferation of embodied workers.

Capitalist Universality: Undifferentiated Bodies, Equal Accumulative Potential

Just as liberal democratic theory posited an abstract individual with the capacity to contract into the French national body, liberal political economy argued that both the economy and the laboring body could be extracted from other social spheres and institutions. Both doctrines took abstract individualism as their starting point, and the contemporaneous existence of these two universalist doctrines—the first of potential citizenship, and the second of potential labor—raises a number of important questions about the relationship between the nation-state and a global economy. For example, was the simultaneous development of universalist understandings of labor and citizenship serendipitous, or were these two entities mutually constitutive? What is the significance of the concurrent development of a bounded nation-state and a transnational capitalist economy?[5] How does the immigrant's fitness for citizenship relate to his or her role in the national economy, and conversely, is fitness for citizenship a necessary precondition for permanent employment in France? To answer these queries we must first outline the relationship between liberal economics and mass international migrations.

In France as in other modern industrialized states, a liberal immigration policy dominated between 1840 and 1914, corresponding with the dominant economic system of laissez-faire capitalism.[6] Migrations were virtually unregulated by the state, and foreigners were generally recruited at the initiative of private industry. The liberal stance on immigration was clearly articulated by the distinguished economist Émile Levasseur of the École Libre des Sciences Politiques in two articles in 1884 in the laissez-faire journal *L'économiste français*. Levasseur described a world in which workers and goods circulated freely, unencumbered by national barriers and to the benefit of all people: "As free and unfettered commercial intercourse between two countries is advantageous to both, for by the exchange of commodities the producer and consumer are both benefited, so also must the unrestricted circulation of the human race be advantageous to all countries concerned."[7]

According to Levasseur, the benefits of mass migration were "conferred upon the human race at large," and thus it was not possible to calibrate the value of immigration from the standpoint of the individual foreign worker.[8] This is because the liberal doctrine of economic productivism was theorized in global terms: according to its proponents, it was in the interest of all humankind to fully develop the world's productive resources. Like other liberal economists, Levasseur argued that unrestricted migrations would facilitate this goal by providing labor power wherever it was needed, in any part of the world. But the doctrine of economic productivism had colonial referents as well, for it established that Europeans had the right to compel people of color to develop the natural capital of their lands, ostensibly for the benefit of all people.[9]

In contrast, opponents of laissez-faire economics argued that the strict regulation of migrants, along with a protectionist economy, would alleviate competition for jobs and goods within the borders of the French nation-state.[10] In their view the priorities of the national economy and its workforce overrode the cosmopolitan pretensions of economic liberalism. This was by no means the dominant position on international labor migrations in the period preceding the First World War. At this time, Richard Kuisel has argued, the doctrine of *étatisme*—premised on a centralized state-controlled economy—had "few advocates and no theorists."[11] Owing to both the weakness of organized labor in France and the job openings created by depopulation, economists and labor experts were less inclined to espouse étatisme's more parochial perspective. Instead, depopulation prompted them to cautiously advocate a liberal migration policy. Much like pronatalist demography, which juxtaposed industrialized and underpopulated nations with prolific but unmodernized states, a liberal vision of immigration presumed that shortages in one nation would be offset by surpluses in another. In this mutually dependent world-system, human and natural capital was to move osmotically to regions of lesser concentration.

The reign of economic liberalism ended with the outbreak of the First World War, when the exigencies of the wartime economy required implementing full-scale regulation. Government ministries enlisted the help of employer cartels to recruit and distribute foreign labor from Europe and overseas, resulting in the importation of approximately 662,000 immigrant workers, about half from the French colonies and China.[12] Official sources counted 78,566 Algerians, 48,995 Indochinese, 36,941 Chinese, 35,506 Moroccans, 18,249 Tunisians, and 4,546 Madagascans. As for the approximately 330,000 European workers who came to France during the war, the majority were Spaniards, along with some Portuguese, Italians, and Greeks.[13] The substantial influx of foreign workers in this period generated a myriad of pseudoscientific inquiries into the productivity and particular talents of a racialized labor force.[14] The conclusions reached by these studies had resonance beyond the circumstances of the wartime economy: we will see that after the peace, they were employed to argue for the necessity of *white* immigration to France.

In the interwar years the continued demand for foreign labor sustained the liberal paradigm until at least the early 1930s. Social scientists, representatives of government ministries, and labor experts affiliated with the League of Nations upheld the view that demographic decline must be considered in an international context, with surplus populations in some countries compensating for depopulation in others. This reading of international population politics was in keeping with the productivist imperative of classical liberalism, which assumed that a more equitable distribution of resources across the globe would allow all people to lead richer and more productive

lives. Mario Gianturco, spokesman for the International Labor Organization (ILO) of the League of Nations, explained that while some nations
were blessed with an abundance of capital and raw materials, others were
endowed with a robust population, a form of "human capital," which was
equally valuable.[15]

In his influential study of foreign labor in France, the geographer Georges
Mauco also highlighted the interdependent nature of the global and national
economies. As explained in chapter 1, Mauco relied heavily on the work of
pronatalist demographers like Arsène Dumont, and thus characterized modern civilization by depopulation, upward social mobility, and a dependence
on foreign immigration. Employing Dumont's notion of "social capillarity,"
Mauco explained that France needed immigrant labor in unskilled or insalu-
brious jobs which native-born workers would no longer accept. As a result,
Mauco was unwavering in his belief that only by importing foreign workers
could France sustain its economic vitality.[16]

By gauging the value of human labor in an international framework,
critics like Mauco and Gianturco included both the empire and less developed European nations in the transnational circulation of bodies, goods,
and capital. Because production required raw materials and human labor to
create surplus, in depopulated nations the labor of male citizens would have
to be supplemented with that of foreigners and, in some cases, native-born
women. Mauco insisted that to promote the economic prosperity of all countries, the particularity of national interests had to be transcended, for "all
national labor is an international collaboration," of which the French nation
was only a part. In the interests of regulating and rationalizing production,
Mauco argued, international migrations must be coordinated by supranational organizations like the ILO.[17]

Professor William Oualid's analysis of global migrations most clearly explained the paradoxes underlying the French understanding of immigrant
labor, which simultaneously championed the individual's right to migrate
and the nation's need to protect its citizenry from "inassimilable" elements.
A former attaché of the Labor Ministry and director of the Foreign Labor
Service during the war, Oualid was an expert on the foreign labor force and
its productivity, distribution, and integration. In an article entitled "Le droit
migratoire" (1930), Oualid upheld the liberal position by lamenting that in
industrialized nations like the United States, the laissez-faire policies of the

nineteenth century were gradually being replaced by quotas and other restrictions. According to Oualid, this had the effect of sacrificing the rights of the vast majority of people for the benefit of the few: "If the great human community has as its duty the best possible exploitation of the universe, is it legitimate that nations overflowing with capital, and endowed with the products of the soil and substratum, assume the right to monopolize their exploitation, and forbid access to populations in excess? Similarly, do they have the human right to close their market of supplies to nations lacking in foodstuffs and materials?"[18] Oualid's critique of the restrictive immigration policies of the United States and other "Anglo-Saxon" nations reflects his endorsement of the liberal principles of productivism, unrestricted circulation of human and natural capital, and individual rights, which as we can determine from the title of his article includes the right to migrate. To reconcile the fates of industrialized nations and those endowed with surplus population, workers must be free to exercise their right to migrate within an interdependent world economy. In his view, the tenacious particularisms of national identity and nationalist sentiment undermined these universalist objectives.[19]

Oualid claimed that in France (and also in Belgium) the right to migrate was most fully respected, thus allowing for the "full blossoming of the human personality" and "free circulation . . . devoid of egoism and particularism, guided by the general interests of humanity alone."[20] Lacking quotas and other restrictions, the French example balanced the interests of individual nations, the international economy, and human beings endowed with the right to migrate. Nevertheless, Oualid's sometimes liberal and universalist vision of global migrations did place limits on which foreigners should be permitted entry, for he did not wish to see receiver nations like France become outlets for "undesirables." Here the particularisms embedded in Oualid's understanding of French culture, French nationality, and the French citizen become apparent. While Oualid stated that it was unacceptable to reject foreigners on the basis of nationality, race, and religion, as the United States did, he affirmed that receiver nations of immigrants retained the right to enact measures protecting their "physical integrity, economic equilibrium, moral unity, and intellectual and social standard," all qualities that he termed "objective."[21] Oualid was seemingly unaware of the racialized character of the categories he had enumerated, and he did not explain how these standards could be met without resorting to discrimination of some sort. Thus Oualid respected the worker's right to migrate and opposed quotas along American lines as unduly discriminatory. But at the same time, he conceded that not all difference was advantageous to the French nation, which must protect its citizenry and patrimony from the inassimilable.

European Work Science: Jules Amar
Racializes Industrial Output

Before the onset of mass immigration in the latter part of the nineteenth century, foreign workers in France were predominantly male artisans and skilled workers from Spain, the Netherlands, and the German and Italian states. Early-twentieth-century studies of the preindustrial mode of production characterized and differentiated foreign populations with reference to the property of skill. According to these accounts, foreign labor tended to cluster in particular sectors of the economy: for example, the court artisans of the Old Regime aristocracy consisted of Italian and Spanish glassmakers, precious metal workers, silk weavers, and furniture makers. Meanwhile the Dutch predominated in shipbuilding, naval construction, bridge building, and engineering, as did the Germans in the furniture trade and printing, and in metallurgy as miners, casters, blacksmiths, silversmiths, and goldsmiths.[22]

According to one study of the labor process, the foreigner possessed a "special aptitude" for, or a "natural disposition" toward, the type of skilled labor performed.[23] Essentialized inclinations to engage in one kind of work were explained through recourse to a sort of geographic determinism, tempered with a modest respect for the social structures of a given people. Thus the soil, climate, diet, education, and political institutions combined to create a laboring body with a naturalized capacity for a specific trade.[24] However, we will see that as the mode of production changed to accommodate the needs of modern industry, the facility with which unskilled or semiskilled workers performed fragmented tasks became the most salient category of analysis. By the second half of the nineteenth century, the growth of heavy industry and the factory system created new jobs while rendering others obsolete. French workers vacated positions they now deemed undesirable, and immigrants assumed those abandoned posts. The mining, processing, handling, and transportation industries in particular welcomed the arrival of new immigrants.[25]

By the middle of the nineteenth century workers from Italy, Belgium, Spain, Switzerland, and Germany could be found in unskilled and semiskilled labor, as well as the artisanal trades.[26] Those from less developed European nations generally assumed the most onerous unskilled jobs. The Italians dominated the building trades, working as painters, glaziers, plasterers, excavators, masons, and well diggers; they also contributed substantially to the public works projects of this period, building railroads, canals, and tunnels. The Spanish generally followed the same trajectory as the Italians, while the Belgians, who hailed from a more industrialized state, were less prevalent in heavy industry; they were concentrated instead in metals and textiles, especially the spinning, weaving, and hosiery trades. The Germans also rejected heavy or unskilled labor in favor of jobs in commerce, metalworking, and textiles. Similarly, the Swiss worked in the commercial professions and the hotel industry, and as engravers, watchmakers, and woodworkers.[27]

As the pace of rationalization accelerated in response to the needs of the wartime economy and the dictates of pre-Taylorist work science, immigrants to France were overwhelmingly male factory workers, rather than skilled artisans. In the words of Mauco, an "immigration of quantity" had replaced an "immigration of quality."[28] As a consequence, studies of foreign labor no longer focused on the property of skill and made reference instead to the discrete gestures of a fragmented labor process. Particularly important examples include the productivity studies of Jules Amar, as well as others carried out in various industries and factories over the course of the First World War. We will see that as the language of labor was altered by rationalization, work scientists and industrialists increasingly sought to calculate optimum output for racialized bodies.

Before the gradual introduction of Taylorism in the late 1920s, the dominant productivist paradigm in France derived from the pan-European school of work science, which generated numerous studies in the interest of promoting maximum productivity.[29] While both work science and Taylorism were devoted to rendering workers more efficient, work science focused on human energy and fatigue while Taylorism emphasized time and profit.[30] Jules Amar, one of the most important theoreticians of work science, was also the author of a wide range of social-hygiene interventions on topics like alcoholism, tuberculosis, prosthetics, and eventually Taylorism as well. Amar's work is a prime example of the rationalist impulse to reduce the labor process to its most infinitesimal gestures in order to promote industrial productivity. In so doing, his analysis also revealed how the very building blocks of labor reflected the worker's essential and racialized nature.

Amar began his career in the laboratory of the physiologist Georges Weiss at the Paris Faculty of Medicine. In 1913 he was chosen to head the Laboratoire de Recherches sur le Travail Professionel, attached to the Conservatoire National des Arts et Métiers. His first significant contribution to the debate on how ontological difference influenced levels of energy, fatigue, and productivity was a pre-war study commissioned by the French Ministry of War, which evaluated the capacity of North Africans for industrial labor in order to determine their fitness for conscription.[31] Amar subsequently devoted a large portion of his book *L'organisation physiologique du travail* (1917) to observations of French, Italian, Annamite, and Kabyle workers, insisting that race, in addition to climate in the country of origin, had a profound influence on productivity.[32]

Amar therefore sought to compare, contrast, and ultimately hierarchize labor performed by immigrants from the colonies with that of white Europeans. "Annamites" referred to the inhabitants of the Annam province of Indochina, while the "Kabyles," as noted in chapter 1, were non-Arab North African Berbers. Amar included Italian and native-born French workers in his comparative study. Both his method and his findings contradict Anson Rabinbach's claim that work science viewed the human organism as a "productive machine, stripped of all social and cultural relations."[33] Instead, Amar's experiments were intended to demonstrate that African and Asian bodies could not rival European ones with regard to endurance, the speed of neuromuscular response, and energy expenditure.

The laboring body had never been the neutral, unmarked subject of an allegedly disinterested scientific discourse but rather a racially embodied entity endowed with a variable capacity for work. Amar's estimation of Italian workers is a case in point. In his words, because the Italians belonged to a "race" and "culture" similar to those of the French, they were the most suitable candidates for assimilation. However, the Italian worker's ability to adapt to the specific needs of factory production was less certain. While Amar remained faithful to the idiom of work science, documenting levels of energy, fatigue, and productivity in a distant and disinterested tone, he nevertheless described Italian labor as fundamentally different from its

5. Amar's Racial Taxonomy of North Africa: "Arabe du Sud, Nègre, Kabyle." In Jules Amar, *L'organisation physiologique du travail* (Paris: H. Dunod et E. Pinat, 1917).

French counterpart: "The Italian . . . lacks strength. He works intelligently, but with a certain nonchalance; he does not have the continuity of effort that our modern industries require. He proceeds blow by blow, managing his energy resources much more than the French worker . . . His labor, which is never feverish, continues from early morning to late in the evening. Thus for him, our system of rationalization, *which requires a minimum presence in the workshop and a maximum of production*, would be a difficult application."[34]

From 1907 to 1909 Amar carried out a "scientific study" of the labor power of various North African populations, which he grouped into the explicitly racial categories of "southern Arab," "Negro" (*nègre*), and "Kabyle" (figure 5).[35] To determine which factors ameliorated the productivity of workers, he measured their varying levels of energy and fatigue while they pedaled on an "ergometric monocycle" (figure 6). In modern industry,

6. "Kabyle on an Ergometric Monocycle." In Jules Amar,
L'organisation physiologique du travail (Paris: H. Dunod et
E. Pinat, 1917).

Amar explained, "speed is a precious factor which presupposes a neuromuscular disposition to react without delay."[36] By reducing the work process
to its most rudimentary level—stimulus response—Amar determined that
the Moroccans and Kabyles, who were "more nervous" than other Arabs,
worked at a speedier pace than the indigenous people of Tunisia, whose
listless gestures were nearly impossible to accelerate.[37] Nevertheless, when
brute strength was the decisive factor in the optimum performance of the
task, Amar insisted that the Arab was the best choice: "stronger than both
the Berber and the European, the Arab is well suited to either agricultural
work, or the sort of unskilled labor which requires continuous exercises with
weights of twenty to thirty kilos."[38]

Amar concluded that of all colonial workers, only the Kabyle was appropriate for industrial work, which required rapid movements punctuated with short and frequent stops. His preference for Kabyles over other North African populations is unsurprising, given the prevalence of the "Berber myth" described in chapter 1, which cast the Kabyle as whiter and more assimilable than other immigrants from the Maghreb.[39] Employing the data he amassed from his experiments, Amar assigned precise numerical values to demonstrate that colonial workers possessed different proclivities for factory labor: "In considering all the various aspects of production during the workday, one could estimate that five Kabyles are worth six good Arabs. It is the same for the Moroccans and the Negroes. The Kabyle's endurance appears to be very great, and his productivity is, in effect, the highest. This endurance is evidenced above all in his ability to repeat the same work, several days in a row, without seeming to suffer from it . . . But the Moroccan, and even more so the Negro, can only serve as an unskilled laborer."[40]

Thus Jules Amar, the most important practitioner of the French school of work science, quantified the productivity of European and colonial labor in an explicitly comparative framework. Under the rubric of scientific observation, Amar further rationalized the labor performed by differentiated bodies, whether Italian, Arab, Kabyle, or "Negro." As a result, he provided a racialized assessment of their capacity for labor, according to which French labor was deemed most productive, and some workers were destined only for unskilled jobs. We will see that the First World War intensified the process of quantification which had begun with Amar's experiments, as the mobilization of European, colonial, and French women workers provided work science with ample opportunity to compare a range of laboring bodies.

Fragmenting the Labor Process: Rationalizing Work and the Body

The economic arrangements of the Great War signaled the decline of the liberal order. Shortly after the war's onset, state intervention in the economy began in earnest, though it was only fully realized in the 1950s.[41] The mobilization of male citizens for battle exacerbated the labor shortages of the pre-1914 period, generating further demand for immigrant labor to toil on French farms and in the factories. Mauco reiterated the productivist paradigm when he observed that "with the impossibility of finding adequate labor in France, the government naturally turned to the colonies, and to China, the great reservoir of human material."[42] Between 1914 and 1918 approximately 300,000 workers from Algeria, Indochina, China, Morocco, Tunisia, and Madagascar were brought to France, in addition to 330,000 European workers from Spain, Italy, Portugal, and Greece.[43] We will see that wartime documents produced by government ministries, employer cartels, and various factories constructed a racial order whose primary mode of differentiation was between whiteness and color. These texts repeatedly distinguished the "white workforce" (*main-d'œuvre de l'immigration blanche*) from the "colonial and Chinese workforce" (*main-d'œuvre coloniale et chinoise*).[44] Like pronatalist discourse, wartime experiments evaluating worker productivity hinged on the critical distinction between white immigrants and foreigners of color.

In the context of the enforced rationalization, French employers, work supervisors, and representatives of the Ministries of War, Labor, and Armaments generally agreed that foreign labor was "more or less useful, depending on its origin."[45] The metaphor of hierarchy was so prevalent that wartime documents are replete with comparative charts, lists, and numerical quantifications of productivity. For example, the War Ministry's Colonial Labor Service Organization, the government body responsible for bringing colonial workers to France, observed that "three Kabyles furnish approximately the output of two Europeans."[46] In a similar vein, the employer consortium of the coal mining industry (Comité Central des Houillères de France) sent a survey to its various associations in 1916 to assess their needs for foreign labor. The survey made no effort to begin with a level playing field and assume a socially neutral laboring body. Instead it requested that each company rank foreigners according to its preferences, and with reference to an implicitly hierarchized list provided by the consortium which began with the Belgians, Italians, and Spaniards. Unsurprisingly, the Slavs and the Greeks ranked just behind these three groups, while North Africans and Asians brought up the end.[47]

While the hierarchies constructed by industrialists and emissaries of the Labor Ministry were extraordinarily nuanced, the primary distinction with which they began was between white and nonwhite labor. White workers were described as more productive and better skilled, whether because of superior training or innate ability. But the demographic argument analyzed in chapter 1 was also critical to their reception. Because white European workers were considered more assimilable, they could contribute to the stagnating French population and serve as citizens as well as workers. In 1914 a letter from the Labor Ministry's Foreign Labor Service to a chief of staff in the Ministry of Armaments contained the following observations: "It seems that we will have to make a choice, or at least establish an order of priority, with regard to the different categories of labor power. It would be best to consider colonials as a reserve from which we can draw if needed . . . As often as we have the choice, it would be preferable to direct our efforts toward white labor which, first of all, is of better quality, and second, is much more assimilable. Our colonials who have been introduced into the metropole and other colored men will become a source of difficulty both here and in the colonies, while on the contrary, white labor can help us reconstitute our population."[48]

In their detailed study of foreign labor during the First World War, Lieutenant Colonel Lucien Weil and the economist Bertand Nogaro, an attaché of the Labor Ministry who would later be elected to the Chamber of Deputies, explained that wartime recruiters only sought colonial labor when faced with an inadequate supply of French women, prisoners of war, and European workers.[49] Their account explicitly documents the differential treatment of white and colonial workers in terms of recruitment, housing, discipline, work contracts, salaries, and sociability. As Tyler Stovall has shown, immigrants of color were subject to *encadrement*, or regimentation, from the moment they arrived in France, forced to live and work apart from their French and European counterparts to ensure their productivity and forestall social unrest.[50] The isolation of the colonial workforce was an effort by French authorities to circumvent racial conflict, as well as an indication of their predetermined refusal to assimilate these workers.[51] They unsuccessfully attempted to discourage relationships between men of color and French women,[52] a theme to which we will return.

Lucien Weil concluded that although immigrant workers of color had generally been "helpful" during the war, their productivity varied in accordance with the different aptitudes of each race. For example, in studies which compared the output, work discipline, and stamina of North African workers, the racialized distinction between Arabs and Kabyles carried far more weight than whether they were Algerian, Moroccan, or Tunisian. According to Weil, the "robust," "sober," and "energetic" Kabyles were well suited to factory labor, while members of the "Arab race" were more productive in an agricultural setting. Weil also observed that the Madagascans were good manual laborers who worked earnestly and conscientiously, even if their productivity was substandard in comparison to French workers. Weil's assessment of Indochinese workers centered on their perceived docility and submissiveness, although in the context of capitalist work discipline, these qualities were considered desirable. He applied a logic of internal fragmentation to Indochinese workers, describing immigrants from the Tonkin province as stronger and more robust and those from Conchin and Annam as more skilled. Weil made similar distinctions with regard to the Chinese: although nearly all Chinese workers in France at this time were employed as unskilled laborers, he claimed that the northern Chinese were hardier and more diligent than those from the South, who were known not only for their unruliness but also their "propensity for collective violence."[53]

One labor inspector for the war industries suggested that rather than complain about the quality of the foreign labor force, industrialists should acknowledge that maximum productivity could only result from an understanding of the immigrant's character and particular aptitudes.[54] General Pierre Famin, the War Ministry's director of colonial troops, issued a similar directive with regard to employing Chinese workers. In his view, optimum output ultimately depended on French comprehension of the intrinsic strengths and weaknesses of the "Chinese character." Workers from northern China, whom he described as "adaptable, intelligent, patient, meticulous, dexterous, and hardy," required appropriate housing and foods similar to those from their native land in order to perform adequately in French factories.[55]

Famin also argued that work discipline should be administered in accordance with an immigrant's particular nature. He explained that while Chinese immigrants were "easy to manipulate" they were also exceedingly proud, and thus employers and supervisors must remember to reward workers and not simply focus on their regulation. Although they must immediately correct the Chinese worker's mistakes and discipline him when he idled, they should do so far from his co-workers and in a "firm but measured voice," to avoid humiliation before his peers. Famin pointed out that to the Chinese, outward displays of anger signified a lack of self-control, and thus a visibly irate French supervisor was nothing but a "Barbarian" in the eyes of his employees. As for the quality of the work accomplished by Chinese immigrants in French factories, Famin was grudgingly optimistic: "One must remember that Asians in general, and the Chinese in particular, do not have our sense of precision. Only slowly will we teach them our habits. Through patience, and by giving small rewards to the team leaders and interpreters of the most punctual and disciplined groups, we will obtain from Chinese workers the best productivity, and witness the disappearance of the small errors they customarily commit."[56]

Throughout the wartime documents, the verdict on Indochinese workers was mixed: their "agility" was typically offset by a "lack of physical vigor."[57] One factory report attested that although the Indochinese worker was "without a doubt a liar and a petty thief," he was nevertheless an intelligent laborer, both adaptable and easy to lead. Moreover, employers could compensate for the frailty of Indochinese workers by assigning tasks proportional to their strength.[58] A report issued by the employer consortium of coal mine owners reached similar conclusions: although the Indochinese were agile and adaptable, they were also physically weak. For this reason they should be assigned to tasks which required skill and dexterity, but very little bodily strength.[59] This perceived combination of agility and frailty led observers to characterize Indochinese labor as "feminine" in quality. According to one factory representative in the armaments industry, workers from Indochina were best suited to small mechanical tasks which required care and precision, the work typically given to women. For example, he claimed that Indochinese workers could be entrusted with simple mechanical work like cutting, supervising machine tools, manufacturing medium-weight pieces, and any procedures which required some dexterity.[60]

The disparity in productivity between white and nonwhite workers was further explained by the observation that Africans and Asians, unfamiliar with western notions of industrial time and work discipline, were unfit for factory labor in France. The newspaper *L'Humanité*, then an organ of the Socialist Party, lamented: "What sort of productivity can we hope for from those accustomed to working at their leisure, as they please, with the nonchalance of the primitive races, for whom time does not count, and whose level of physical strength is generally inferior to that of Europeans."[61] However, as we have noted, many employers also described colonial and Chinese labor as docile, adaptable, and easy to lead, thus suggesting their hope that it could be molded to the demands of the factory system.

Despite their bold conclusions, wartime documents are ultimately inconsistent in their observations of foreign labor.[62] For example, one report explicitly acknowledged that the value of different immigrant populations varied from factory to factory: while one employer might praise Spanish workers, another rated them as unsatisfactory, and while some factories preferred Kabyle workers, others claimed that prisoners of war were most productive.[63] A report in 1917 from the armaments industry concluded that "what it costs to transport Portuguese workers to France is not worth what they produce," for only a "feeble output" could be expected from workers whom it described as "indolent" and "lacking in vigor."[64] In contrast, a report in July 1916 praised Portuguese workers for being "hardy" and "very easy to lead," also noting with approval that they assumed dangerous and tedious tasks without uttering a word of complaint.[65]

These discrepancies did not deter contemporaries from concluding that the experience of the Great War had amply demonstrated the futility of continuing to recruit African and Asian labor in peacetime.[66] Postwar studies were also somewhat inconsistent in their evaluation of foreign labor power, but data increasingly distinguished a temporary workforce of color from assimilable European migrants. In 1919 Joseph Lugand explained that neither Taylorism, nor mechanization, nor recourse to female labor could fill the "mortal hole" in the French economy: further refining the division of labor or the means of production could not compensate for a population deficit, and thus importing foreign labor was absolutely essential to the rebuilding of French industry. But Lugand insisted that to obtain workers of high quality, it was necessary to consult wartime data. Following the findings of the Labor Ministry's Foreign Labor Service, he ranked in descending order the economic productivity of various foreigners when compared to the normative category of the French male worker:

1) Italians: Very good workers, docile, steady.
2) Spanish: Very good workers. Nomadic tendencies.
3) Portuguese: Good workers. Docile. Able to do hard labor.
4) Greeks: Docile, intelligent, specialists, not able to do hard labor.

5) Moroccans: Very good agricultural laborers.

6) Kabyles: Somewhat good workers (at least since 1916, as those previously recruited left much to be desired . . .).

7) Southern Chinese: Robust and docile.
Northern Chinese: Mediocre, undisciplined.

8) Annamites: Good for skilled labor, a quasi-feminine labor force.

9) Workers from Madagascar and Martinique: Docile and physically weak.[67]

In more racially explicit language, Bertrand Nogaro of the Labor Ministry's Office of Economic Studies advised in May 1918 that after the war, foreign workers should consist of "immigrants of the white race, whose children are able to assimilate fairly well."[68] Two weeks later he reiterated this position to the office, stating that it would be "opportune to favor the immigration of foreigners of the white race" who could be assimilated quickly.[69] A comparable report from the Ministry of Armaments claimed that workers who were "members of the white race and hence assimilable" should be encouraged to remain in France, aiding in both the nation's economic recovery and in reconstituting the French population.[70] These documents return us again to the demographic imperative described in detail in chapter 1. According to this logic, foreign workers were to be judged with reference to both their productive and their reproductive value, and whiteness was a necessary precondition for assimilability.

Thus in the immediate aftermath of the war, a temporary workforce consisting of Africans and Asians was increasingly distinguished from migrants from Europe with the potential to be assimilated into the French national body. A new set of studies and analyses sought to illustrate the "insurmountable obstacle" faced by French employers who hired workers from the "vast reservoir of men in the colonies." In the words of the political economist Édouard Catalogne, "It would be in vain to hope for fusion with racial elements so different from us, who will never be able to blend [s'amalgamer] with the rest of the population. In the end, this fusion is not even desirable. The palpable alteration of the race that would ensue, on both a physical and moral level . . . could only have the most serious repercussions for the destiny of the nation."[71]

By the interwar years the language of labor had successfully incorporated both productivism and racial hierarchy. For example, the immigration expert André Pairault of the École Polytechnique remarked that after 1919 it was typical to find immigrants from "ten or twenty different races" in the same factory or workshop, although the "productivity of each type of foreigner in the industries where they work side by side is not the same."[72] This modified idiom reflected contemporary concerns such as the need to quantify productivity, the physical constitution of the worker's body, and the discrete gestures of which the rationalized labor process was composed. However, the abstract universalist categories prevalent in the heyday of economic liberalism had been abandoned in favor of racialized language. Moreover, the deskilled condition of factory labor was highlighted in countless texts which identified the ideal worker as robust, disciplined, and sober, in contradistinction to the "undesirable," who was described as weak, unstable, and unhealthy (figure 2). This blend of productivist, rationalized, and racialized language is clear in the responses to a survey conducted in 1937 by the employer consortium of coal mine owners. When asked to comment on the productivity of their colonial laborers, industrialists indicated almost unanimously that the output of North Africans was inferior to that of French and other European workers owing to a "less robust constitution," the "clumsiness of their movements," and the "slowness of their reflexes."[73]

The same report employed precise numerical language to signify the scientificity of its claims. It stated that the productivity of North African workers never surpassed 85 percent of what had been accomplished by the "ordinary labor force," and more typically remained at about 60 percent. While French observers conceded that poor diet was one reason for lower productivity among North Africans, the more important factor was the "nonchalance inherent to their race." The report concluded that the "very mediocre" productivity of North Africans in French mines proved that they should only be employed as manual laborers.[74] An ethnographic study of the Moroccan labor force in France reached similar conclusions: "[It] possesses no special aptitude, but can do a bit of everything, although modified by a coefficient greatly inferior per unit, thus reducing its aptitude to one-third or one-fourth of that of the European laborer. The Moroccan works unmethodically, however simple the task, and lacks initiative. All of this is added to an often poor physiological state, thus keeping the typical Moroccan worker from providing a satisfactory productivity."[75]

Thus interwar studies of foreign labor continued to calculate productivity differentials for racialized workers. Georges Mauco described a series of experiments comparing the output of Arabs and Poles working in both supervised and unsupervised conditions. While under surveillance—which was an essential part of the rationalized labor process—the productivity of Poles nearly doubled, while that of Arab workers tripled.[76] Data of this sort reaffirmed the notion that immigrants of color made for an indolent and undisciplined labor force, and justified the need to supervise all workers, regardless of race, in the interests of maximum efficiency.

But above all, these productivity studies upheld the conclusions reached during the First World War, during which the poor quality of colonial labor was affirmed. A survey of sixty thousand workers in the metallurgy industry was conducted between 1927 and 1929, ranking foreign labor power in the following order: Belgian, Italian, Spanish, Polish, Portuguese, Russian, and North African. Comparing both the high and low end of the scale, Mauco observed that "the number of Belgian workers rated as satisfactory was four times higher than North Africans."[77] Similarly, William Oualid compared the "technical value of various racial groups" in French coal mines, noting that the output of North African workers was only 25 to 50 percent of the French figure.[78]

A final example is provided by William Oualid's article in 1929 for the *International Labor Review*, a publication affiliated with the International Labor Organization of the League of Nations. In this account Oualid analyzed data from an inquiry made in 1926 by a "large motor car works in the Paris district" which employed over seventeen thousand workers, more than five thousand of whom were foreigners. To illustrate what he called the "Comparative Technical Value of Foreign Workers," Oualid included a chart which aptly demonstrates the mutual imbrication of rationalized and racialized logics (figure 7).[79] We can see that universalist abstractions had no place in Oualid's argument, which juxtaposed a differentiated labor force with a fragmented labor process. Along the Y-axis he listed "nationalities in order of general value" in a predictable sequence which privileged whiteness and cultural proximity. At the apex were the Belgians, Luxembourgers, Swiss, and Italians; followed by the Czechs, Yugoslavians, Russians, Poles, Chinese, Greeks, and Arabs. Embodied workers were plotted against the categories most salient to the new system of production, such as physical

COMPARATIVE TECHNICAL VALUE OF FOREIGN WORKERS EMPLOYED IN A MOTOR-CAR FACTORY

Nationalities in order of general value	Number of foreigners employed	Physical fitness	Regularity in work	Output on time work	Output on piece work	Character and discipline	Satisfaction given	Facility in understanding French	General classification	
									Total marks	Average (maximum = 10)
Belgian and Luxemburg	297	10	8.1	8.1	10	6.8	10	10	63.0	9.0
Swiss	109	10	7.5	8.1	9.2	8.1	8.5	8.1	59.5	8.5
Italian	427	7.5	7.5	6.2	7.8	5.3	8.5	8.7	51.5	7.3
Czech and Jugoslav	162	8.1	6.2	6.8	7.1	6.2	8.5	4.3	47.2	6.7
Russian	994	8.7	7.5	4.3	7.8	6.8	8.5	3.1	46.7	6.6
Spanish and Portuguese	296	5.7	7.5	4.2	6.6	5.7	9.1	7.1	45.9	6.5
Polish	295	8.7	6.8	6.2	8.5	6.5	5	3.1	44.8	6.4
Armenian	411	6.2	6.8	2.8	6.6	7.8	8.	5.6	43.8	6.3
Chinese	212	4.3	7.1	5	8	8	8	2.1	42.5	6.1
Greek	141	5.6	5	3.7	5.8	6.4	5.7	4.3	36.5	5.2
Arab	1,730	1.2	4.3	1.2	3.2	2.8	4.2	3.7	20.6	2.9
Total	5,074									

7. "The Occupational Distribution and Status of Foreign Workers in France." In William Oualid, *International Labor Review* 20, no. 2 (August 1929), 161–84.

fitness, discipline, productivity, dexterity, and an economy of time. Thus the discourse of productivity racialized workers' bodies, removing them from the realm of socially abstract labor power.

Conclusions: Toward a Segmented Labor Market

In the end the neutral and universalist language of political economy blended with a racialized and particularist idiom. While the demographic crisis and the wartime demand for labor might have tempted employers, labor recruiters, and government representatives to view all bodies as potential creators of surplus, instead they soon distinguished between European labor and colonial labor, whose productivity and skill they systematically devalued. In the *Revue de l'immigration*, a journal published for French employers of foreign workers, abstract human capital was equated with idealism, or a failure to recognize the reality of embodied identities: "Except in dreams, you cannot reason as a citizen of the world. As the member of a particular continent, country, or race of a certain color, you cannot force others to do your thinking. All people must examine their problems from the place where they are situated. It falls to us to study these phenomena from three standpoints: that of whites, of Europeans, and of French people."[80]

Racial discourse was intended to reconcile the contradictory aims of production and reproduction by particularizing abstract human capital to create a category of assimilable workers. Not only did the racialization of socially abstract labor produce surplus value and generate profit; it also permitted the regeneration of the "French race" in keeping with an ideal of biocultural sameness. Clifford Rosenberg has persuasively argued that racialized discourses of the labor process most strongly influenced government policy in the immediate aftermath of the war: French authorities expelled virtually all colonial workers from the metropole, and in the early 1920s they negotiated a series of bilateral treaties with white European nations like Italy, Poland, Spain, and Czechoslovakia.[81] The liberalizing elements of French Republicanism, along with the ideology of "Greater France," would not permit the implementation of quotas along American lines that denied colonial migrants the "right to migrate." Nevertheless, we have seen that employers, work scientists, and representatives of government ministries never considered foreign labor in a colorblind manner, or with reference to the universalist language of abstract human capital. Instead, because the French nation required both productive workers and potential citizens, a biocultural definition of belonging emerged which privileged white European immigrants at the expense of colonial subjects.

The stakes of the "demographic crisis" for the economy and citizen body in early-twentieth-century France were enormous. Immigration functioned as a site of racialization which sought to bridge the potentially conflicting demands for productivity and assimilability. We will continue to explore how historical actors, social movements, and specialized forms of knowledge attempted to address the various paradoxes immanent in French Republicanism and its citizen body, first by turning to the question of race mixing and interracial unions in colonial and metropolitan space.

Chapter Three

HYBRIDITY AND ITS
DISCONTENTS

For the medico-scientific community of early-twentieth-century France, the circulation of human capital between metropole and colony and among European nations demanded a nuanced explanation of the consequences of métissage (race mixing), an explicitly racialized form of embodiment.[1] By exploring how physicians, scientists, and racial anthropologists characterized métissage, the viability of métis offspring, and the foreigner's capacity for assimilation, I expand upon my earlier arguments regarding whiteness as a necessary precondition for citizenship in Republican France. Just as pronatalists and work scientists called for white immigration to meet the nation's productive and reproductive exigencies, so too did men of science distinguish race mixing "between whites" from what they considered a more perilous form of métissage: that of whites and people of color. This chapter therefore considers how late-nineteenth-century and early-twentieth-century race science portrayed interracial unions of all kinds, along with their perceived consequences for the national body. Remaining true to the racial idiom of the period, I examine relations between French people and their colonial subjects, as well as those between "whites of different races." I therefore insist that the "white race" was an intelligible category in Third Republican France, one which operated both as a cohesive whole ("whiteness" as opposed to "color") and as a fragmented entity of different populations which were white to different degrees.

Republican race science emerged from nineteenth-century anthropology, eventually evolving into a homegrown school of eugenic thought devoted to improving the quality and quantity of the French population.[2] It generated knowledge about the intimate consequences of immigration and colonization; namely, how the movement of people across national and imperial boundaries facilitated a wide range of domestic and sexual arrangements. According to these racializing discourses, the offspring of these unions, whether in the metropole or the colonies, profoundly influenced the nation's racial stock. As a consequence, physicians and anthropologists proclaimed that "métissage between whites" was the only viable crossing, and formulated a logic of white endogamy in the interest of reinvigorating the "French race." By distinguishing racially hygienic admixtures from degenerate ones, race scientists contributed to an internally consistent yet paradoxical conception of nationhood which, like Republican political theory, had both universalizing and particularizing components. I will show that race scientists remained committed to universalist optimism when evaluating race mixing between French citizens and white Europeans; they described these unions as eugenically sound, and fully French by the second generation. In contrast, they responded to métissage between phenotypically distinct races with a virulently particularist biological determinism, thus fully rejecting the premise that the nation could assimilate its nonwhite colonial subjects.

In this chapter I examine how Republican race science deployed organicist metaphors of nationhood derived from blood-based understandings of racial identity. I suggest that this was neither a corruption of Republican universalism nor inconsequential to its formulation of the citizen body; instead, organicist and assimilationist metaphors of nationhood were two sides of the same coin, for French Republican political theory was simultaneously composed of particularizing and universalizing elements.[3] I therefore argue against a rigid distinction between ethnocultural (hence particularist) and contractarian (hence universalist) understandings of national identity, because both have been critical to French understandings of the nation and its citizenry. I therefore show how social-hygiene, medical, and eugenic discourse in this period comfortably borrowed from the language of Republic universalism *and* blood-based ethnoculturalism when focusing on the consequences of intimate relations between French people and various immigrants.

In contrast, contemporary scholarship has emphasized an overwrought distinction between the "French" and "German" models of citizenship, the former ostensibly based on universalist principles and practices and the latter on particularist ones.[4] According to this view, the assimilationist and contractarian vision of the French nation is set apart from the organicist metaphors of nationhood typically associated with German romantic nationalism, which privileged the *Volk* and its lineage over the universalism of the Enlightenment and the French Revolution. Taken to its logical conclusion, the Republican vision held that in theory, all foreigners, despite their differences, could assimilate if they were willing to assume the cultural patrimony of the nation. This is because Republican universalism placed great faith in the power of the French language, schools, soil, and women to render immigrants culturally similar to the French. However, as I will demonstrate, organicist metaphors of nationhood were not inimical to Republican discourse, nor were they a "marginal" contribution to the early-twentieth-century immigration debate, as Gérard Noiriel has claimed.[5] Instead, in the debate on immigration and métissage, social critics freely employed both particularist and universalist elements to explain the stakes of racial mixing. The hybrid nature of this vision is critical to understanding the transition from liberal democracy to the Vichy state, as it redirects our attention to the relatively wide currency of biologism during the Third Republic. That is, essentialist notions of community were generated within Republican culture and institutions, and with reference to both foreigners and colonized people. While an anti-parliamentarian and explicitly racist regime like Vichy both extended and more formally institutionalized these ideas and practices, it cannot be credited with inventing them.

I begin by briefly considering the eighteenth- and nineteenth-century precedents of the debate on métissage, which occurred before the phenomenon of mass immigration further complicated perceptions of race mixing. Earlier works generally emphasized race mixing between whites and people of color, and of course their immediate context was European expansion into Africa and Asia. However, colonial instances of race mixing must be juxtaposed with their metropolitan counterparts, for as Emmanuelle Saada correctly suggests, the framing of the "*métis* problem" in the French empire "should prompt us to rethink certain metropolitan practices—especially in the realm of immigration policy."[6] I therefore emphasize that métissage was a concept which resonated throughout Greater France, and that it was a parallel discourse with both metropolitan and colonial referents. I therefore focus here on the far less familiar case of métissage within the French metropole by analyzing the work of several early-twentieth-century physicians, eugenicists, and racial anthropologists on the immigrant question. Through a close reading of these texts I demonstrate how race scientists combined assimilationist and organicist metaphors of nationhood to imagine a reinvigorated national body. Like the pronatalists examined in chapter 1, men of science argued that métissage among whites could function as a "blood transfusion" to resuscitate a depopulated nation, while mixing with "racially distant" groups produced unsound offspring and precipitated further decline. Thus a public debate on embodied migrations was again refracted through a particular form of specialized knowledge: in this case, eugenic science and its associated disciplinary locations. The effect was to facilitate the emergence of a Republican and pronatalist race science which posited that white immigration could bridge the ideals of assimilationism and the social reproduction of the citizenry.

Degeneration and Colonial Prohibitions

Questions regarding the possible dangers or benefits of métissage, as well as the civic and biological fitness of the métis, were not new to the early twentieth century. Racial theories that had developed in the previous two centuries were modified or redeployed to convey acceptable forms of hybridity, and hence the parameters of the Republican citizenry. As early as the eighteenth century scientists like the esteemed French naturalist Georges Louis Leclerc de Buffon sought to determine two things: whether métis offspring were "viable," and whether they inherited the best qualities from their parents or were instead "vehicles of degeneration."[7] Thus from its earliest incarnation the question of métissage was posed in biopolitical terms: Was the mixed-race individual infertile? And if not, was he or she doomed to be sickly, mentally unstable, criminal, and degenerate?[8] For some, like Buffon, métissage was an advantageous practice, as he believed that the offspring of mixed-race unions inherited the best traits of each parent.[9] According to this particular understanding of métissage, "lower" races could be gradually improved through successive crossings with members of the white race.[10] This position is generally associated with the doctrine of monogenesis which, without necessarily abdicating white supremacy, claimed that the various races descended from a common origin.

The polygenist counterargument gained momentum in France around 1850.[11] Scientists who professed the plural origins of humanity, like the physician and anatomist Paul Broca, along with other practitioners of a burgeoning nineteenth-century ethnographic science, were far less optimistic about the viability of mixed-race unions.[12] Generally speaking, these men described the métis as infertile, degenerate, and contaminating, and métissage as a regressive reproductive practice which ultimately encouraged the "fatal mediocratization of the species."[13] This was of course the infamous thesis of the Comte Arthur de Gobineau in his treatise *Essay on the Inequality of the Human Races* (1853): those racial groups which remained the most "pure" were also the most hearty, fecund, and prosperous; crossbreeding inevitably brought about the abasement of the "superior" race; and métissage destines a race to degeneration, depopulation, and eventually demise.[14]

Before the labor shortages of the First World War facilitated both European and colonial migration to the metropole, the question of métissage was most carefully considered with reference to the colonial empire. In the earliest phases of colonization in Africa and Asia, interracial unions between white men and women of color were either tolerated or actively encouraged.[15] Above all, this was due to the paucity of white women in the colonies. Colonial policy makers — and particularly those associated with the economic administration of the empire — believed that European women's constitutions were too feeble to subsist in the tropics; moreover, to import white women was a costly endeavor which would diminish the profitability of the imperial enterprise. As a result, concubinage with an African or Asian woman "formed the dominant domestic arrangement in colonial cultures through the early twentieth century."[16] The *"petite épouse"* (concubine; literally "little wife") served to acclimate European men to their colonial environment and provided a safer sexual outlet than native prostitutes who, as we will see in chapter 4, were considered likely carriers of venereal disease.[17] Only in the first two decades of the twentieth century did white endogamy become the prevailing sexual and domestic paradigm.

There were a variety of reasons for this shift. For one, colonial administrators increasingly viewed native women as contaminating elements with the power to purge European men of their civilized western mores. A white man living with an African or Asian concubine was frequently said to have "gone native" and as a result, forfeited his uncontested claim to a white European identity.[18] This was especially problematic because colonial rule was predicated on a clear demarcation between whiteness and color, civilization and savagery, ruler and ruled. As a consequence, ambiguous identities which defied the rigid binarism of the colonial taxonomy were interpreted as impediments to imperial rule.[19] Particularly interesting for our purposes is the perceived power of women in domestic space to transform the identity of men. In the colonies, intimate life with native women "decivilized" European partners, while in the metropole, as we have seen in the discussion of the debate on pronatalism, French women were to "civilize" immigrant husbands and instill in them the cultural competencies of Frenchness. I will return to this theme in chapter 5, in which I discuss independent nationality for married women, and how French politicians, feminists, and jurists characterized the household's impact on national identity. For now, I emphasize the parallel consequences of domestic life in the metropolitan and colonial contexts, where indigenous women were granted the power to either civilize or decivilize men.

Interracial sex also became a contentious issue once its reproductive potential was scrutinized.[20] As we will see in chapter 4, a somewhat different language was employed when discussing commercial rather than procreative sex, for commentators generally ignored the possibility that commercial sex could also lead to conception. If we focus squarely on interracial unions which racial theorists believed were most likely to produce offspring, we note the prominence of biopolitical definitions of the nation and its citizenry. The scientific community, along with interested colonial administrators, widely debated the dangers that métis children posed to national health, warning of their degenerate physical and mental state and their pernicious effect on the population as a whole. The supposed degeneracy of mixed-raced individuals had grave political consequences: male métis were viewed as potential revolutionaries who might one day stake a claim to the civic rights associated with French blood. As for the métisse — the female personification of racial hybridity — her degeneracy manifested in sexual licentiousness and often a proclivity for prostitution.[21] In defiance of imperial binaries, mixed-race children thus quite literally embodied the interstitial spaces of the colonial world. For contemporary observers, the indeterminacy of métis identities rendered mixed-race people degenerate, unpredictable, and dangerous.[22] Similarly, by the interwar period interracial sex in the colonies was labeled a subversive practice which threatened white prestige and reflected European degeneracy.[23]

Racial Mixing in the Metropole

Turning now to metropolitan France, we will see how European and colonial immigration reframed the issue of interracial sex and its possible trajectory toward marriage or reproduction. In contradistinction to the eventual ban on mixed-race unions in some of the French colonies, marriages between white French citizens and people of color had never been illegal in the metropole during the history of the Third Republic. For brief periods in the eighteenth and nineteenth centuries, however, these unions were forbidden: a ban in 1778 on what we would now term "mixed marriages" faded into the backdrop amid the turmoil of the Revolution;[24] in addition, Jennifer Heuer has recently unearthed material on a ban in effect between 1803 and 1819.[25] Nevertheless, before the First World War the primary arena for the debate on interracial unions and mixed-blood children was the empire. This focus was to change dramatically with deployment of colonial troops on metropolitan soil, and the urgent call for both white and nonwhite laborers to replace French men in the fields and factories. Wartime recruitments and conscriptions for work in the French metropole amounted to 662,000 men, almost half from the colonies and China.[26] The overwhelmingly male immigration in this period, in tandem with the shortage of French men on the homefront, subjected the interactions of French women with foreign men, whether white or of color, to closer scrutiny. We have seen how pronatalist critics looked upon relationships with white European immigrants most favorably. As for French women's relationships with men of color, both the general public and a variety of social critics judged them morally suspect and racially unsound.[27]

The factories of the First World War did not initially segregate the sexes, thus encouraging social reformers like Ghénia Avril de Sainte-Croix to describe the workplace as a breeding ground for indecent behavior. In her words, young French women who lived and worked with Indochinese laborers had "compromised their morality" by submitting to the "worst of all temptations."[28] That colonial men had access to French women in metropolitan brothels provoked vociferous protests from the general public, middle-class reform groups, and to a lesser degree the French police, as we will see in chapter 4. Relations between men of color and French women, whether prostitutes or "respectable" women, were the catalyst for a number of popular skirmishes during the war years.[29] Hence the mass migration of foreign men to France reinvigorated the debate on métissage, and situated it firmly within a metropolitan context. That is, the social consequences of immigration and empire generated analogous discourses on race and reproductive practices which resonated throughout Greater France.

Particularly after 1915, with a growing number of French men dead, held captive, or away at the front, the rate of marriages between French women and European immigrants accelerated greatly, from 3,317 in 1913 to 5,929 in 1917 to 7,745 in 1918, or 4.3 percent of all marriages in France in that year.[30] By 1920 27,000 marriages between natives and foreigners were contracted, 70 percent of which were composed of a French woman and a foreign man.[31] From the First World War to the early 1920s the majority of these unions were between French women and Belgian men, although after 1926 marriages with Italian men took the lead, with significant increases in unions between French women and Spaniards and Poles.[32] Men from these nations, we have seen, formed the bloc of "assimilable whites" preferred by pronatalists, work scientists, and other participants in the immigration debate. But demographic statistics also indicate a dramatic increase in unions between French women and colonial men. According to one study, marriages between French women and Algerian men accelerated after 1926, once the colonial presence had been more firmly established in the factories of the metropole: "Accustomed to seeing North African men for several years already, French women did not refuse them when asked for their hand in marriage."[33] Another study claimed that seven hundred Algerian men married French women in 1930, while another five thousand lived in concubinage (*unions libres*) with a French partner.[34] And as for what may have been more casual associations, in an issue of the women's magazine *Eve* in 1920, the novelist Charles-Henry Hirsch asserted that "thousands" of French women had engaged in relationships with "black men" during the war.[35]

Critiques of métissage put forth in this period were largely a response to the increased visibility of interracial contact during the war, whether in factories, brothels, or spaces of leisure. Just as the colonial setting generated its own debate on racial mixing, so too did foreign immigration to the French metropole. While the concept of métissage between two white individuals was not particularly salient in the colonies, in the context of mass immigration to the metropole it was widely employed by members of the medico-scientific community and contributed significantly to the discourse on race hygiene. In the popular newspaper *Mercure de France*, Dr. René Martial explicitly reminded his readers that the term *métis* did not uniquely apply to the offspring of Europeans and people of color. According to Martial, one of the most prolific writers on race and immigration in this period, the child of a Dutchman and a Frenchwoman was also of "mixed race," although this particular hybrid was perfectly assimilable and could be integrated into the French nation, unlike someone with African or Asian blood.[36] Thus although not all métis were equally assimilable, the language of race mixing was liberally employed by experts like Martial to connote various forms of human intercourse. And faced with the troubling predicament of demographic decline, race scientists also advocated métissage between whites as a means to repopulate the ailing French nation.

Immigration as a "Blood Transfusion"

Biological understandings of race had a strong institutional basis throughout nineteenth-century Europe and specifically in France.[37] I have therefore suggested that the inquiry into the quality of mixed-race unions was not new to early-twentieth-century scientific circles but rather was reinvigorated by the presence of white and nonwhite foreigners in France, in addition to evidence of métissage in the colonies. Moreover, the resurgence of blood-based understandings of Frenchness was facilitated by what Robert Nye has described as the widespread use of an "organicist discourse of national health" in late-nineteenth- and early-twentieth-century France, according to which the nation's viability was expressed in terms of the medical model.[38] Social ills such as depopulation, alcoholism, tuberculosis, and venereal disease indicated the sickliness of the national body, and demographic decline necessitated selective racial mixing until a population surplus could be achieved. One further consequence was physicians positioning themselves as experts in the expanding realm of social hygiene, and increasingly presuming that the immigrant question was a logical extension of their specialized knowledge.

In seeking a biological understanding of degeneration and revivification, medico-hygienic texts described immigration in organicist language, labeling it a "blood transfusion," a "cellular transplant," or even an "interracial grafting."[39] So too did Dr. Georges Dequidt of the Ministry of Hygiene and Dr. Georges Forestier, a departmental health inspector. At the annual meeting of the Société de Médecine in 1926, they warned that because immigration amounted to a "massive transfusion of foreign blood," the "future health of the race" would be gravely compromised if the government did not assume a regulatory stance toward international migrations.[40] Their biological determinism stemmed from their conviction that both the French race and the white race must be preserved. Like the pronatalist critics examined previously, Dequidt and Forestier linked the consequences of mass migration to a state of white demographic panic. They also believed that international migrations were the product of civilization's ebb and flow, and that overcivilized nations like France suffered from depopulation because of their widespread degeneracy. In keeping with the pessimism of late-nineteenth- and early-twentieth-century demographic discourse, Dequidt and Forestier claimed that immigration to the United States and modernized European nations indicated the "twilight of our Western Civilization and the decline of the white race."[41] They framed the immigrant question in a racially defensive and essentialist language which pitted whites worldwide against people of color.

The organicist metaphor of nationhood was most forcefully argued by prominent members of the French medical community: professors at the Paris school of medicine, Nobel laureates among them. Several of these men were involved in founding the Société Française d'Eugénique (FES) circa 1913, and a few would come to assume administrative positions under Vichy, from which they continued to articulate the blood-based racial taxonomies they had espoused before the Second World War. Their views on immigration, interracial sex, and mixed-blood offspring are often downplayed in scholarly accounts of immigration to France, if not completely omitted from them.[42] However, eugenic discourse on immigration vividly testifies that particularist definitions of national affiliation flourished in the first few decades of the twentieth century, and were well within the purview of Republicanism.

In contrast, a strictly universalist position promoted race mixing in those cases where assimilation was preordained as possible. Because assimilation was predicated on cultural homogeneity, its proponents believed that by participating in institutions like the Republican school system and the army, and by mastering the French language and other markers of cultural community, foreigners would be transformed into Frenchmen just as peasants from the provinces, in the course of the nineteenth century, had been brought under the aegis of the centralized state.[43] However, owing to the shortage of French men and the overwhelmingly masculine quality of the first waves of immigration to France, advocates of the Republican model of civic incorporation focused their attention on the integration of *male* foreigners, who were also to be assimilated by marriage to a French woman. As I argued in my analysis of pronatalist discourse, Republican ideology vested female nationals with the power to transmit the French cultural patrimony to their spouses and children.

The assimilationist view of race mixing was also sustained within the French scientific community by the persistence of Lamarckian, rather than Mendelian, theory. Because French biologists, physicians, and racial anthropologists remained devoted well into the 1920s to Lamarck's theory of the heredity of acquired characteristics, their concerns regarding the foreigner's adaptability to a new environment were alleviated, or at the very least deferred.[44] But in the 1930s, with the introduction of Mendelian genetics to France, and in a climate of mounting xenophobia heightened by economic depression and the rise of the far right, scientific writings on immigration took an especially essentialist turn.[45] Nevertheless, the logic of *jus sanguinis* — or blood-based notions of civic inclusion — had been present in immigration debate throughout the first half of the twentieth century, and was a critical part of the Republican definition of citizenship.

The organicist metaphor of nationhood was most aptly phrased by the provincial intellectual, anthropologist, and eugenicist Georges Vacher de Lapouge,[46] whose work is a clear example of how biopolitical concerns regarding the quality and quantity of the population intersected with the immigrant question. As early as 1887 Lapouge argued that métissage within France had resulted in degeneration and depopulation because it produced offspring who were less fertile than the racially pure.[47] Although an outsider without a proper institutional base — Lapouge was in fact more widely respected in the United States, Germany, and Brazil — by the mid-1920s he was cited frequently by respected members of the French public health community. For this reason William Schneider reminds us that Lapouge was not simply resurrected in the late 1930s and 1940s by Vichy supporters: his work had found an audience more than a decade earlier among the medical community of the Republican regime.[48]

Lapouge provided the introduction to the French translation of Madison Grant's *The Passing of the Great Race* (1916), undoubtedly one of the most influential American expressions of the eugenic view of immigration. In it Lapouge stressed the relevance of Grant's essentialist account of race to French society, reminding the reader of the ontological certainty of both race and gender:[49] "A nation is a family . . . a biological ensemble, a material thing, and not a juridical fiction, but economists, statisticians, and jurists, who confuse the quality of a Frenchman with the rights which are attached to him, seem to have forgotten this. A prince, a king, a minister, or a parliament can no more make a Frenchman from a Greek or a Moroccan than they can bleach the skin of a Negro, widen the eyes of a Chinaman, or turn a man into a woman."[50]

A number of well-placed physicians espousing social-hygiene principles agreed with Lapouge that the nation was a "biological ensemble" rather than a territory guided by abstract rights in which any person could eventually prosper by adhering to those rights. It follows that not all foreigners were equally suitable to biologically regenerating the nation, and hence it was essential to assess the ontological contribution of various immigrant groups. For example, Drs. Dequidt and Forestier warned that because immigrants possessed certain "irreducible ethnographic characteristics" (*caractères ethniques irréductibles*), France must not simply view foreigners as the "bearers of riches," no matter how desperately it needed their labor. Dequidt and Forestier explained that immigrants possessed "mental, moral, and physical defects" which promoted "racial degeneration" and the "nation's disintegration." For this reason they advocated the careful selection of foreigners in accordance with the principles of eugenic science: "We are aware that rapid degeneration strikes the products of métissage between different races. Knowledge of the precise and well-established laws of eugenics would lead us to a policy of selective immigration."[51]

F.-L. Blancher of the FES, like the pronatalists, industrialists, jurists, and Republican politicians we have examined thus far, remarked upon the need to reconcile the "economic and social aspects of immigration," or in the terms of my analysis, immigration's productive and reproductive value. In this regard he claimed that the particular question of assimilation fell squarely "under the jurisdiction" of the FES and its members.[52] Similarly, the pediatrician Georges Schreiber, who served as secretary general of the FES, defended the authority of the organization in matters related to immigration. He announced at a meeting in 1922 that the society should investigate whether "eugenically undesirable elements" were among those foreigners who crossed French borders daily.[53] And Georges Papillaut, an FES member who was also vice-president of the Société d'Anthropologie,[54] one of the primary institutional bases for scientific racism in France, believed that it was the FES's "prerogative" to "issue a verdict" on the "racial selection of immigrants." Not all mixtures were equally sound, he explained, and thus it was necessary to determine in which cases "propagation" was "desirable." For Papillaut, the whiteness of a given population was critical. In his estimation only members of the "productive white races" could meet the nation's interrelated demands of immigration, assimilation, and social reproduction.[55]

Dr. Eugène Apert, a pediatrician specializing in childhood hereditary diseases, served variously as secretary general, vice-president, and president of the FES. He provided one of the most nuanced understandings among French eugenic theorists of racial difference, putting forth a tripartite vision which first distinguished whites from nonwhites, and then bifurcated whiteness to differentiate Western Europeans from Jews, Levantines, North African Berbers, and Eastern Europeans. Of course we have seen this sort of racial taxonomy before, namely in the work of pronatalist critics and work scientists who also regarded whiteness as a category which could be fragmented and internally hierarchized. Like his colleagues, Apert argued that mass immigration to France required careful deliberation of the consequences of racial mixing, for not all forms of métissage were equally salubrious. For example, the mixing of Catalans with the French population in the Roussillon region of southern France—a form of métissage between closely related white populations—was far superior to the "degenerate" unions which had formed between African and Asian soldiers and "lower-class French women."[56] To evaluate various crossings, Apert held that one must identify three very different modes of racial mixing, in accordance with the dictates of eugenic science.

The first was métissage between "remote" varieties of the human race, namely whites with Africans or Asians. Apert cited the work of the Nobel laureate and physician Charles Richet, one of France's most prominent eugenic thinkers, to claim that the introduction of "black or yellow blood" into France constituted a "crime" against the human species as a whole.[57] Although Apert conceded that some of these children were indeed "very pretty,"[58] they necessarily inherited the worst characteristics of each parent's race. Because degeneration was the only possible outcome of such mixing, Apert concluded that "no yellow or black blood may mix with French blood."[59] Thus Africans and Asians should only be permitted to immigrate if native French citizens and white foreigners could not meet the demands of the army and the national economy.[60] As a last resort, France could harness the productive value of colonial men, but at the risk of undermining the nation's racial stock by introducing nonwhite elements. Apert's fellow eugenicist Georges Schreiber, in his response to Apert's presentation at a meeting in 1924 of the FES, urged the French to emulate the United States and Canada by insuring the "white colonization" of the nation.[61]

But Apert did not assign equal weight to all members of the white race. He distinguished métissage involving "related whites" from métissage between French citizens and "more distant white populations." While people from "central" and "oriental" Europe—North African Berbers, Levantines, Balkanites, and Slavs—were "fundamentally white,"[62] they differed greatly from other whites in "physical and intellectual aptitude, physiognomy, character, productivity, intelligence, and aptitude for work and progress."[63] Apert therefore concluded that the French should only mix with "related members of the white race" with whom "fusion" easily occurred. The Belgians, Italians, and Spaniards formed the core of this group; they assimilated rapidly, and when they reproduced with the French the resulting "mixed population" was of "good quality."[64] Apert therefore upheld the critical importance of white endogamy to French immigration policies, explaining that the "introduction of foreign subjects of the white race adulterates the [French] race much less."[65] Given the deficit of native French births, he concluded that Belgian, Italian, and Spanish immigrants could increase the national population without substantially modifying the "qualities of the race."[66]

According to Dr. Albin Faivre, the immigrant question forced the French medical community to decide whether its task was simply to protect the population from an influx of pathological elements or to work more generally to safeguard the "purity of the race."[67] Physicians and racial anthropologists employed the term *immigration sanitaire* to describe both the charting of particular diseases among immigrant communities and something closer to racial hygiene. Immigration sanitaire therefore gauged the foreigner's propensity for assimilation in accordance with the medical model, especially the repercussions of mixing his or her blood with that of the "French race," and hence the quality of the foreigner's reproductive capital.[68] In the interest of public health, proponents of immigration sanitaire argued that all immigrants should be monitored for syphilis, malaria, intestinal parasites, and the like, but ideally a racial selection should precede an immigrant's screening for physical and mental diseases.

The medico-scientific community defined assimilation as a "biological problem" with analogous enactments in the plant and animal worlds.[69] As a consequence, they argued that human races followed the same generative laws as flora and fauna, and just as the haphazard crossing of two breeds of sheep might produce substandard offspring, human métissage, if practiced indiscriminately, would result in degenerate children.[70] This genre of racial theory was a recapitulation of Gobineau, who several decades earlier had argued that "human crossbreeding" invariably led to racial degeneration. Physician-eugenicists warned of the "instability of the *métis*" and the incoherence of their "psychic state."[71] Borrowing metaphors from the sciences of arboriculture and zootechny (animal breeding), they claimed that national health depended on the prudent introduction of racial elements which least contaminated the existing "French race."

Of course a eugenic vision of immigration policy contradicted the assimilationist strain within French Republicanism, as well as the universalist longings of a liberal democracy. This observation did not escape the members of the French medical community writing on immigration, who remained untroubled by the particularist and essentialist premises upon which their analyses rested. For example, Drs. Dequidt and Forestier complained that at the International Conference on Immigration, Emigration, and Colonization in Rome in 1924, little consideration had been given to the relationship between immigration and racial hygiene. They blamed this omission on the International Labor Office of the League of Nations, which because it was "steeped in egalitarian humanism" was incapable of comprehending the profound significance of human difference with regard to the consequences of international migration.[72] Dr. René Martial also typified this anti-universalist backlash when he warned that "human cross-breeding is not an operation to be practiced by chance. To want to unify humanity by racial mixing is utopian, a vain hope, it is to wish that all the world spoke Esperanto."[73] According to Martial, only those who had been duped by the "myth of the equality of the races" could ignore the importance of racially selecting prospective immigrants before they gained entry to France.[74]

Martial's work on "interracial grafting," Taylorism, venereal disease, prostitution, and insanity corresponded neatly with the heyday of Foucault's social-hygiene state, and as the author of several dozen books and articles on immigration, most of which appeared in the major medical journals of the day, he saw his opinions regarding race and immigration widely circulated in the popular and the medical press. A member of the French Legion of Honor and the Academy of Medicine, and a professor at the Institute of Hygiene at the School of Medicine, Martial was able to continue his career under Vichy at the Institute of Anthroposociology, an organization created by the General Commissariat for Jewish Questions.[75] Martial stressed that French blood was not "pure," as even the most strident eugenicists were forced to recognize, because it had been elaborated since Gallo-Roman times by successive crossings with the Latins, Celts, and Ligurians.[76] It was therefore not the aim of French immigration policy to safeguard racial purity, which had never actually existed in France; instead, over the course of several centuries, the "French race" had been constituted through a long history of mixing among whites. Rather than aspire to a false ideal of racial purity, the goal was to promote *le bon métissage*, or appropriate racial crossings. What Martial described as the *race résultat français* (the resulting French race) was the product of sound and hygienic racial crossings throughout the ages. The nation's health therefore depended on altering this combination as little as possible through the judicious addition of foreign blood, selected in accordance with eugenic principles.[77]

On the whole, French commentators associated the concept of racial purity with German understandings of race and nation, and for this reason they strove to differentiate their racial model from one they viewed as historically inaccurate and ideologically repugnant.[78] The organicist metaphor of nationhood therefore acknowledged that the "French race" was in fact of "mixed blood." According to Jacques St-Germain, it was the harmonious result of centuries of invasions and crossings with the Franks, Burgundians, Celts, Scandinavians, and Basques. But this was also a history of métissage among whites, and St-Germain warned that the "French race" would not have been the same if those invaders were "Negroes" (*nègres*), "Asiatics" (*asiatiques*), or "Levantines" (*Levantins*). For this reason he concluded that future mixings should only occur with immigrants of "compatible blood," by which he meant white European immigrants. Employing Martial's terminology, he asked: "Is not our *race résultat* successful because it results from the fusion of compatible races and bloods? Must we accept all racial mixings or, on the contrary, can we select those that we want? Why can't we formulate an immigration and naturalization policy that is one of racial interventionism [*dirigisme racial*]?"[79]

Dr. Louis-Laurent Pinon also affirmed that while métissage had played a critical role in French history, the "resulting French race," though a product of mixing, must forever remain a white race. Pinon listed two primary means by which a nation might go about selecting potential immigrants. The first presupposed that there existed superior and inferior races; it was therefore a "racist model" which "opposed all métissages." In contrast, the second model viewed all races as equal, and recognized that to some degree all human populations were the product of various crossings. According to Pinon, French immigration policy adhered to the second model. It was not "racist" because it freely acknowledged the historical admixtures which had given rise to the French race, and because it recognized the social and economic advantages that hybridity might have in the nation's future. But by privileging white hybridity, Pinon masked the racism inherent in *both* of the models he put forth. He therefore concluded that for the "resulting French race" to remain ontologically sound, immigration policy must bar the entry of Africans, Asians, and Levantines, whom he described as "morphologically" and "psychologically" distinct from the French.[80]

Hybrid Metaphors of Hybridity

According to Raymond Millet, author of a widely cited book on immigration to France between the wars, opponents of all forms of race mixing could trace their heritage to Gobineau, who held that métissage always occurred to the advantage of the "inferior race." In contrast, Millet claimed that proponents of assimilation followed another nineteenth-century racial thinker, the historian and critic Hippolyte Taine, who believed that nation fashioned race, and that all "[the nation] touched would become French."[81] Like contemporary analyses of race and nation which juxtapose the French and German examples, Millet clearly distinguishes the assimilationist camp from one which draws on a blood-based and mixophobic tradition. But this binary logic cannot adequately explain the intricacies of the Republican position, for as Gary Wilder has argued, French Republicanism simultaneously contained both universalizing and particularizing elements.[82] This doubled vision of the citizenry is reflected in the medico-scientific community's concurrent use of assimilationist and organicist metaphors. As a result, men of science could assert the irreducible difference of people of color and the impossibility of their assimilation, while at the same time maintaining that the French race was a mixed race, and that traditionally Republican methods of assimilation would suffice for white Europeans.

Take, for example, Dr. Victor Storoge, who contrasted the French and American experiences of immigration. He explained that in the United States, the "problems" caused by the "arrival of the colored races" demonstrated the need for an "ethnographic verification" (*contrôle ethnique*) of foreigners before they were granted entry.[83] But this precaution was not necessary in France, where immigrants were traditionally drawn from "diverse branches of the white race" and were therefore more assimilable. With the immigrant pool restricted to white Europeans, Storoge maintained that Republican methods of assimilation would be adequate to guarantee their integration. Above all, he held that French authorities should encourage "familial crossings" with French women, whose assimilative power over foreign men was widely noted. In addition, the state must focus its efforts on integrating the second generation through the mechanisms of the Republican school system.[84]

Similarly, in a text published in 1926 by the jurist Jean Bercovici, assimilationism and biological determinism were combined to explain the medico-hygienic repercussions of immigration. For Bercovici race could be understood in both "cultural" and "physiological" terms. However, the cultural dimension of race—in his words, race as a "community of aspirations which constitutes a people"—was far more important than a physiological (or organicist) definition which viewed race as a "community of origins." Bercovici's preference for a cultural understanding of race seemingly affiliates him with the contractarian and universalist position devoted to Republican assimilationism. However, as he elaborates further, we see that Bercovici reserves this culturally grounded definition for "individuals belonging to the white race," as they alone can mix with and assimilate into the French population. In contrast, only with "much caution" and "in very limited numbers" should "exotics of the black race, or yellow-skinned people with thick lips and slanty eyes, [be permitted] to settle in France."[85] Having established whiteness as a necessary precondition for immigration to France, Bercovici applauded the work of Republican institutions like the Foyer Français, an organization responsible for teaching French language and culture to foreigners, in keeping with assimilationist logic.[86]

The concurrent deployment of organicist and assimilationist metaphors also characterized a report issued by the French Academy of Medicine, in 1926. It suggested that in spite of the French nation's "well-known power of assimilation," an influx of foreigners from different races had transformed the immigrant question into a "biological problem" of a "scientific order." For this reason, the report claimed that immigration should be studied with reference to current research on acclimation and crossbreeding, notably in the field of zootechny.[87] In keeping with the medical model, the report also likened immigration to a "cellular transplant" and a "blood transfusion," and claimed that assimilation would only occur if the "transplanted elements [were] as close as possible to the autochthonous ones, and thus able to adapt easily to their new humoral milieu."[88]

The report concluded that assimilation was a "mutation" which different races were more or less capable of performing. While there were few obstacles for members of the "diverse branches of the white race," Africans and Asians were impervious to the effects of traditional methods of assimilation. According to the academy's report, only foreigners who were "ancestrally close" to the French, such as northern Italians, Belgians, and Canadians, should be encouraged to migrate. Men from these nations could enter "familial crossings" with French women who, because of the man shortage which followed the Great War, could only hope to found a family through marriage to a foreigner. The report also held that Republican mechanisms of integration were adequate for white European migrants, who would easily assimilate as long as they "settled permanently upon French soil, spoke . . . our language, adopted our customs, received our culture, crossed with the autochthonous population, and sent their children to French schools."[89] In contrast, the report claimed that Africans and Asians endangered the "physical and intellectual qualities" of the French "patrimony," and thus that their integration was utterly impossible.[90] Finally, the report placed the question of assimilation in an international context, reporting that in Argentina, one of the most important destinations for immigrants in the early twentieth century, the powerful influence of the school system was largely responsible for assimilating the children of white European immigrants. Meanwhile, in the United States, which had been forced to receive both white immigrants and foreigners of color, the inassimability of Africans and Asians was responsible for the "serious affair of the colored races" (*grave affaire des races de couleurs*).[91]

A final example is provided by the *Revue de l'Immigration*, a journal directed at French employers of foreign workers. In an article in 1930, the law professor André Pairault sought to explain how immigration might affect the "future of the race." He insisted that the "massive influx of exotics" into France made this question all the more germane, since once African and Asian workers had settled in the metropole it was only a matter of time before they entered into "mixed unions" with French women. To determine whether these immigrants threatened to "compromise ethnographic unity" (*compromettre notre unité ethnique*) and "transform [French] mores and culture," Pairault claimed that one must first distinguish between two different understandings of race.[92]

The first was a "morphological definition" which included skin color, cranial structure, hair type, and the like: these are the components of what we would now term "phenotype," or the physical manifestations of race. A second definition took into account "ethnographic" (*ethnique*) and "linguistic" elements, in addition to "social considerations" such as a people's standard of living, religious beliefs, and political and economic institutions. Pairault held that while the "somatic particularities" (i.e. phenotypical characteristics) of race could not be ignored, more important was the "ensemble of a people's social and religious traditions." Moreover, race was a "dynamic" construct, or an "expression of collective life" which continuously changed throughout human history. Here Pairault seems to privilege a socially constructed and historically contingent definition of race over the essentialism of his "morphological" definition.

Pairault also highlighted the mixedness of the French and other European populations, claiming that owing to multiple "ethnographic crossings" (*croisements ethniques*), most Europeans were already "to some degree *métis*."[93] He thereby conceded that métissage was an integral part of the European past, and moreover a potentially reinvigorating practice if it were carried out selectively. In contrast, immigration could have a "nefarious" influence on race if it introduced elements with a dramatically different "physical constitution, language, religion, and degree of civilization." By including physical constitution on this list, Pairault retained a hybrid definition of race composed of both somatic and cultural qualities. According to this logic, because Africans and Asians possessed a "completely distinctive psychology," their immigration endangered the racial composition of European nations.

Pairault concluded that there was no need to be pessimistic about the future of the "French race," because recent immigrants belonged to consanguineous races and therefore possessed "great affinities" with the native population: "The Italians are Latins who quickly assimilate in the Midi. The Spaniards in the Bigorre and Roussillon are practically at home . . . and the Belgians, particularly the Walloons, are only slightly different ethnographically [*ethniquement bien peu différenciés*] from our people in the Nord. Finally, the Poles, the most Latin of Slavs, have always manifested profound affinities with the French nation." Pairault therefore maintained that like all living entities, race evolves according to the influence of the foreign elements it absorbs. Métissage is thus the natural trajectory of human history, and a salutary practice as long as it occurs uniquely among white populations. If France recruited immigrants from Italy, Spain, Belgium, and Poland, "degeneration" and "decadence" could be avoided. While white immigration might alter the precise composition of the French people, Pairault contended, the French nation and its patrimony would continue.[94]

Conclusions: "We live in the same house,
but we did not build it together"

According to Dr. René Martial, members of the *race résultat français*, which had been elaborated over the past 4,500 years by successive transplants of Ligurians, Celts, and Latins, "[have] built a house in which other people want to live." But if men and women of "old French stock" (*de vieille souche*) wished to remain "masters" in their home, the racial selection of immigrants was necessary to avoid random and potentially degenerate crossbreeding.[95] Race consciousness was nothing more than a means to protect the nation's inhabitants and their progeny, or an acknowledgment that while some foreigners had the capacity to rejuvenate the anemic French blood, others could only poison it. In Martial's words, with a clear understanding of the "biological aspects of immigration," the French could carefully "select the tenants of the house [they had] built."[96]

In the medico-hygienic discourse on immigration, civic incorporation was predicated on cultural *and* biological sameness, thus attesting to the hybrid nature of the Republican vision, with assimilationist and organicist elements. Racial theorists argued that the selection of foreigners must begin by distinguishing members of the white race from people of color, and that the continued mixedness of the French race would only be viable if it consisted of métissage among white populations. As for immigrants of color, Dr. Louis-Laurent Pinon of the Paris Faculty of Medicine observed that the "particularism" of Africans, Asians, and Levantines rendered them "physically" and even "morally inassimilable."[97] By coding immigrants of color as necessarily particularist elements, Pinon placed them outside the universalist paradigm which equated assimilation with cultural homogeneity, and characterized colonized people as impermeable to the ideological and cultural work of the "French melting pot."

According to French eugenicists and other racial theorists representing the medical and scientific community, individual rights and reproductive obligations were not incompatible values. Early-twentieth-century French eugenics was strongly influenced by both pronatalism and Lamarckian genetics, which mitigated the call for negative eugenic measures such as anti-miscegenation laws, sterilization, or a virulently racist immigration policy.[98] Besides, the liberalizing aspects of French Republicanism would not permit such flagrant violations of individual rights; for this same reason, throughout the entire history of the Third Republic interracial marriages and interracial sex were never forbidden in the metropole. Nevertheless, Republican race science defined *le bon métissage* as white endogamy alone, and thus only white European foreigners were considered acceptable candidates for assimilation and the social reproduction of the citizenry. Republican race science, like Republican political theory, was simultaneously liberalizing and racializing. While it conceded that métissage was a racially unsound practice and that people of color were inassimilable, interracial unions were only banned in colonial space, and never in the metropole. In the following two chapters we will examine concrete examples of métissage within the metropole: first with regard to interracial prostitution, and then in terms of mixed marriages. In both cases we will see how Republican politicians, feminists, and social reformers attempted to reconcile individual rights and reproductive obligations, and how an ideal of gender complementarity, rather than a universalist vision, dominated the immigration debate.

Chapter Four

BLACK MIGRANTS, WHITE SLAVERY

Métissage in the Metropole and Abroad

This chapter analyzes racialized narratives of sexual danger deployed in the campaign against "white slavery" (*la traite des blanches*). Its focus is the brothel, in metropolitan France and overseas, while its female subject is the prostitute rather than the citizen mother heralded by populationist discourse. I therefore move from the pronatalist discussion of procreative sex, analyzed in detail in chapter 1, to the abolitionist crusade against recreational sex performed as commercial exchange. The embodied migrations central to this story are twofold: I begin with the movement of French women overseas to labor as prostitutes, and then return to the example of colonial migrants in the metropole, whose relationships with white women were scrutinized by feminists, social reformers, the military, and the police. We will see that French critics projected anxieties about national health, racial hygiene, and gendered notions of respectability onto the issues of white slavery and regulated prostitution.[1] They called for the vigilant policing of racial boundaries which had been destabilized by mass immigration, and a protective stance toward French women who had too literally exploited the possibilities of individual agency.

As I argued in chapter 1, the "demographic crisis" facilitated the veneration of the virtuous mother and scorn for *la femme moderne*. We have seen how pronatalist discourse denounced the selfishness and lack of patriotism of French women who, despite the nation's population deficit, chose to remain childless and profit from their freedom. "White slavery," or the alleged entrapment of women and their sale into prostitution abroad, was another vehicle through which this tremendous anxiety about female autonomy was expressed. According to its opponents, women who removed themselves from sites of paternalistic control placed themselves in jeopardy and compromised their reputation. By emphasizing the omnipresence of moral and sexual danger, social reformers endorsed a conservative understanding of the gender order in which all women, but especially independent, modern women, teetered on the brink of whoredom.

Opponents of regulated prostitution also incorporated French men into their critique by maintaining that male participation in commercial sex exacerbated demographic decline. In their view, French men who frequented prostitutes wasted their reproductive capital by engaging in sexual acts intended only to satisfy libidinal urges rather than repopulate the nation. Furthermore, by exposing themselves to syphilitic contamination — as it was invariably the prostitute who was considered its source — French men spread the disease to their wives and endangered a citizenry already plagued by depopulation. I have argued that the "demographic crisis" worked to decenter masculinity by promoting an image of the nation and its male citizens as effeminate. The campaign against white slavery also reflected this troubled masculinity in its efforts to reinscribe the paternal authority of French husbands, fathers, and the state. By depicting public space as treacherous and corrupting, abolitionists sought to restrict the movement of women nationally and internationally, and to return their reproductive capital and affective labor to the family and the nation.

I begin by explaining the logic behind the "French system" of regulated prostitution, as well as its "abolitionist" critique. I then link the proliferation of white slavery narratives to the prevalence of international migrations, and especially to the French public's concern for women traveling overseas who could compromise personal and national reputations. By relaying how the police, the military, and social-hygiene reformers grappled with the question of sex between white prostitutes and colonial men, I demonstrate how the debate on métissage that we examined in chapter 3 was concretized in a particular national and imperial setting. The explicitly racialized rhetoric employed in this debate is central to my analysis, as it deliberately equated the prostitution of (white) women with the enslavement of people of color.

The effect was to underscore women's problematic position in a Republican narrative which apotheosized both the autonomous individual and gender complementarity. If prostitution was enslavement, the prostitute was by definition a dependent being. Like the slave she was not fully human, and therefore unworthy of universal rights. But to free women from prostitution by reenclosing them in domestic space was to uphold dependency of another sort, a gendered dependency which defined female citizenship in terms of women's particularity, and with reference to their embodied experience.

The "French System": On Regulation and Rights

According to the standard white slavery narrative, innocent French girls were duped, often with promises of marriage or employment, and sold into prostitution overseas by traffickers portrayed sometimes as French but more often as Jews, men of color, or foreigners. The growth of the popular press, in addition to the public's newfound fascination with the *faits divers* — stories of murders, scandals, and crimes of passion — provided the campaign against white slavery with an irresistible momentum.[2] But the debate on white slavery was also a product of the age of mass migrations. In the early twentieth century an immense emigration of largely young, poor, and working-class men to all parts of the globe created in some regions an imbalance between the sexes. According to Alain Corbin, this surplus of men generated a demand for prostitution in regions to which female immigration had not yet occurred.[3] Likewise, the transportation revolution greatly facilitated international travel; the steamship in particular expedited the movement of immigrants from continent to continent. A French delegate to the Congress on the White Slave Trade of 1899 maintained that "elements of civilizing progress" such as the "multiplication of colonies, the development of trade routes, and the increasing connections among people thanks to new modes of communication" were the "active agents that created and propagated the white slave trade."[4] The modern and profoundly mobile world described at the Congress was one in which civilization had generated both progress and social disintegration. Arguments against prostitution, like those condemning neo-Malthusian reproductive practices, made use of degeneration theory and its view of civilization as a state with both positive and negative effects. Critics of white slavery contended that even though the state of civilization had brought about significant benefits, like improved trade routes, communications, and transportation, it had also facilitated traffic in women, and thereby promoted their dishonor.[5]

Social reformers focused on the state's sanctioning of sex work through the doctrine of "regulationism." Between 1802 and 1946 prostitution in France was not legal per se but "regulated": prostitutes had to register with the police and submit to regular venereal inspections. Justice was meted out not by the French judiciary but rather by the Morals Police (Brigade des Mœurs), which had full regulatory discretion and often acted arbitrarily,[6] sometimes arresting and detaining women without a warrant. For example, all prostitutes considered symptomatic of syphilis were locked in venereal wards like the infamous Saint-Lazare prison in Paris until their symptoms had abated. But most importantly, prostitutes were subject to a body of law made for and applicable to them alone. Feminists involved in the crusade against regulated prostitution singled out this particular injustice as a flagrant violation of the prostitute's individual rights.

Regulation was predicated on the notion that sexual abstinence was ultimately impossible for men, and that prostitution was a necessary evil that should be contained rather than forced underground. In his widely cited early-nineteenth-century study of prostitution, Parent-Duchâtelet maintained that without the outlet provided by prostitution, sexually frustrated men would prey upon honest women; similarly, Dr. Louis Fiaux wrote in 1880 that the maison de tolérance (a regulated, or literally "tolerated" brothel) functioned as a "seminal drain."[7] But regulation was also a means of ordering society: by "marking" the prostitute, it sought to make clear the distinction between honorable women and the "fallen." In this regard regulation was a paternalistic and protective mechanism for shielding virtuous women and innocent children from vice. But most importantly, regulation gave men access to commercial sex that its proponents held was hygienic, orderly, and likely to be disease-free.

Abolitionists in France were not calling for the absolute prohibition of prostitution, but rather an end to the state's mediating role in promoting sex work, which was likened to the role of a procurer. The separation of the brothel and the state would require a ban on regulated maisons de tolérance as well as criminal punishments for procuring. In both Europe and the United States adherents of the movement chose to call themselves "abolitionists" to invoke the immorality and injustice of the African slave trade and position themselves within a lineage of righteous crusaders. This connection had special resonance in France, where Republicans cherished the nation's reputation as a vanguard in the manumission of black slaves. The oxymoron of "white slavery" cast the prostitute as the quintessential victim because white people were not supposed to be colonized or enslaved. That is, both the prostitute and the slave were beings untouched by Revolutionary values; lacking individual liberties and human agency, they were condemned to a life of unfree labor.

French feminists invoked Revolutionary ideals of individual rights and universal equality to argue against regulated prostitution, a tactic they would also employ in their battle for independent nationality, as we will see in chapter 5. However, this strategy only highlighted the "paradoxical" position of French women in the Republican order.[8] While far from being enslaved, French women were citizens without voting rights, and dependent rather than independent because of the restrictions of civil law.[9] Nevertheless, feminists remained undaunted; they insisted that regulated prostitution was illegal, as it established an extraparliamentary system which deprived prostitutes of the rights they too had been granted by the Declaration of the Rights of Man and Citizen in 1789. In the words of Marcelle Legrand-Falco, an ardent suffragist and member of the Conseil National des Femmes, a middle-class feminist organization, the regulationist system was the "quintessence of arbitrary," a "violation of individual liberty," and a "cynical violation of the Rights of Woman."[10] Moreover, since the turn of the century, feminists like Ghénia Avril de Sainte-Croix had maintained that regulation followed a double standard of morality because it focused its disciplinary mechanisms upon the prostitute and not her client.[11] The call for a single moral standard (*unité de la morale*) was yet another feminist plea that a universal — and not particular — model be applied to women as well as men. Avril wrote: "We do not want a woman, whoever she is, to be subjected to the laws of exception. Like man, she is a human being with a right to her integral autonomy, and we protest against every kind of regulation that, under the pretext of safeguarding the health of men, or even the family, sanctions and consolidates the principle of a double morality for the two sexes."[12] State-sanctioned prostitution thereby underscored the contradictory meanings attributed to French women's bodies. For example, if national and nationalist discourse depicted women as embodiments of Republican virtue and at least in theory as recipients of universal rights, how could some women be subject to arbitrary laws, inspections, and imprisonments? And how was the French woman's individual liberty to be reconciled with the social value of reproduction and the exigencies of the procreative family?

Whitewashing the Slave Trade

By the 1920s and 1930s female immigrants had become increasingly visible in Europe and the Americas, generating new anxieties about the movement of women across national boundaries. The campaign against white slavery was a direct consequence of the migration of European women; in turn, the nation attempted to extend its paternalistic control overseas to safeguard the honor of its female members.[13] French and other European reformers acknowledged that female migration was sometimes warranted, especially if it reunited families which had been split apart by the immigration of male heads of household to foreign lands. For this reason they demanded that legal measures be implemented to insure the safety of female migrants and their children. The League of Nations backed this call for reform, and article 7 of its Convention on the Traffic (1921) called for the surveillance of women and children traveling by sea unaccompanied. Signatories to the convention were to post flyers in ports and train stations warning women of the potential dangers of the trade, and providing information on housing and other forms of assistance.[14] National and international attention was therefore centered on the alleged *entrapment* of women, often in port cities and at border crossings, and their sale into a life of "ill repute." The victims were ostensibly forced onto trains and steamships, transported to South and Central America, North Africa, and East Asia, and sold into prostitution. White slavery was thus the cruel inverse of immigration: female nationals were wrenched from their native land, forced to migrate and sell their labor.[15]

Initially the term "white slavery" referred to procuring practiced by brothel owners and suppliers within France who sought to recruit and replenish their staff, typically for work within regulated brothels. French abolitionists employed a broader definition: they argued that regulated prostitution in any individual nation directly fed the traffic in women abroad, and thus they saw white slavery as encompassing "forced" prostitution both within national borders and beyond them. Abolitionists in France and their allies at the League of Nations emphasized the critical link between national and international networks of prostitution. In their view, women were first entrapped in their native country and forced to engage in commercial sex, and later sold to traffickers who circulated them across the globe in accordance with the laws of supply and demand. Opponents of the early-twentieth-century trade were well aware of the important role of late capitalism in transforming the nature of prostitution. The social reformer Paul Gemaehling claimed that "as part of the commercialization and industrialization of modern life, procuring now shows all the characteristics of a methodically organized commerce . . . with ramifications across the entire world."[16] Similarly, the feminist newspaper *L'Œuvre* wrote: "The traffic in women is an organization that extends throughout the world and has considerable amounts of money at its disposal. Women are sold, exchanged, and resold from brothel to brothel and from country to country."[17]

Like "abolitionism," the term "white slave trade" is deeply inflected with racial meaning. By emphasizing the whiteness of the abducted woman, Europeans could imagine that one of their own was forced to prostitute herself to foreigners, and even to men of color. As Donna Guy has explained in her groundbreaking study of Buenos Aires, the white slave campaign was "explicitly racist" because it presumed that all white women in foreign brothels had been coerced by immoral men, and that no white woman, no matter how desperate, would willingly engage in commercial sex with a man of color.[18] Abolitionists exploited this racialized rhetoric by equating the prostitution of women with African slavery, defending the analogy on the ground that "white slavery" referred to a similar "form of commerce."[19] Meanwhile, the anti-trade press described traffickers as "slave drivers" (*négriers*) and the women they transported as "human merchandise" and "objects of pleasure and commerce."[20] It was not until 1921 that the League of Nations officially substituted the term "traffic in women" (*la traite des femmes*) for "white slavery" (*la traite des blanches*), a term which, the organization acknowledged, appeared to neglect the entrapment, exchange, and prostitution of women of color in a worldwide network of vice.[21] As the Dutch delegate to the International Conference on the Traffic of 1921 explained: "It was never intended that we should concern ourselves only with white women. Still at first there was so much to be done that we began by dealing only with the White Slave Trade and not with that in coloured women."[22]

According to several commentators, the lives of prostitutes were actually worse than those of African slaves. A report of the League of Nations in 1927 proclaimed that "as long as there remains a single creature submitted to a slavery more ignominious than ever was that of blacks, the voice of women will rise to demand the end to an institution that dishonors Humanity."[23] Another leading abolitionist voice was the League for the Uplifting of Public Morality (Ligue pour le Relèvement de la Moralité Publique), a mostly male and overwhelmingly middle-class reform association whose stated goal was to infuse democracy with morality.[24] Its secretary general Emile Pourésy spoke of the "hypocrisy" of contemporary protests against slavery in Ethiopia when women in France were also enslaved. He explained that while African slaves worked amid the beauty of nature, under the tropical sun and to the singing of birds, prostitutes were mercilessly locked in brothels and denied access to the outside world.[25]

Police records overwhelmingly describe sex traffickers as white metropolitan Frenchmen. However, in the popular press traffickers were distinctly racialized as Jews, Corsicans, southern Italians, or sometimes men of color. According to an article in *La Grande Revue* in 1902, the large majority of sex traffickers were "Levantines, Galician Jews, and South Americans."[26] Tales in mass circulation newspapers of white slavery played on cultural anxieties and fomented public outrage. Unsurprisingly, the portrayal of sex traffickers as Jews or men of color roughly corresponded with waves of anti-Semitic protest in France, as well as colonial migration to the metropole. Historians have documented the explicit anti-Semitism of the white slavery campaign in an international context, along with its stereotypical portrait of the Jewish trafficker.[27] French commentators also resorted to a number of long-standing depictions of Jews — as salacious, in control of international capital, and ultimately disloyal to any nation in which they resided — to associate them with the problem of sex trafficking.[28] On the whole, social reformers perpetuated the racialized analyses of white slavery which appeared in French newspapers. Gemaehling, a professor at the University of Strasbourg and president of the League for the Uplifting of Public Morality, accused Jewish cartels such as "Zwy Migdal" of maintaining the "route to Buenos Aires," the most popular destination for prostitutes in the first half of the twentieth century. According to Gemaehling, Jewish involvement in the trade was responsible for its "capitalist and internationalist character."[29] Anti-Semitic rhetoric easily lent itself to the particularities of the white slave narrative:

because of the long-standing belief that Jews were involved in international conspiracies, networks were already in place for trafficking women across the globe. Similarly, Jewish lust for profit was purportedly so great that a price could even be placed on the honor of young French women.

Colonial men were also singled out for their alleged role in promoting sex trafficking. Like the vision of French women entrapped and traded by venal Jewish men, the idea that men of color had helped to "defile" white women fueled popular anxieties about colonial migration to the metropole. Before a Parisian audience, Gemaehling lamented that France had "abolished the *traite des noirs*" (traffic in black people) only to replace it with the "*traite des blanches*" (traffic in white women). According to a transcript of Gemaehling's speech, the crowd roared with disapprobation when he noted that in France, it was most frequently black men who organized the white slave trade. He further goaded his audience with the story of a brothel in an eastern French city, staffed by twelve white women and run by a black madame. But most egregious of all, in Gemaehling's words, was that the brothel catered exclusively to a black clientele.[30]

White women in general and French prostitutes in particular were in demand for the international trade. In 1910 the abolitionist newspaper *Le Relèvement Social* claimed that "procurers from the entire world come to Paris to supply themselves."[31] More than two decades later, in 1937, the Temporary Union against Regulated Prostitution (Union Temporaire contre la Prostitution Réglémentée), an abolitionist umbrella organization with 300,000 individual members and more than eighty member associations, corroborated this view in its petition to the French Senate. In this document representatives of the Temporary Union stated that most of the prostitutes contributing to the "worldwide plague" of white slavery hailed from France. Women were first recruited in Paris, where they may or may not have spent time in a regulated brothel, and eventually sent to Marseilles, Bordeaux, and other ports before embarking to South America and especially the "Sin City" of Buenos Aires.[32]

The "*franchucha*," according to the well-known sensationalist reporter Albert Londres, was an Argentine expression which, owing to the prevalence of French prostitutes in Buenos Aires, simultaneously connoted "French woman" and "woman of ill repute."[33] There are a number of reasons to discount Londres's lurid account of the sex trade in Argentina.[34] Especially significant is his overt anti-Semitism, reflected in his scathing portrayal of Jewish traffickers and his more sympathetic depiction of French ones.[35] However, the "truth" of Londres's account is less interesting than the depiction of a phantasmatic Buenos Aires that he conveyed to a French reading public already voraciously consuming stories about the trade. Londres's French audience found his account captivating precisely because he described Argentine brothels teeming with French women forced to engage in interracial sex for pay.

The *casas francescas* — or French-inspired bordellos — were important features of vice culture in Buenos Aires. Police archives contain business cards from brothels with quaint names like La Petite Bordelaise, La Nouvelle Maison Française, and Le Moulin Rouge, a "Maison Spécialement Française."[36] Likewise, the French military attaché assigned to document the traffic in women in Argentina and Uruguay reported that "in this world of gallantry, French women are the most sought after because of their spirit, and the ill-perceived reflection of Paris they supposedly convey. The best-known pleasure zones of Buenos Aires are called Le Pigalle and Le Casino, and French is the language most commonly spoken there."[37]

Donna Guy has argued that Buenos Aires was the "ideal target" for European reformers concerned with sex trafficking because of its predominantly male population, in addition to a substantial presence of female immigrants. Regulated prostitution had existed in Argentina from 1875 to 1936; as in a number of Latin American countries, Argentine reformers (*higienistas*) had been inspired by French writings on social hygiene.[38] An official study presented to the League of Nations in 1927 corroborated reports in the popular press that French women prevailed among registered foreign prostitutes abroad. According to its findings, French women accounted for 45 percent of registered prostitutes in Montevideo, 75 percent in Buenos Aires, and an astonishing 80 percent in Rio de Janeiro.[39] Both journalists and representatives to international congresses on the trade maintained that of all women, French prostitutes were the most desired and the highest paid: Londres claimed that French prostitutes in Buenos Aires could charge five pesos while Polish women could only ask for two. In any event, European prostitutes always fared better than indigenous ones, who were forced to sell their labor for the lowest price of all.[40] Similarly, the French representative to the International Conference against the Traffic in Women of 1910 reported that traffickers sold French women to South American procurers for 7,000 francs, while Chinese and Japanese women fetched only 1,000.[41]

If statistics indicate that French women were overrepresented among foreign prostitutes in most nations, is it true that they were the most desired? While this question cannot be answered with any empirical certainty, it is crucial to remember that "white slavery" was an extremely protean concept, one which could be adapted to fit a number of nationalist, paternalist, and imperialist narratives. I will address the imperial resonance of white slavery shortly; for now let me emphasize that white slave narratives were deployed in many countries for similar reasons: in the hope of curtailing the sexual and economic freedom of all women, and their ability to move about locally, nationally, and internationally.[42] Nevertheless, France had the dubious privilege of being the country which had exported regulated prostitution to the rest of the world. In the course of the nineteenth century and the early twentieth, what was referred to as the "French system" was implemented in a number of nations, including Russia, Mexico, Sweden, and Argentina, as well as in the French colonies, protectorates, and mandates.[43] Foreigners most likely considered the French prostitute the most authentic representative of the "French system," and easily associated her with Parisian red-light districts and other powerful signifiers of vice culture.

Despite the orientalist fantasies which had captivated the French erotic imagination at the turn of the century,[44] in the literature on sex trafficking it was the white prostitute who received the highest acclaim. The journalist Henri Champly, whose account of the sex trade in Shanghai in 1933 was meant to complement Londres's study of Buenos Aires, regretted that the French imperial presence in Asia had encouraged "commerce in white women among Asian men" (*la commerce des Blanches parmi les Jaunes*).[45] According to Champly, it was not only Asians but all men of color who succumbed willingly to the *Vénus Occidentale*: a prostitute in Montmartre explained to him that French women have an irresistible appeal to men of color, and "the darker the man the more he desires us . . . right down to the pure African."[46] According to Champly, French women were the most attractive members of the most attractive race: "the great beauty secret of white women is a harmony, an equilibrium which shines from inside to outside and from the soul to the body, and French women have the greatest percentage of this charm."[47]

While regulationists believed that the "French system" maintained the boundary between respectable women and the fallen, abolitionists argued that on the contrary, the notoriety of French prostitutes abroad demeaned the nation and its women as a whole. Abolitionists lamented that the regulationist system, which by the interwar years had become increasingly rare outside Greater France, had damaged French standing in the eyes of the civilized world. In addition, the conspicuous presence of French women in overseas brothels had compounded this dishonor. In a letter to the Ministry of Foreign Affairs, a French diplomat in Guatemala complained that French prostitutes there had "misrepresented the morality of the French woman."[48] The feminist Maria Vérone, a practicing attorney and ardent suffragist affiliated with the left-leaning Ligue Française pour le Droit des Femmes, shared this opinion. At a function hosted by the Temporary Union against Regulated Prostitution in 1934, she called the crowd's attention to the unfortunate impression that French prostitutes left with international observers: "This is why, gentlemen, they think that all of us French women are for sale, and that it is only a question of price."[49] Similarly, in the Temporary Union's annual bulletin in 1936 it was noted that a man who could pay for a *francesita* in a remote South American town was likely to "imagine he could do the same with any French woman."[50]

Such fears reflect the bourgeois feminism of the Temporary Union and its members, along with their desire to see all French women's bodies conform to the norms of middle-class respectability.[51] By affirming that the prostitute's indecency could be generalized to include all French women, feminist abolitionists accepted the gendered social and spatial constraints which dictated that any "public woman" was morally suspect. Feminist abolitionists never challenged the image of the virtuous citizen mother so dear to the Republican gender order. For them the very existence of regulated prostitution was an impediment to women's rights, because the "enslaved" prostitute highlighted the profoundly unequal status of men and women in the nation: she was the polar opposite of the enfranchised woman, if not an argument against her enfranchisement. For this reason, Gemaehling reminded members of the Temporary Union that as long as there existed in France an "official organization of female slavery, it would be impossible to demonstrate that all French women deserved full citizenship rights."[52]

Abolitionists forcefully argued that the trade in women violated the prostitute's rights. Because they depicted the prostitute as a victim rather than an agent, abolitionists never considered the possibility of the prostitute's "right to work." According to anti-trade rhetoric, women did not willingly choose to prostitute themselves but were forced to do so, and forced by self-serving procurers rather than poverty.[53] There is no reliable documentation of how many women were sold into prostitution, kidnapped, or duped by the promise of marriage or "respectable" work overseas. Such women surely existed. But in France, Alain Corbin has concluded that the abducted virgin or woman transported overseas against her will was a "rare exception," just as Judith Walkowitz holds that there is little evidence supporting the sexual slavery of British girls and women in this period.[54] The fact remains that *any* woman migrating alone at this time was immediately considered suspect, and as for the "victims" of the trade, they were most likely prostitutes traveling abroad in search of more lucrative work. If one views prostitution as labor and prostitutes as workers, it follows that they too circulated in a global economy which demanded women's work as well as men's.[55] In this light, the feminist scholar Marjan Weijers makes the excellent point that "whereas men who migrate tend to be viewed as active, adventurous, brave and deserving of admiration, for the same behavior women are pictured as passive, foolish and naïve, deserving either rescue or punishment."[56]

To insist that white slavery was forced prostitution denies the prostitute's volition, along with her economic and sexual agency. By clinging to the model of the prostitute as an innocent victim, feminist reformers endorsed the traditionalist vision of the gender order praised by bourgeois reformers and cultural conservatives.[57] However unwittingly, they colluded with ideological allies and opponents to formulate a discourse intended to limit women's access to public space. After all, the anti-trade campaign had been galvanized by cultural anxieties about female independence — hence its persistent reference to life outside the domestic sphere as perilous and morally corrupt. Similarly, female agency was written out of the white slave narrative in order to describe a chaste and redeemable virgin who, once saved, could be reintegrated into the family and the state, and thereby could return her reproductive capital to the nation.

While abolitionists claimed that they wanted to free prostitutes from the conspicuous surveillance of the regulated brothel, their solution also required the vigilant monitoring of women, who were now to be watched over in ports, at train stations, and aboard steamships. A letter issued by the Ministry of Interior in 1919 regretted how the traffic in French women to Argentina and Uruguay discredited "France's reputation abroad." In response, the ministry called for the "attentive and efficacious surveillance" of steamships departing for the Americas.[58] In 1921 the feminist Ghénia Avril de Sainte-Croix reported to the League of Nations that "young emigrant girls" faced a number of "moral dangers" aboard boats catering to the transport of migrants. She documented a "lack of surveillance" on these ships, where men traveling in first class "could easily enter third-class areas" and "[strike] up conversations with female emigrants." Sainte-Croix claimed that during the course of their journey young women were "indoctrinated" by unscrupulous men with more lucrative offers of employment.[59] According to the Canadian delegate to the League of Nations international conference of 1921, the steamship was a dangerous and unsupervised space where women lost good sense and succumbed to their darker side: "The cause has not yet been definitely settled as to why so many women and girls traveling on a steamship forget the careful consideration of their reputation and person without which they drift very close to the borderland of undesirability. It may be their first freedom from the restraint of homelife, or the escape from toil irksome and unpleasant, into a temporary condition of ease . . . it is a fact too patent to be overlooked that a percentage of women and girls, unaccompanied by father, mother, or husband, do commit indiscretions during a sea voyage which they know are really transgressing propriety if not something worse."[60]

Abolitionist propaganda described in menacing language the imminent danger of sexual servitude. For example, a flyer posted by the Temporary Union in Paris read: "Young girls, young women, watch out!!! Be wary of men or women you don't know who are on the lookout for you." If they required assistance, women were encouraged to contact either the Temporary Union or one of the Catholic, Protestant, or Jewish agencies devoted to the protection of young women, whose addresses were listed at the bottom of the page.[61] Similarly, another flyer designed for the ports of Marseilles carried the following warning: "Young women, young girls, beware! In Marseilles more than anywhere else you risk falling into a trap from which you will never escape. Be watchful because with every step and in every instant you risk becoming the victim of unscrupulous people."[62]

Although abolitionists professed to work for the emancipation of the prostitute and, by extension, of French women in general, abolitionism was an alternative form of subjugation which sought to place women under the scrutiny of social reform agencies, churches, and synagogues, or their families. According to this view, "benevolent" forms of surveillance were preferable to the medical and police surveillance that women endured under regulation. The French prostitute abroad had removed herself from two critical sites of paternalistic control: the family and the French state. Anti-trade discourse therefore focused on curtailing particular freedoms and re-inscribing social control. As a consequence, the French crusade against traffic in women cannot be divorced from pronatalist political culture which demanded a stark distinction between recreational and procreative sex. The stream of French women migrating abroad, whether to work as prostitutes or otherwise, amounted to a loss of reproductive capital; in the words of one abolitionist, each girl abandoned to white slavery was a mother lost to the nation.[63] And because both the popular press and abolitionist discourse portrayed the "victim" of white slavery as an innocent and abducted virgin, it was easy to envision that before her fall, she might have assumed the so-cially sanctioned role of the citizen mother. In contrast, the French woman irreparably lost to the trade was depicted as the antithesis of respectability. Her visibility degraded female compatriots in the eyes of the international community, while her conspicuous "enslavement" undermined Republican feminists' claims for rights and the reproductive agenda of the Republican state. Like the "Malthusian couple" who shirked its civic duty to procre-ate, the prostitute promoted depopulation and accelerated national decline: asocial, syphilitic, and degenerate, she only sapped the nation of potential births and further infected the social body.[64]

Separate but Equal? French Prostitutes
and North African Men

We have seen that mass immigration fostered the debate on white slavery by calling attention to the movement of women across national borders, and by transporting male migrants to all parts of the globe. The surveillance of female subjects was the concern not only of regulationists advocating an extralegal and medico-hygienic authority over prostitutes, but also of abo-litionists seeking to reestablish paternalistic control over the family and the state. But imperial rule also demanded the active policing of colonized subjects. As a result, the police and the military—who along with the medical profession were the key proponents of regulation—focused their disciplinary gaze upon colonized men along with female prostitutes. While a primary feminist critique of regulation was that it monitored the bodies of women alone, in the case of colonial subjects who visited white prostitutes, another kind of regulation was at stake. The police took care to note the use of French brothels by foreigners, especially those from North Africa. Similarly, the French Army's High Command—which was not unfamiliar with the question of its soldiers' access to prostitution—specifically addressed the problem of how to safely supply colonial soldiers with sex workers.[65]

In 1914 a "Morals Brigade" was created within the Paris Prefecture of Police by fusing two earlier units devoted to monitoring vice within the city. The new unit was responsible for inspecting maisons de tolérance, as well as investigating and prosecuting traffic in women, pederasty, the drug trade, pornography, and clandestine prostitution. The Morals Brigade collected detailed information on local bordellos, including whether they catered to French men, foreigners, or both. Documents left by the brigade claim that North Africans in particular were the primary patrons of the infamous *maisons d'abattage*, in which prostitutes serviced multiple clients for a minimal fee. (In French, to work "*à l'abattage*" means to do something quickly and without care.)[66] Prostitutes working in these houses saw thirty to fifty men a day for a fee of six to ten francs each, which included a towel and bar of soap.[67] Alain Corbin describes the maisons d'abattage as the product of early-twentieth-century political economy, offering "Taylorized coitus" and "conveyor belt sex."[68] One such example was the brothel at 8, boulevard de la Chapelle, which was carefully monitored by the police after a complaint that at this address the "body of each unfortunate woman was passed over by an average of fifty [North African] men each day." The letter requesting police attention to this matter indulged a rather hackneyed phantasm of black male sexuality when commenting on the genitalia of the brothel's clients: because they were "hung like mules" (*montés comme des mulets*), North African men had "deformed" the "poor French women" who worked there.[69] Again and again, both proponents and opponents of regulated prostitution relied on prurient observations—if not outright fantasies—of the sexual practices of colonized people.

Dr. Alfred Lévy-Bing's report to the Ministry of Public Health in 1935 observed that a number of maisons d'abattage charged French men a higher rate than "Arabs." A madame explained to Lévy-Bing that this was due to the Arab's satisfaction with a perfunctory visit ("l'Arabe monte et déscend") while "the French man takes his time."[70] Her understanding of the differences between French and Arab sexual practices is clear. Even with a prostitute the French man remained bound to the rules of seduction and reciprocal pleasure, while the Arab satisfied his basest carnal instincts. Surely it was for this reason that Madame Augustine Keller provided her French clients with a set of clean linens, but Arabs with only oilcloths and undersheets.[71] Lévy-Bing even noted that Arab clients would not indulge prostitutes working à l'abattage with a bit of petroleum jelly when in need: "If I point this out," he self-consciously insisted, "it is uniquely to show the tolerance acquired by the genital organs of these women, thanks to their long training."[72] Lévy-Bing's report therefore contrasted the bestial and excessive desire of colonial men with that of Frenchmen who, even in the context of commercial sex, comported themselves in a civilized and even chivalrous manner.

Not all prostitutes accepted work from North African men. Some brothels refused them admittance, while others were opened with the express purpose of administering to their needs. Still other maisons de tolérance practiced a "separate but equal" form of segregation, such as the establishment in the Parisian suburb of Saint-Denis described by Lévy-Bing, which was literally divided in half. Separate entries for French and colonial men ended in segregated bars, while separate stairways led to rooms on different landings. When asked why such strict segregation was necessary, the madame explained to Lévy-Bing that French workers did not want to mix with the brothel's North African clientele.[73]

While Josephine Blais's establishment at 162, boulevard de Grenelle refused to receive either Algerians or Moroccans, a number of neighboring ones did, such as the infamous brothel which opened on 12 June 1930 at 43, rue Frémicourt.[74] Residents of the quartier loudly protested this particular maison de tolérance because it catered exclusively to North Africans, thus providing colonial workers with reason to come to their neighborhood and commit "scandalous acts" in the streets.[75] The establishment was also discussed at length by members of the Temporary Union and the League for the Uplifting of Public Morality. Émile Pourésy, the league's secretary general, complained that at the rue Frémicourt the immorality of prostitution à l'abattage was compounded because its clientele was not white. He disdainfully explained that at this particular brothel, "in three days, twelve white women could share one-thousand Arabs [*Sidis*], at the rate of sixty to seventy each day."[76] Of course Pourésy's calculations are imprecise, given his penchant for hyperbole and his desire to sensationalize the issue.

On a similar note, at a meeting of the Temporary Union in February 1931, Marc Sangnier strongly objected to the French government's legal sanction of brothels like the one on the rue Frémicourt in which "white slaves" (*les esclaves blanches*) were made available "for the pleasure of Negroes" (*pour la jouissance des nègres*). He argued that the rue Frémicourt brothel had tarnished France's reputation as a colonial power in the eyes of the "civilized world." According to his logic, while the Colonial Exposition of 1931 was meant to showcase the glory of the French empire and its civilizing mission, the rue Frémicourt establishment revealed its bankruptcy. Sangnier deeply regretted that international spectators to the exposition would also have the opportunity to view the regulated brothels of Paris, not to mention the one at the rue Frémicourt, which had been "specially organized for colored people to have their pitiful needs met."[77]

In response to numerous individual complaints and a petition signed by 130 residents of the quartier, the Morals Brigade responded with round-the-clock surveillance, but found no evidence to corroborate the protests.[78] A report in November 1930 confirmed that indeed the brothel was extremely busy. According to the report, each prostitute saw ten to twelve men on weekdays and twenty-five to fifty on weekends, hence a total for the establishment of 150–200 clients during the week and 400–500 on Saturdays and Sundays (note that these estimates are far more modest than Pourésy's, although they too do not add up properly). In any case, the Morals Brigade did not document any increase in street fighting or lewd behavior in the neighborhood.[79] Toeing the regulationist party line, Prefect of Police Chiappe instead praised the brothel for diverting colonial men from clandestine and unregulated prostitutes who were likely to carry syphilis.[80]

Like the recruitment of colonial men to work in French factories during the First World War, the stationing of colonial troops in the metropole provided a new context in which French fears of métissage could be expressed.

This uneasiness with the practice of interracial sex is reflected in the military's surveillance of prostitution for colonial troops in France. According to army officials, access to prostitution was of supreme importance because colonial soldiers deprived of a sexual outlet threatened the safety of French women. Of course the French Army had long made the same argument to justify the brothel visits of white soldiers, and we cannot say for sure whether it was made with more vehemence on behalf of colonial men. Thus during the First World War, French General Headquarters ordered that the use of brothels be "discretely encouraged" for *all* soldiers. Initially this meant that public officials such as the police should allow more brothels to be created; however, throughout the course of the war the army took a more active stance on managing commercial sex and thereby became the "new master of regulation."[81] In 1918 General Mordacq, chief of staff (*chef du cabinet*) of the War Ministry, issued orders allowing brothels to be established near encampments that were far from urban areas and lacked easy access to prostitutes. When buildings could not be rented or requisitioned to serve as brothels, the army corps of engineers was charged with building new ones.[82]

According to army officials, the potential consequences of commercial sex differed for metropolitan and colonial troops. But in practice, the army command was troubled by relations between African soldiers and *any* white women, whether or not they were prostitutes. "There is something amoral about French women, prostitutes or not, submitting to the caprices of *indigènes*," wrote General Guntz of the 13th Infantry Division.[83] A report in 1935 expressed concern that the lack of "indigenous" women would encourage colonial soldiers to leave the barracks and seek out French women, whether in regulated brothels or among the general population. For example, when the 22nd Regiment of Algerian infantrymen (RTA) left Verdun for Toulouse in 1931, a letter to the chief of the Overseas Division (Section Outre-Mer) confirmed that seventy French women had tagged behind the regiment. But even more disturbing was that "respectable" French women, some of whom were married or "young women of the bourgeoisie," had joined the convoy following the colonial troops.[84]

The High Command was convinced that these liaisons undermined military discipline and damaged the nation's prestige in the eyes of its colonial subjects, but it also warned that denying North African men sexual access to

28. *Au Camp d'Arbalou l'Arbi   Le B M. C.*

8. "The Camp at Arbalou l'Arbi, le BMC." n.d. [probably 1925]. Postcard, personal collection of the author.

women would encourage homosexuality. Ann Stoler has commented on the "absent presence of the dangers of homosexuality" in metropolitan anxieties about interracial sexuality,[85] and while such conspicuous silences also punctuate French Army documents, in this case the fear of same-sex relations was made explicit. The report concluded that to safeguard the reputation of white women, sustain army morale, and hinder the practice of homosexual sex, local brothels must hire North African prostitutes, or *bordels militaires de campagne* must be installed inside the barracks.[86]

The bordels militaires de campagne (BMCs) — or "military brothels in the field" — were ambulatory prostitution units provided by the army to minister to French and colonial troops in the colonies and mandates (figure 8). As for the use of BMCs in the metropole, it appears that they were only established in the occupied Rhineland, where they were available to colonial soldiers as part of the recreation provided by the so-called Moorish cafés (cafés maures). "Indigenous women" — probably North Africans, although this is not specified in the documents — were given round-trip tickets to Europe along with a financial bonus to work as prostitutes. In 1921 the government funds which had subsidized their travel dried up, and shortly thereafter the Rhineland BMCs were terminated.[87]

BMCS are distinguishable from makeshift brothels by their itinerant nature, with tents, bedding, and women traveling as part of an advancing army convoy. Peripatetic prostitution is not unique to the BMC; mines and other industrial sites have long employed similar forms of commercial sex. What interests me in particular is which sexual arrangements the BMCs sanctioned and which they sought to impede, as well as how proponents of regulated prostitution characterized the sexual desire of French and colonial men. Within metropolitan France access to regulated maisons de tolérance would typically circumvent the need for BMCs. However, because army officials attempted to segregate colonial soldiers and white prostitutes, and because some sex workers refused nonwhite clients, the army command was forced to revive its discussion of the BMC in the metropole.

A note to the First and Third Bureau of the Army's Chief of Staff in 1935 warned that the principal effect of denying colonial men access to brothels was to "multiply in a worrisome fashion contacts between French women and indigenous men." The document explained that "cases of marriages and concubinage between French women and North African men were augmenting each day," and for this reason North African prostitutes should be recruited to work in French brothels, or BMCs installed in the barracks.[88] Colonel Massoni of the Eighth Regiment of Moroccan Infantrymen (*tirailleurs*) feared the "serious social consequences" of allowing his soldiers to frequent European women. He therefore suggested to the city government of Belfort that an annex be attached to the local maison de tolérance to house North African prostitutes who would cater exclusively to his troops.[89] A report in 1935 claimed that to inhibit the possibility of marriage between indigenous soldiers and French women, "special" establishments staffed by Arab women and reserved for colonial troops were necessary. Sexual segregation would safeguard "French prestige" while accommodating Arab men who, according to the report, "could not live without women."[90]

Intelligence collected on North African troops also warned of the growing number of liaisons between *indigènes* and French women. The regimental commander (*chef de corps*) was to "oppose as much as possible such marriages by refusing them authorization except in exceptional cases," "exert a vigilant surveillance over colonial troops who could have relations with European women," and finally "not hesitate to order their transfer or repatriation."[91] According to General Nogues, the "easy relations" that French women entered into with colonial soldiers had gravely damaged "French prestige," an expression frequently employed to convey both sexual respectability and fitness for imperial rule.[92] Officials at another camp insisted that to maintain French authority, relations between North African men and white women, even if they were prostitutes, had to be suppressed. Army intelligence suggested that the majority of rapes committed against French women in North Africa were the work of indigenous men who had once lived in the metropole, where they had become accustomed to the company of white women. To avoid such problems in the future, army officials held that "from now on we must take the necessary measures to see that contact between our colonial troops and white women is practically abolished."[93] Another report cautioned that to avoid sexual or romantic relationships between European women and men of color, the Army Command must "use all means necessary" to divert the energies of colonial soldiers to local maisons de tolérance.[94]

In theory, to staff metropolitan BMCs and brothels with North African women was to legitimize the subjugation of colonial women's bodies. However, through a surprising twist of events, the Army's plan to import colonial women for sex work in metropolitan France was thwarted by the League of Nations. The League's Subcommittee on the Traffic in Women and Children provided the legal basis to block the "trade in women" within Greater France. The International Convention of October 1933 included an injunction against transporting a woman over the age of majority to another country "for the purposes of debauchery," even with her consent. The pertinent article specified that its use of the term "country" was meant to include the colonies, protectorates, territories, and mandates of each signatory.[95] As France was one of eighteen nations to ratify the convention, the Army High Command gradually came to realize that recruiting African women to work as prostitutes in the metropole would be in flagrant violation of international law.[96] The intervention by the League of Nations in the debate over white slavery demonstrates how the construction of gendered notions of respectability and racially appropriate sexual exchanges transcended the boundaries of the imperial nation-state, with "transnational communities" like the League of Nations and the international feminist movement further complicating the question of sex trafficking.[97]

For French abolitionists the traffic in French women to the colonies was at least as pressing as the traffic in women to France. Paul Gemaehling resoundingly praised the League of Nations Convention of 1933 because he believed that it would eradicate "a particularly repugnant form of the trade: the recruitment of French women, destined to be delivered to our Asian and African subjects." [98] In the colonies sexual relations between European women and men of color were cast as particularly dangerous because of a widespread belief in the imperial fiction that European prestige depended on the presence of virtuous and inaccessible white women. According to both abolitionists and the Army High Command, the white woman's sexual availability was a threat to imperial rule, and allowing colonial men to have access to French prostitutes undermined the very foundations of empire. Expressions of this sentiment in abolitionist discourse appeared in the newspaper *L'Abolitionniste*, which lamented the French state's role in promoting the degradation of its female citizens by institutionalizing the regulated brothel: "When the French state bureaucracy [*l'administration française*] itself opens these hovels for the use of our workers and colored soldiers, in which French women are delivered to them for a price . . . it undermines respect for white women which, up until now, had been one of the undisputed foundations of our civilizing initiative." [99]

In a similar vein, a reader of the popular newspaper *Le Temps* described the white woman as the "most magnificent symbol of [French] prestige," which conferred upon the nation its "right to colonize." But now that racial boundaries had been abandoned in the colonies, the white woman's authority was on the wane: "Up until today, she had been a veritable goddess in the eyes of a dying barbarism." [100] The social reformist newspaper *Le Relèvement Social* asked how the supposedly "superior race" could maintain its standing in the eyes of the "so-called inferior race" if it "delivers its women for a few pennies to men of all races and all colors?" "It would be lamentable," the article continued, "if in their ignorance these poor people mistook this orgy of blood, incoherence, and debauchery for civilization!" [101]

Needless to say, the BMCS were a focus of abolitionist attacks, as was the earnest support that the military gave to prostitution as a whole. To Émile Pourésy, the BMCS were one further example of how the French were "poisoning rather than civilizing" the colonized: "How do we expect black, yellow, and brown men to respect honest women when for five francs or even less, they can approach a woman who is the same color as a doctor, an officer, a general, or a governor."[102] Once again, the Temporary Union against Regulated Prostitution emphasized the French government's complicity in the matter. Not only could a man of color enter the BMC and "pay a minimal sum for a white woman," but that woman had been placed at his disposal by the regulationist French state.[103]

The Temporary Union claimed that according to reports from French army officers, colonial men who frequented the BMC no longer respected the wives of European civilians and military leaders. While white women had "once been perfectly safe among the natives [indigènes]," since the extension of the "French system" of regulated prostitution to the colonies, they no longer were.[104] Army commanders also believed that to protect French and European prestige, BMCs in the colonies must be stocked with "indigenous" women.[105] As for French soldiers in the colonies, they had access to the BMC without regard to the race of the prostitutes working in them, although they were generally open at different times for colonial and metropolitan soldiers.[106] At least one BMC had separate entrances for each group "so as not to disturb the European clientele that frequents this establishment."[107]

Abolitionists also charged that France was abdicating its civilizing mission by exporting prostitution to the colonies, protectorates, and mandates. According to the Temporary Union, the "scandal" of regulated prostitution had been introduced into Syria and Lebanon in the 1920s against the protests of the native population.[108] General Gouraud commissioned Robert Tucci, a café owner in Beirut, to create for French troops a chain of brothels over which the French tricolor proudly flew.[109] For this task Tucci received an advance of 100,000 francs which he used to set up 18 brothels staffed by 200 women in Aleppo, Damascus, Beirut, Tripoli, Ham, and Homs. By the time of the League of Nations study in 1932 of trafficking in the East and Far East, 207 maisons de tolérance were counted in the Levant.[110] Regulation continued in the French concession of Shanghai even though by 1933 other western occupiers as well as the Chinese had abolished it.[111] And remarkably enough, the report of two French colonial physicians nonchalantly referred to implementing regulated prostitution in North Africa as part of France's policy of "peaceful penetration" (l'œuvre de pénétration pacifique).[112]

9. "Casablanca: A Calm Night in the City of Love." ca. 1920. Postcard, personal collection of the author.

It was in the Maghreb that France constructed an extremely ambitious disciplinary apparatus sustained by the medical, juridical, and military sectors of colonial society: the so-called reserved quarters (*quartiers réservés*), (figure 9). The first, Bousbir, was built in Casablanca in the early 1920s: occupying 24,000 square meters, it housed approximately 200 inhabitants. There was only one entrance, guarded by the police and the military, and its mosaics, fountains, and arcades invoked in the eyes of one observer "an Eden straight out of *One Thousand and One Nights*."[113] To accommodate their clientele and the prostitute-inhabitants who were generally confined to this space, the reserved quarters of several North African cities contained a number of shops, a hammam, a movie theater, a smokeshop, and a "Moorish café."[114]

This particular feature of colonial urbanism reflected the common interests of metropolitan social hygienic reform and colonial policy. Christelle Taraud even suggests that Bousbir exemplified the wish to apply in Casablanca what had failed in Paris in the preceding century, during the heyday of regulation.[115] In the reserved quarters the ordering of the city and the management of sex went hand in hand. In accordance with regulationist logic, these enclosed "cities of love" segregated the brothel and its prostitutes from good society and honest women, while at the same time ostensibly containing the spread of syphilis. This Manichean distinction was crucial in North Africa, where colonial authorities claimed that it was especially difficult to label and control prostitution. According to Dr. Jean Bulliod, the veil concealed the differences between prostitutes and "ordinary" women, thereby obscuring this critical social division.[116] Another factor was the conviction of metropolitan observers that all colonized women were libidinous and wanton. Thus in Christian Houel's work on marriage, adultery, and prostitution in Morocco, published in 1912, he noted that "in the heart of all Muslim women is a whore who sleeps . . . If men did not keep them locked up or oblige them to go out veiled and in groups, there would be no Muslim woman who did not prostitute herself."[117]

While regulationists were eager to point out that prostitution and syphilis predated colonialism, the abolitionist League for the Uplifting of Public Morality painted an idyllic pre-colonial world inhabited by noble savages without any interest in paying for sex, thereby insinuating that colonialism had perverted the colonized.[118] Émile Pourésy inverted colonial morality by claiming that the white man was the enemy of the black man, and the civilized the enemy of the savage.[119] He described regulated prostitution as a "form of barbarism," deftly reversing the imperial binary of a civilized metropole and savage colonies. By bringing regulated prostitution to the mandate of Cameroon, Pourésy argued, the French nation had unmistakably demonstrated how "the greatest enemy of black civilization is white civilization."[120] In the same spirit Paul Gemaehling charged at a meeting of the Temporary Union in February 1931 that by participating in the "commerce of human flesh," France had failed in its duty to bring "civilization" to benighted parts of the world. In fact Gemaehling claimed that by aiding and abetting the traffic in colonial women, French authorities had violated the Versailles Treaty, which in his words called for its signatories to fight injustices, abolish forced labor, and come to the aid of the weak and uneducated.[121]

The League for the Uplifting of Public Morality maintained that France had also forgone its custodial responsibilities by assisting in the construction of Marrakech's reserved quarters, where it had introduced the regulated prostitution of Muslim women into a country placed under its protectorate.[122] According to Pourésy it was an "unspeakable hypocrisy" for France to believe that it had been "designated by Heaven to civilize the entire universe with its sub-savage mores [*mœurs de sous-caraïbes*]."[123] He wrote: "If it were the Moroccans who had come to France to civilize us . . . would they have set up the BMC or the reserved quarters for whites? Do you believe that if the indigenous people of our 'immense and magnificent colonial empire' . . . possessed a city like Paris, they would set up official houses of prostitution where black women were at the disposition of white men, as one now finds there: regulated brothels organized by whites for blacks, where at any hour they are sure to find white women of the people to satisfy their sexual desires . . . And we are surprised when black men no longer respect either white men or white women? When and how have we ever respected blacks?"[124]

The comments of social reformers like Gemaehling and Pourésy should not be understood as indictments of colonialism per se. Reformers feared that a degenerate France was exporting a degenerate colonial ideology which had relinquished its moralizing mission, and ignored the importance of race hygiene. What was described as "indiscriminate" racial mixing symbolized the dissolution of bodily boundaries and the subversion of established hierarchies. The reserved quarters were a case in point. Although regulationists heralded them as modern, hygienic, and rational, to abolitionists they invoked sexual chaos and perversion, a space where "French and above all Muslim women were penned in to perform sexual services for Muslims, whites, blacks, and Asians [*jaunes*]."[125] Likewise, a study of regulated prostitution in East Asia revealed that in Saigon more than eighty-one European women were working for Annamite and Chinese clients. Regulation had thereby reversed imperial rule by facilitating the "slavery of white women by yellow men" (*l'esclavage des blanches par des jaunes*).[126] Thus when the League of Nations in 1933 extended its ban on the "traffic in women" to the colonies, protectorates, and mandates, Gemaehling celebrated the event as nothing short of "progress": "For the first time, the trade in so-called consenting adult [*majeure*] women will be suppressed by an international convention . . . and will make disappear from our colonies a particularly repugnant form of the trade: the hiring of French women, destined to be delivered to our African and Asian subjects . . . One hundred years after the abolition of the enslavement of blacks by whites, we see in France the trade in white women by black men."[127]

DANS LE BLED
FAUTE DE GRIVES...!

10. "Dans le Bled: Faute des Grives . . . !" ca. 1910. Postcard, personal collection of the author.

Conclusions: Sex Work, Sexual Practices, and Nation Making

Absent from these debates was any discussion of relations between French men and colonized women. These interracial liaisons were not simply unproblematized in abolitionist and regulationist accounts but entirely unmentioned. Even abolitionists believed that prostitution was a necessary evil, and thus did not question the Frenchman's right and need to obtain commercial sex. Neither did abolitionists or regulationists question his right, as part of the colonial sexual contract, to have access to colonized women's bodies, even if they were perceived as substandard replacements for white women (figure 10).[128] This is because "colonial sexual prohibitions were racially asymmetric and gender coded."[129] Women of color were considered part of the spoils of imperialism, and white men's access to them signified the right to rule rather than a challenge to the social and racial order. While historians of empire have demonstrated that concubinage with indigenous women threatened white prestige and symbolized European degeneracy,[130] commercial sex consisted of little more than a fleeting encounter between the prostitute and her client. As a consequence, the transitory sexual act had less potential to subvert a white identity already at risk in the colonies, far from France and deeply immersed in an unfamiliar climate, culture, and mores.

Abolitionists and regulationists agreed that interracial sex between French women and colonized subjects dangerously undermined the authority of white imperial rule. Abolitionists framed their arguments against regulated prostitution by referring to its corruption of an ostensibly beneficent civilizing mission, and the shame that it brought to all French women in the eyes of a global audience. Even regulationists believed that interracial commercial sex should be eradicated or, at the very least, restricted to a racially and geographically segregated environment. I have remarked upon this obsession with white endogamy in concurrent debates on pronatalism, work science, and racial mixing. Similarly, both abolitionist and regulationist accounts of prostitution sought to minimize, if not eliminate, intimate contact between white women and men of color.

Thus for all participants in the debate on sex trafficking, the integrity of the imperial nation was reflected in the sexual modesty of white women. But abolitionists in particular followed the culturally conservative logic of pronatalism by privileging gender complementarity, the traditional family, and by extension the civic duty of reproduction. Proponents of regulation acknowledged that prostitution was labor and, as such, that it should be rationalized and carefully monitored. In contrast, abolitionists were concerned with restoring the family unit by repatriating French women and realigning the relationship between the sexes.[131] That is, the conflicting Republican imperatives of production and reproduction resurfaced in the campaigns for and against regulated prostitution. On the one hand, regulationism spoke to the exigencies of national production and its impulse to rationalize a gendered and racialized labor force. On the other hand, abolitionism employed an emancipatory rhetoric to demand the freedom of "enslaved" prostitutes, along with their safe return to the haven of the family.

As for French women, they were ultimately caught between these contradictory discourses on the social and sexual order. Should they be free to migrate and practice their trade, or was freedom only possible once they had been liberated from prostitution? Should French women be permitted to circulate in public space and across national borders, or should they be returned to the home, where their productive and reproductive capacities could best serve the nation? These very tensions were already embedded in the logic of Republicanism, which oscillated between its concern for the autonomous individual and its glorification of the procreative family. The campaign against white slavery only unmasked these contradictory impulses, forcing feminists in particular to make arguments about women's freedom in terms which emphasized women's social value to reproduction. By relying on racialized metaphors of dependency, feminists argued that regulated prostitution had deprived French women of key universal rights. But this enabled a gendered notion of dependency which repositioned women in domestic space and reinscribed paternal authority.[132]

Chapter Five

INTERMARRIAGE,
INDEPENDENT NATIONALITY,
AND INDIVIDUAL RIGHTS

The Napoleonic Civil Code of 1804 broke with the tradition of both Old Regime and Revolutionary France by dictating that a French woman who married a foreigner must assume her husband's nationality, and that he alone could transmit nationality to their offspring. While several articles of the Code decreed that wives were subordinate to the authority of their husbands — in Napoleon's words, "the woman belongs to her husband just as the fruit tree belongs to the gardener"[1] — I am most interested in articles 12 and 19, which dictated the nationality of married women. Before the promulgation of the Law of 10 August 1927, which revised the Code's stance on women's civil status, French women who married foreigners were automatically divested of their native nationality. Such marriages were not a rare occurrence in early-twentieth-century France, especially after the casualties of the Great War, which exacerbated a century-old pattern of demographic decline. With 1.4 million men dead and 700,000 women widowed, many French women turned to the pool of eligible foreign bachelors. In the decade of the 1920s alone, more than 100,000 legal marriages were contracted between French women and foreign men.[2] Between 1900 and 1926 more than 190,000 French women became foreigners by marriage, only 30,000 of whom regained French nationality by the naturalization of their husband, his death, legal separation, or divorce. The census of 1926 counted close to 150,000 French-born women who had become foreigners by marriage, of a total of one million foreign women. Native-born French women therefore represented 6.5 percent of the foreign population, and 15 percent of all foreign women.[3]

From these statistics alone it is clear that the question of independent nationality for French women married to foreigners would assume a prominent place in interwar political discourse. But this was even more true in the midst of what contemporaries described as a "demographic crisis," returning us to the problem of how to reconcile the biopolitical demands of the nation with a historically contingent vision of French racial identity. As I have demonstrated, a wide range of social critics sanctioned the marriage of French women to white European foreigners in the hope that immigrant husbands would become Frenchmen, and the children of these unions would repopulate the ailing nation. Pronatalists, industrialists, work scientists, and eugenicists argued for "*métissage* among whites" to restore the nation's demographic capital. In a similar vein, politicians and jurists in favor of independent nationality for married women maintained that if the state were to harness the demographic potential of the family, female nationals could not be expatriated upon marriage, and any children they bore had to be officially incorporated into the French national body. They therefore argued that because the patriarchal authority enshrined in the Code conflicted with the nation's populationist aims, the time was ripe for the Code's revision.[4]

The racialized limits of populationist discourse were evident in all deliberations on reform. While only a small number of the marriages in question were between French women and nonwhite men, fears of métissage between phenotypically distinct partners intersected with discussions of women's legal rights and status within the nation. Once again, social critics understood the whiteness of foreigners as a critical indicator of their potential to constitute normative French families capable of sustaining the national future. Pronatalist demography privileged the reproductive capital of white Europeans, work science confirmed that they were more productive laborers, and medico-hygienic discourse on immigration reaffirmed that race mixing between whites and people of color resulted in degenerate and inassimilable offspring. Even with regard to ostensibly non-procreative forms of sexuality such as prostitution, interracial unions were described in a language of condemnation and containment. Similarly, the feminists, jurists, and politicians who campaigned for the Code's reform also underscored the importance of white endogamy, describing relationships between French women and non-white men as racially unsound and potentially dangerous.

The continued salience of reproduction to the national narrative is clear from the way the French parliament ultimately framed the Law of 10 August 1927 as a populationist measure to reverse the trend of French demographic decline. In contrast, feminists arguing for independent nationality employed the Republican rhetoric of equality and individual rights to stake their claim.[5] In the end feminists won the battle, but not on their own terms. Because the debate on independent nationality brought to light the conflicting imperatives of Third Republican political culture — the family *and* the individual, reproductive obligations *and* civil liberties, abstract equality *and* embodied subjectivities — it allowed its various interlocutors to unite in a common goal for entirely disparate reasons. The populationist dictate would be crystallized in the legal form of the Law on French Nationality of 1927. Thereafter women's citizenship status was officially linked to the demographic demands of nation.

To juxtapose the feminist and pronatalist positions, I trace the passage of the law in the French parliament and examine the arguments of practicing attorneys and law professors from across the nation on independent nationality for married women. I also explore the crusade for this reform of the Civil Code in the feminist press, namely in the pages of France's feminist newspaper with the largest circulation, *La Française*.[6] The paper's feminist politics were moderate, anti-militant, and Republican; it is therefore a representative forum for this question because the campaign for the reform of married women's civil status was overwhelmingly carried out by middle-class and secular feminists.[7] Bourgeois feminists, many of them lawyers themselves, were active in the debate on independent nationality as part of their general project to reform the Napoleonic Code. They argued that men and women, by virtue of their shared humanity, were entitled to equal rights, and that French law must reflect this equality by employing universal categories applicable to all. Thus feminists, jurists, and parliamentarians called upon jurisprudence, as a specialized form of knowledge, to substantiate this critical debate on embodied migrations, just as the social commentators we examined earlier referred to the disciplines of work science, racial theory, and social-hygiene reform to express their versions of a racialized national narrative. The arguments formulated by feminists, jurists, and politicians against expatriating married women revealed the complicated relationship between the marriage contract and the nationality contract in early-twentieth-century France, as well as the intertwined destinies of familial obligations and citizenship status in the Republican nation-state.

These are the discursive parameters of a debate that had very real consequences for the women and men subject to these laws. The crusade for independent nationality reflected the belief of feminists and jurists that it was no longer appropriate to subsume a woman's nationality under that of her husband. This belief was part of a greater shift in the juridical conceptualization of gender roles, as the doctrines of coverture and legal incapacity, which subsumed the married woman's civil identity under that of her husband, were gradually replaced with statutes affirming her individuated status.[8] However, the discussion in parliament, the feminist press, and faculties of law across the nation was carried out in tandem with, and in response to, the experiences of French women married to foreigners. Politicians, prominent feminists, and newspaper editors received letters from women all over France laying claim to the nationality they believed was their birthright. In these accounts French women aired their grievances, solicited advice, and urged politicians and feminist leaders to continue the fight for independent nationality, thus demonstrating how profoundly they were touched by the protracted discussion of the bill in parliament. What feminists described as the "odious" and "sorrowful" consequences of the law are evident in the following letter sent by a woman from Nantes: "A Frenchwoman by birth, my greatest desire is to become French again by law. I have never recognized the nationality legally attributed to me, that of my Polish-Austrian husband, and I never will. A Frenchwoman I am, and a Frenchwoman I will remain despite it all."[9] She then implored the newspaper to continue its campaign for independent nationality on her behalf, and for all French women in the same predicament.

Patria Potestas *and the Juridical Ascription of Gender*

The stakes of the debate on independent nationality were rooted in the legal status assigned to women by the Napoleonic Civil Code of 1804. The portions of the Code that pertained to the family were based on the Roman-law tradition of *patria potestas*, or the right of the father as head of the family. Domestic relations were governed by patriarchal authority and a unitary conception of the family rather than an egalitarian one, in which the personalities and interests of individual members were valued more than the collective existence of the family.[10] Like the codes developed in other continental European nations in the eighteenth and nineteenth centuries, the Napoleonic Civil Code in its effort to achieve comprehensiveness treated the relationship between husbands and wives in great detail.[11] Articles pertaining to marriage were generally framed in the spirit of complementary but unequal roles for men and women, such as article 213, which held that a woman owed her husband obedience in return for his protection.[12] Similarly, article 214 dictated that "the wife is obliged to love her husband, and to follow him wherever he judges it appropriate to reside," granting the husband sole authority in determining the marital domicile. In the spirit of reciprocity, however, he was required to "receive her and to furnish her with all that is necessary, according to the ability of his station."[13] Some articles were particularly devastating to female independence, such as the infamous article 1124, which defined the married woman as legally incapacitated, and hence a perpetual minor before the law.[14]

Articles 12 and 19 dictated the nationality of married women. Article 12 granted French nationality to a foreign woman upon her marriage to a French man, while article 19 divested a French woman of her nationality when she married a foreigner, thereby expatriating her.[15] Among liberal feminists the attack on derivative nationality — a legal status derived solely from the civil identity of one's husband — was part of a greater movement to free women from the subjugation of the Civil Code. French feminists did not all agree that suffrage was the supreme goal of feminism; many were equally concerned, if not more, with the other restraints placed upon women by civil law. They therefore demanded that the Code — which some described as a "a heap of odious, stupid, and ridiculous articles" — be modified to promote civil equality between the sexes.[16] In their view all people, regardless of sex, were entitled to the rights which originated in their shared humanity. Feminists arguing from the liberal tradition thus held that those rights enjoyed by men must also be extended to women: if men could serve on juries, sign contracts, dispose of their own incomes, and so on, women should be able to do the same. And if men had the right to choose their nationality, it was unjust to obligate women to abdicate their own.

The logic behind the practice of derivative nationality for married women was to insure that husband and wife were subject to the same laws with regard to their marriage and its possible dissolution. If more than one body of law could be called upon to dictate the affairs of a theoretically united household, the potential for juridical chaos was great.[17] Other explanations for this practice invoked the New Testament, in which Christ declared that through marriage, two beings became one, and thus should be united in all regards.[18] This notion was also explained in more secular terms. In a harkening back to the Aristotelian idea that the state was no more than an agglomeration of families, it was argued that disharmonious households would seriously compromise the strength of the state. The Civil Code therefore prescribed that husbands and wives have the same nationality because any division within the home could undermine its proper functioning. In accordance with both "nature" and juridical tradition, it was the husband's nationality that the wife was to share.[19] In addition to assuming her husband's name and official place of residence, a married woman was also obligated to receive his nationality.[20] The individual interests of the woman were subordinated to the collective interests of the family and by extension the state, which required a unified household to insure the stability of its governance. Thus while traditional legal doctrine held that nationality could not be forced upon an individual — "*la nationalité ne s'impose pas*" — an exception was made for the married woman, in the interests of the collective good.[21]

The predicament of French women was far from unique. At the beginning of the twentieth century, women across the globe were legally expatriated upon their marriage to foreign men. In most cases the law of the husband's country instantly granted the wife his nationality, but when it did not, a married woman might actually find herself in the predicament of possessing no nationality at all.[22] In the United States, a self-proclaimed nation of immigrants, marriages between foreigners and nationals were far from uncommon, and the struggle for the independent nationality of married women therefore assumed a special significance.[23] In England and on the Continent, jurists, feminists, and politicians faced similar challenges in reconciling family and citizenship law.[24] The debates extended to Europe's colonial empire, where the possibility of "mixed marriages" between European women and colonial men, in addition to raising the contradictory relationship of subject people to the imperial nation-state, further muddied the juridical status of the husband and wife in question.[25] In short, any nation whose interpretation of family law was indebted at least in part to the Napoleonic Code would have to grapple with its legacy: the expatriation of female nationals upon their marriage to foreign men.[26]

Toward the end of the nineteenth century the international feminist movement had begun to question this premise. The Soviet Union declared in 1918 that female nationals who married foreigners could retain their native citizenship, and in the course of the 1920s similar statutes were enacted in the United States, several Latin American nations, Turkey, China, and Persia. By 1930 about half of the world's women could maintain a nationality different from their husband's after marriage.[27] In France it was article 8 of the Law on French Nationality of 1927 that overturned this particular manifestation of patriarchal prerogative. It provided that a French woman who married a foreigner retained her French nationality, unless she expressly declared her desire to acquire that of her husband, in accordance with the laws of his country.[28]

French feminists and their allies employed liberal democratic understandings of the individual as a rights-bearing subject to make their case for independent nationality. They suggested that a more modern way of envisioning the family taxonomy was to view women, like men, as individuals who were entitled to rights and endowed with the knowledge to express consent. Feminists argued that independent nationality was one step in their "juridical emancipation," as freedom from the restrictions imposed by civil law — in addition to economic, social, and political liberation — were the laudable and necessary goals of feminism.[29] They also claimed that if nationality was indeed a "contract" between state and citizen, this principle had been abandoned by the requirement that a woman assume her husband's nationality *ipso jure*, or by the law itself.[30] That is, the voluntary nature of the contractual agreement had been invalidated because the law demanded that married women take a particular course of action: they had to assume their husbands' nationality. But most importantly, feminists argued that to force a woman to relinquish her native nationality and assume another without her consent was a scandalous violation of her individual liberty. This was the backbone of the feminist argument against articles 12 and 19 of the Civil Code.

Feminists thus cast independent nationality as one of many rights to which women, as individuals, were entitled. This line of reasoning, however, explicitly juxtaposed women's individual rights with the collective interests of the family, a potentially volatile argument to uphold in the political culture of the interwar years. We have seen that according to the populationist rhetoric of this period woman's reproductive duties took precedence over her individual rights, and the excessive individualism of men and women had resulted in a degenerate and depopulated France. Pronatalists believed that women became citizens through motherhood rather than formal political participation, and that the domestic sphere rather than the public realm of politics was their natural and appropriate place. So while feminists viewed independent nationality as one further step toward civil equality and ultimately enfranchisement, pronatalists equated female citizenship with reproductive obligations that would benefit the collective good.

The claim to an independent nationality by virtue of individuated status was further complicated by the fact that in France married women were legally incapacitated until 1938, and no adult woman could exercise the right to vote until 1944.[31] While American feminists could move logically from their enfranchisement to the demand for an independent nationality, and found that politicians were far more sympathetic to their cause after the Nineteenth Amendment had been ratified,[32] French feminists could not make a similar claim. They called for, and were granted, an independent nationality at a time when married women could not even plead in court, act as guardians, administer property, or enter into commerce or the professions without the consent of their husbands.

Unsurprisingly, the internal contradictions of French Republicanism were reflected in its legal discourse, which was ultimately unable to accommodate the persistent problem of gender difference. Indeed, many of the complications that French feminists faced in their battle for independent nationality stemmed from their reliance on Republican rhetoric, which despite its purported universalism defined women as citizens without voting rights, and as individuals with differentiated, child-bearing bodies. Given these "paradoxical" representations of female embodiment, one returns to the question eloquently posed by Joan Wallach Scott in her account of modern French feminist arguments: Did, or even could, the abstract individual immortalized in Republican discourse refer to women?[33] If women could not effortlessly embody the disembodied form of the abstract individual, were they really entitled to individual rights, such as the right to determine their own nationality? Similar questions which emerged during the discussion of independent nationality are still germane to contemporary debates in feminist political theory, such as those centering on the issue of contract and consent. For example, if nationality is understood as a contract between state and citizen, could women, represented by men and deprived of key civil rights, act as contracting agents with the nation?[34] If the ability to consent to the terms of the social contract is the foundation of modern democratic theory, could women, whose rights and freedoms were legally curtailed, have that ability to consent?[35] And finally, because the franchise had not yet been extended to French women, how salient is formal political participation to the title and practice of citizenship?[36]

We will see that the feminist demand for independent nationality was eventually met, for reasons unrelated to the individual rights of French women. This is evidenced by the way French politicians ultimately framed the law of 1927, which rather than construing independent nationality as the necessary consequence of equal rights, cast it as a populationist measure designed to increase the number of French nationals. While feminists had called for independent nationality as early as 1869, only with the death of nearly 1.5 million men in the trenches did the debate gain momentum in the French parliament.[37] Because it permitted the retention of female nationals who would otherwise assume the nationality of their spouses, it provided an immediate corrective to the demographic decline that politicians had so vociferously lamented. Other articles of the law of 1927 facilitated the naturalization of foreigners and granted French nationality to children born in France of French mothers with foreign husbands. Its overtly populationist concerns were to privilege collective obligations over the radically egalitarian promise of individual rights.

To win this silent consent is to make use of all
the violence permitted in love . . .

— Rousseau, *Politics and the Arts*, 85.

The argument for civil equality based on the individuated status of women was made possible by a more modern understanding of marriage within a number of secular discourses. Although the infamous article 213 of the Civil

Code preserved the supreme authority of the husband, by the early twentieth century a considerable debate had emerged in juridical circles with regard to women's civil rights, as well as the purported infallibility of the Code.[38] Jurists explained that while marriage had once been understood as the union of a man who rules and a woman who obeys, in its modern incarnation marriage was to reflect the reciprocal duties and rights of each partner.[39] The husband remained preeminent to ensure the proper functioning of domestic life, but jurists, politicians, and feminists believed that in modern marriages, the man's authority should no longer to be exercised monolithically:[40] each spouse should be entitled to retain his or her personal status, as the family was an association and not a union.[41] In this light, derivative nationality was a profoundly anachronistic and inequitable practice. Thus a bill in 1919 proposing independent nationality in the Chamber of Deputies noted: "feminists and jurists currently agree that the former rules of our Civil Code, with regard to the nationality of the married woman, no longer correspond to the mores or the mentality of the present day."[42] Similarly, the jurist and deputy Félix Liouville (Union Républicaine et Sociale, Seine), the law's spokesman in the Chamber, invoked the more egalitarian spirit of modern marriage in response to a letter from the editors of the feminist newspaper *La Française*: "You have called to my attention the desire of the numerous readers of *La Française*, who wish to see the immediate passage by Parliament of the bill concerning a married woman's nationality. How can I refuse *La Française* and its kind readers the very legitimate satisfaction they deserve? If we have established the rights of women, I do not know what right is more sacred than her being the only one to have her nationality at her disposal . . . There was a time when this change of status made sense, when we were your lords and masters. But today, we think of you as associates contributing to a common life, an equal but different tribute, and thus it is assuredly shocking that in spite of yourselves, you can be divested of a nationality which is dear to you. One can love a man, and continue to love one's country.[43]"

Those in favor of independent nationality, as well as those opposed to it, noted that the spirit of the bill was more in keeping with modern jurisprudence, which increasingly favored the interests of the individual over those of the family.[44] Legal scholars pointed out that feminism had facilitated this shift by insisting that women were also individuals, and therefore entitled to individual rights. But as we have seen in our discussion of pronatalist demography, early-twentieth-century social critics held that "individualism" was responsible for both progress and degeneration. Feminism and individualism, they believed, were intimately related, and feminists, along with "modern women" and syphilitic prostitutes, had sapped the nation of its reproductive capital. As I have shown, individualism was conceived as dangerous for women because it promoted independence from the family and freedom from patriarchal control. This was precisely the point of René Savatier, law professor at the University of Poitiers, when he claimed that the greatest consequence of female emancipation was the freeing of "the individual from family ties."[45] Previously marriage had been understood as a "fund of common sentiments," and thus a woman who married the man she loved "also married his homeland." For Savatier the alleged commonality of the couple's interests justified derivative nationality, and the ruling in 1927 which put an end to this practice signaled the "collapse of the principle of marital unity."[46]

In contrast, proponents of reform argued that to force a woman to abdicate her nationality was to assume that patriotic sentiment could be cast aside at the altar, and that a woman would grow to love her husband's country by virtue of her love for him. The marriage contract should not be permitted to trump the nationality contract, especially since traditional jurisprudence clearly held that nationality, as a contract between state and citizen, could not be forced upon an individual.[47] Nationality was a civil status which individuals were free to change at will, and which no one could compel them to change against their wishes.[48]

How, then, could such an enormous exception be made for the many thousands of French women who had married foreigners since the promulgation of the Civil Code? The explanation provided by juridical texts further undermined the presumption that women could be defined as individuals, or as the rights-bearing subjects of Republican discourse. Legal scholars claimed that because of the "presumed consent" of the wife, she was divested of her native nationality and obliged to assume that of her foreign husband. In their view, because women were aware that by marrying foreigners they would lose their nationality (though in fact many were not aware), the loss was a "voluntary abdication" rather than a flagrant denial of their option to exercise consent.[49] In this manner, the ostensibly contractual nature of nationality was preserved.[50] By exercising her right to marry whomever she chose, the French woman also expressed, however silently, her will to abdicate her nationality.[51] Presumed consent implied that women were autonomous, fully informed, and competent agents in the moment when they entered the marriage contract. It was therefore proof that women possessed full knowledge of the consequences of their actions and, in accordance with liberal political theory, that they assumed any changes in their legal status voluntarily.[52]

Suzanne Grinberg, an attorney and member of the Union Française pour le Suffrage des Femmes, argued that for this reason women were forced to choose between love for their homelands and love for their husbands.[53] Marcel Sauteraud, advisor to the appellate court of Paris and one of the foremost champions of the bill, exposed the faulty logic behind presumed consent by noting that if a woman were to express her will to the contrary — that is, if she were to declare her intention to remain French, rather than to assume her husband's national status — she would nevertheless be stripped of her nationality.[54] Feminists and their allies therefore recuperated the nationality contract, demanding that it be applied identically to male and female subjects: "Just as it would be unfair to impose the all-powerful will of the husband in the domain of a woman's thought and conscience, so too would it be unfair to sacrifice the profound sentiments that attach her to her country. The juridical will of the wife must be maintained. Nationality is to be retained and disposed of voluntarily: that is the principle."[55]

The Great War, Depopulation, and the "Man Shortage":
Forfeit Your Nationality or Die a Spinster

The experience of the First World War permitted those in favor of independent nationality to base their arguments on concrete examples rather than abstract claims to individual rights. The casualties of the war and the resulting "man shortage" allowed feminist arguments to reach a far greater audience. Pronatalist jurists and Radical politicians, most with tenuous or nonexistent links to feminism, joined in the campaign for independent nationality. All factions of the debate contended that the patriotism displayed by French women during the war entitled them to retain their nationality if they married foreign men. Moreover, populationists argued that to surrender French nationals and their future children in the midst of a demographic crisis was a shortsighted legal precedent.[56] Instead, to combat depopulation French women should be permitted to keep their nationality, raise children who were legally French, and employ their particularly feminine influence to assimilate foreign husbands. Because the demographic calculus of the early-twentieth-century world dictated that strength and prosperity depended on the wealth of a nation's "human capital," the state had an interest in retaining as many of its nationals as possible.[57] Male jurists and politicians therefore incorporated elements of the populationist platform into their argument in favor of independent nationality, and highlighted the particularist role of the citizen mother's differentiated body in propagating and sustaining the nation.

The Catholic pronatalist senator Léon Jenouvrier (Gauche Républicaine, Île-et-Vilaine), author of one of the earliest bills calling for independent nationality, explained in 1918 that at the time the Civil Code was promulgated, marriages to foreigners were relatively rare. However, with a multitude of unmarried allied soldiers stationed on French soil during the war, marriages between French women and foreigners had begun to increase at an alarmingly rapid pace. Jenouvrier therefore asserted that the only way to curtail the loss of female nationals was through reform of the Civil Code.[58] Similarly, Sauteraud explained that because the war had decimated nearly an entire generation of marriageable men, a dramatic increase in marriages with European and colonial men was to be expected. For this reason, independent nationality was essential: with the loss of so many French men in the war, it made no sense to facilitate the expatriation of French women and further exacerbate demographic decline.[59] In addition, Sauteraud contended that independent nationality would serve as added protection against German demographic might, a concern of utmost importance to pronatalist politicians who equated French military defeat with depopulation.[60]

Proponents of the law also insisted that to force French women to abdicate their nationality was a supreme affront to their patriotism, a callous response to the sacrifices they made amid the privations and hardships of the war.[61] Rather than be rewarded for their virtue, French women were transformed into foreigners and ambiguously situated in a nation that would "no longer recognize them as its own." To divest French women of their nationality was to assume that they sought husbands abroad for lack of patriotism rather than a genuine desire to found a family. Instead of praising their commitment to maternal values and the institution of marriage, Sauteraud claimed, the French nation "renounced" its women because they were "not resigned to the sterility of spinsterhood or the instability of concubinage [*unions libres*]."[62] In 1920 Félix Liouville echoed this view in the Chamber: "Why must the wife, whose instinctive tenderness or desire to found a family has led her to marriage, sacrifice the profound sentiment which attaches her to her homeland? Why must she be forced to repudiate the land in which she grew up, the land whose culture and mores have formed her heart and mind?"[63]

French women were therefore forced to make the impossible choice between spinsterhood and the renunciation of their homeland. An article in *La Française* lamented that the Civil Code, "which did not foresee the Great War, has condemned the entire present population of French women. It has inflicted on them a terrible moral dilemma, ignoring their sacrifices, sorrows, and past hardships."[64] Similarly, an article in *Le Matin* warned: "Do not forget that there are currently three million female citizens for whom there are no French husbands. Far from condemning them to spinsterhood and sterility, it is in the nation's interest to facilitate the establishment of their households, on the condition that their children be French."[65] In March 1927 Charles Lambert proclaimed in the Chamber of Deputies that he had received numerous letters from women who were "waiting impatiently" for articles 12 and 19 to be overturned so that they could marry their foreign fiancés. He had also heard from their mothers who, because of the "scruple of patriotic sentiments," were unwilling to consent to their daughters' marriages. One woman wrote that although she had long waited for her daughter's wedding day, she was "attached to her country and wanted above all for her daughter to remain French, and above all that for her grandchildren to be French."[66]

Of course the facility with which French women could exercise their option to marry was particularly important in the cultural context of interwar France, where the unmarried woman was excoriated and the virtues of maternity extolled.[67] Sauteraud warned that the current legislation had the unforeseen consequence of encouraging French women to remain unmarried, whether as spinsters or by living in concubinage with their mates. In his words, the Code's proscriptions were an "obstacle to marriage," which was the "basis of [French] society."[68] The feminist and attorney Maria Vérone of the Ligue Française Pour le Droit des Femmes corroborated this middle-class vision of the family by lamenting that French women in "free unions"

(*unions libres*) retained their nationality because "in the eyes of the legislature, they are single: this is what they call protecting legitimate families!"[69] Vérone illustrated this point with reference to a letter she had received from a French schoolteacher who wished to marry a veteran of the Belgian army. If the couple wed, the woman would become Belgian and thus be forced to give up her teaching post, which was contingent on French nationality. However, if the man were naturalized French, he would lose his army pension. According to Vérone, the couple's predicament exemplified the Code's inadvertent disregard for the institution of marriage and its contribution to the moral problem of concubinage: "The only solution is to live in free unions . . . And this is how they claim to defend the family."[70]

Odette Simon of the French Union for Women's Suffrage, an attorney and frequent contributor to this debate in the feminist press, provided another concrete example of the consequences of the man shortage in France. She told the story of a French woman in her early thirties who supported two children by working as a concierge in a Paris school, with the help of her pension as a war widow and family allowances from the state. When this woman fell in love again and decided to remarry, she had the misfortune of choosing a Swiss electrician who had immigrated to France. If she married the Swiss man and thereby forfeited her nationality, she would also have to relinquish her position at the school, a benefit derived from her former husband's status as a French functionary, and would no longer be entitled to the housing she received in return for her work as a concierge. As for her pension, only the portion allocated specifically for her children would be available. According to Simon, the predicament of the French concierge in love with a Swiss man was but one example of the "poignant consequences" of the Civil Code's stance on a married woman's nationality: "I think . . . there is something odious and cruel in this situation, and we must find a remedy for it soon. Especially at a time when so many young women, because of the disappearance of so many young men, are condemned to spinsterhood or eternal widowhood if they do not marry foreigners."[71]

The feminist newspaper *Minerva* printed a number of similar examples, and was quick to point out that many of the circumstances precipitated by the Code actually "defied reason." Take the case of a French woman married to a Czech who had never been naturalized, even though he had lived in France for twenty-six years: because he served in the French army during the First World War, he was exempt from the *taxe de séjour* while his French-born but legally Czech wife was not. Likewise, a Norman woman who had been married for eighteen years to a Belgian man was forced to pay the *taxe d'étrangère*. The couple lived in Strasbourg, where they were subject to the irony of being surrounded by German women who spoke not a word of French but were exempt from the tax because they had married Alsatian men.[72] And of course the feminist Susanne Grinberg reminded the readership of *La Française* that French women married to German and Hapsburg men had actually been interned during the First World War, and had their belongings impounded.[73]

Independent nationality was therefore construed as a logical response to the demographic crisis. For feminists as well as male proponents of the law, it allowed French women to marry and have children while retaining a nationality which they treasured and which offered them protection. The newspaper *Le Matin* claimed to have received numerous letters from French women who attested to their sincere desire to start a family, but who preferred to "abandon that idea, rather than give birth to foreign children on native soil."[74] For male jurists and politicians in particular, independent nationality assured the retention of female nationals at a time when depopulation was viewed as the most serious of social pathologies. By overturning this provision of the Civil Code, French women would be free to accomplish the assimilative labor which accompanied their prescribed role in the domestic sphere. As we have seen in our investigation of pronatalist demography, Republican ideology granted French women the responsibility of assimilating foreign husbands and half-foreign children. This task was an extension of the gendered duties of citizenship prescribed by the doctrine of Republican motherhood, which viewed the household as the "nursery of the state."[75] According to this vision, the domestic sphere was a transformative space in which immigrants could be made French.

Feminists did not employ this argument to make their case for independent nationality. Rather than base their claim on the particular capacity of a woman's differentiated body to bear children, they called for civil equality by virtue of their fundamental sameness with the rest of the human family. Nevertheless, the primary participants in the immigration debate conceded that the best way to assimilate foreigners was through marriage to French women. Radical politicians extended this notion to the case of independent nationality. For example, Adolphe Landry (Gauche Radicale, Corsica) and André Honnorat (Union Républicaine, Basses-Alpes), the ardent pronatalists who founded the Groupe de Défense des Familles Nombreuses in the Chamber of Deputies, asked the following questions of their colleagues in 1918 in debating a bill proposing independent nationality for married women: "Was it not through the influence of our mothers that, by the reflection of the received impressions of childhood, the true character of nationality—the ensemble of tastes, the tendencies of spirit and sentiment—was formed in each of us? And was it not necessary for this influence to have been singularly penetrating in order to merge the diverse elements that have, throughout the ages, collided upon our territory? Is this not how the exceptionally harmonious form of European civilization, known as French civilization, was born?"[76]

According to this logic, the great talent that French women possessed for molding the national character and cultural competencies of their families should not be jettisoned in the interest of an outmoded vision of marital authority. For example, Professor William Oualid, whose ubiquitous presence in the immigration debate was made manifest through his posts at the Labor Ministry, the Foreign Labor Service, and the Paris Faculty of Law, deemed the current nationality law "profoundly regrettable," as it rested on a "serious misunderstanding of marital psychology." He wrote: "It has been observed many times . . . that in mixed households, the woman exercises the dominant influence, particularly through the education of the children. To deprive a French woman of her nationality when she marries a foreigner is to make her an inferior being in her own country, as well as to forfeit the powerful means of gallicization (*francisation*) she provides."[77]

Eugène Audinet, member of the Institute of International Law and professor at the University of Poitiers, argued that if a couple made France their marital domicile, it was more logical to focus on integrating the foreign husband into the French nation, along with the rest of the family, rather than penalize the wife by forcing her to develop an attachment to a land she did not know.[78] Because it was in the nation's best interest to encourage the naturalization of foreigners residing in France, and because marriage to French women simplified the assimilation of immigrant men on both a practical and a psycho-social level, it was counterproductive to demand that French women renounce their nationality, along with their desire to found a French household.[79]

Thus when faced with mass immigration and depopulation, early-twentieth-century social critics widely debated the issue of marriage between French citizens and foreigners. Demographers, politicians, industrialists, and social scientists held that intermarriage was the quintessential emblem of integration, indicative of the foreigner's willingness to relinquish his or her particularities in favor of the universalism of the French melting pot. Historians in France today have echoed this view.[80] Marianne Amar and Pierre Milza have written that the Law on French Nationality of 1927 is proof of the legislature's conviction that mixed marriages demonstrate a "decisive step toward integration." They argue that the law is a concrete symbol of the faith that French politicians had in the Republican woman's ability to render her household and husband French.[81]

There is no reason to believe that this purported influence could not have extended to any potential mate, whether of African, Asian, or European descent. But as we have seen, a French woman's assimilative talents were presumed to be sharply curtailed if her partner was not white and European. The juxtaposition of civilization and barbarism, so prominent in demographic treatises on depopulation and abolitionist arguments against white slavery, resurfaced in the discussion of marriages between white women and non-white men. Because these unions did not constitute what racial theorists had described as *le bon métissage*, or appropriate and salubrious racial mixing, they were depicted as dangerous, degenerate, and undignified. In contrast, marriages between Europeans involved spouses from the same level of civilization, a civilization with laws that upheld the honor and virtue of white womanhood. Although feminists demanded that the injustices of the Civil Code be rectified, for many observers the gender order of the civilized metropole was preferable to the alleged despotism of African and Asian men. Thus one of the primary arguments in favor of independent nationality was that French women who married foreigners were no longer afforded the protection of the French legal system. According to both feminists and male jurists, this situation was most precarious in marriages between French women and nonwhite men. Like the campaign against white slavery, the fight for independent nationality was framed in terms of protecting white women from the abuses of men of color. Moreover, the feminist movement's explicit condemnation of interracial unions reveals the degree to which eugenic discourse coincided with the social agenda of bourgeois feminism.

Protecting French Women in Less "Civilized" Unions: The "Meta-Husband" of the French State

Proponents of independent nationality unanimously held that because the condition of women was greatly inferior in the colonies, African and Asian women, unlike their French counterparts, were denied the respect and dignity merited by their position as wives and mothers of the nation.[82] French women who married colonial men therefore lost the esteem upon which their role in the French family was based.[83] But more importantly, they lost the legal protection of the French state, as they were now national and juridical subjects of their husbands' country. Life for women outside the European metropole was portrayed as dangerous, exploitative, and lacking in material comforts. In contrast, jurists were certain that within Europe, a more enlightened attitude toward women prevailed. In the words of one legal scholar: "In a number of exotic lands, the condition of indigenous women is undoubtedly inferior to that of European women. By forcing European women to take on the nationality of their husbands, they experience an actual social decline. They fall to the level of 'second-class women,' and risk seeing themselves surrounded by the concubines their husbands can legally bring into the household."[84]

Marcel Sauteraud of the appellate court of Paris believed that a French woman who married an African or Asian debased herself and the nation.[85] However, to outlaw such marriages was in clear defiance of liberal Republican principles: the freedom to marry the person of one's choice was said to be an "individual liberty" and a "natural right."[86] At the very least, legislators could guarantee the protection of French women married to African and Asian men, even if the unions were an affront to whiteness, womanliness, and the racial integrity of the nation. The feminist Maria Vérone claimed that it was "indispensable to provide legal protection for French women who enter mixed marriages," as they had to be safeguarded from the "poor treatment bad husbands could inflict," and the "abuse they could suffer at the hands of an ignorant population."[87] Thus according to Sauteraud and Vérone, the French state had an obligation to continue protecting its female members, rather than abandon them to the legal system of their husbands' homeland.

Polygamy was undoubtedly the greatest fear.[88] As in the debate on white slavery, the sexual life of colonized people was a reflection of their supposed barbarity. Polygamy was further evidence of the excessive sexuality of colonized people, as well as their inability to comprehend the most rudimentary democratic notions.[89] By invoking polygamy, critics of mixed marriages played on anxieties of racial defilement while simultaneously titillating the orientalist imagination. In addition, by disavowing polygamy and deploring its injustices, they contrasted colonial domestic values with those of the allegedly monogamous bourgeois household back in the metropole. It is therefore unsurprising that jurists, politicians, and feminists, in their defense of independent nationality, should have argued on behalf of French women whom they described as prisoners in their North African husbands' harems.

While the feminist Alice Berthet condemned the "terrible adventures of French women married to Turkish, Chinese, and Annamite men," she was especially concerned with the possibility that her countrywomen would turn to "legally polygamous Muslims."[90] Marcelle Legrand-Falco cautioned her readers that North African men who had studied in France would "revert to their primitive mentality" once they returned to the Maghreb. French wives who accompanied their husbands to the colonies were immediately "locked up in a harem" in accordance with "traditional custom." To add insult to injury, they faced the hostility of their husbands' other wives and the women of his extended family.[91] "Once an Arab marries," Maria Vérone professed, a French woman "can expect to be cloistered away like a simple Muslim woman."[92] And in India as well the Maghreb, polygamous households and corporal punishment awaited French women who dared to marry nonwhite men.[93]

French women who wed Chinese men were warned that their husbands would remain obligated to leave France once their work contracts had expired. A French woman would therefore be required to accompany her spouse to China, where she was to "vegetate in misery among the worst possible deprivations." Upon her arrival it was not uncommon for her to find that her husband had previously been married to a Chinese woman, and according to Chinese custom, she was now the first wife's subordinate.[94] For these reasons the French Ministry of Interior issued an advisory suggesting that such marriages only be ratified in the presence of documentation attesting to the Chinese man's unmarried status.[95] The ministry's note was meant to alert those French women who, "smitten with exoticism," were unaware of the "dangers of a moral and juridical order" which might await them in their spouse's homeland.[96]

A letter to Vérone described the plight of one woman, a Parisian chambermaid, who had returned to Algeria with her new husband. To the horror of both Vérone and the letter's author, when the woman presented herself at the city hall to request social assistance, she was in native dress with her eyelid split open, the result of a beating from her husband. According to the observer, the woman had been fed just enough to keep starvation at bay, had been treated cruelly by the women of her husband's family, and had been denied access to the outside world, "locked up day and night in a house without light or air." For Vérone the Parisian chambermaid offered an obvious example of the need to safeguard French women in mixed marriages: "The fact of leaving French women under the protection of French law will certainly not abruptly modify the mentality of the *indigènes*, but they will very quickly learn that they do not have the right to impose native laws and customs on their French wife, who remains under the protection of French authorities."[97] That is, until colonized men had assimilated the lessons of civilized domestic relations, French women could only be protected through recourse to the metropolitan legal system.

For the proponents of what was to become the law of 1927, the cultural differences between metropole and colonies, especially with regard to family hierarchy, women's liberty, and gendered duties within the institution of marriage, could not easily be bridged. For this reason derivative nationality placed French women in an extremely precarious position. According to Sauteraud, a French woman who married another European received a "respectable" nationality in return, and she was therefore safeguarded by a legal system based on civilized and democratic values. However, if she married a man from an "inferior civilization," her "first-rate" French nationality was replaced by one beholden to an inferior set of legal principles, which made no provisions for its female nationals.[98] For precisely this reason independent nationality had to be established. The authority of the French state would then supersede the laws of less evolved judicial systems, acting as a "meta-husband" to French women otherwise subject to the authority of nonwhite men.

"Protection" was often understood with regard to the newly reinstated right of French nationals to divorce their spouses in accordance with the Naquet Law, promulgated in 1884. While for the greater part of the nineteenth century there had been an understanding of marriage as indissoluble, Republican politicians salvaged the Revolutionary definition of marriage as a civil contract that could be terminated by one or both parties.[99] Advocates of independent nationality—and male jurists in particular—fervently embraced this right on behalf of French women, making it a cornerstone of their argument. They pointed to the grave injustice suffered by French women who married foreigners from nations that did not permit divorce, and thus were denied any legal recourse to dissolve their union.[100] Of course this was most frequently the predicament of French women married to Italians, rather than Africans or Asians, as it was Franco-Italian marriages that occurred most frequently in the first half of the twentieth century, and divorce was not available in Italy until 1970.[101] Nevertheless, French jurists deplored the fact that in Muslim and Jewish marriages in North Africa, essentially all the power to dissolve the unions was placed in the hands of the husband: Muslim law allowed the husband to repudiate his wife, while Jewish law refused women the right to initiate divorce without the consent of their spouse.[102] Thus while the call for independent nationality was a crucial component of the larger feminist crusade for reform of the Civil Code, jurists and feminists did not hesitate to claim that civil equality had been more fully realized in France than in nations also subject to the prescriptions of religious law.

Conclusions: Individual Rights and Reproductive Obligations?

The practice of derivative nationality had been easier to justify in a less mobile and more insular world. According to Sauteraud, this "legislative error" had only been tolerated because at the time of the Code's promulgation, marriages between foreigners and French women were relatively rare. However, the combined influence of the demographic crisis, the casualties of the First World War, and the presence of foreign soldiers and immigrants on French soil had irretrievably changed this situation. Sauteraud conceded that with a multitude of men from different "races" settling in France, a dramatic increase in intermarriage was to be expected.[103] In turn, French feminists, legislators, and jurists were compelled to confront the issue of juridical independence for married women and the continued applicability of the Napoleonic Civil Code.

But the debate on independent nationality for married women also unearthed the conflicting assumptions of French Republicanism, a social theory which simultaneously championed individual rights and populationist ideals, universalism and gender complementarity, and family and market values. In the course of reenvisioning the Code's conception of family authority and women's civil status, two primary contradictions were brought to the fore. The first was the abstract universalism of a Republicanism which nevertheless positioned women as its embodied others. While French feminists made demands for independent nationality in traditionally Republican terms, referring specifically to its ideals of equality and individual liberty, it was articulated from their paradoxical subject-position, as citizens who had not been granted key political rights and who were charged with serving the nation through motherhood and other intimate duties.

Second, the justification voiced by French legislators for repealing articles 12 and 19 of the Civil Code aptly demonstrates how the political culture of the Third Republic, while devoted to individual rights, was also supremely concerned with the primacy of the population over the individual. From the moment when the debate on independent nationality entered the French parliament in 1915, it was framed in populationist language which made no reference to the individual rights of women. For example, in 1916 Senator Louis Martin (Gauche Radicale, Var) assured his colleagues that his proposal for independent nationality was unrelated to the question of whether women should be "eternal minors" before the law, thus distancing himself from the feminist demand for reform of the infamous article 1124 of the Code, which defined women as legally incapacitated.[104] Similarly, in their proposal of 1918, the pronatalist senators Adolphe Landry and Auguste Honnorat referred to independent nationality as one of the "most reliable instruments of national defense," because the demographic capital of French women would not be lost upon their marriage to foreign men. Landry and Honnorat further confirmed that populationist concerns undergirded the bill by recalling the sacrifices of French men in the Great War: "Our sons did not die so that their sisters would become foreigners in France, and leave only foreign grandchildren to our mourning households: they died so the French nation would remain after they were gone."[105] And months before the law was passed, the Radical deputy and professor of law André Mallarmé (Gauche Radicale, Alger) reminded the Chamber that the law of 1927 would dramatically increase the number of naturalizations, not only because immigrants would be able to request naturalization more easily but also because French women currently married to foreigners would demand to be reinstated into the national body. He concluded: "In the midst of the formidable tests of the postwar period, [this law] will permit us to reconstitute one of the essential elements of our national weaponry."[106]

The Law of 10 August 1927 also granted French citizenship to the children of French women married to non-naturalized foreigners, and liberalized naturalization procedures by lowering the age of eligibility from twenty-one to eighteen and shortening the waiting period from ten to three years. Unsurprisingly, the law was widely praised by a number of pronatalist organizations, as its potential to contribute to the national population was undeniable.[107] In the words of Justice Minister Louis Barthou, it was a "law of national interest" and a "law of national defense."[108] Thus the specter of depopulation and the assimilative potential of the Republican mother critically informed the decision of French parliamentarians to grant women an independent nationality. Mallarmé, one of the primary sponsors of the bill, repudiated its radically universalizing potential by making it abundantly clear that support for independent nationality was not to be equated with the right to formal political participation: "The reform we propose to the Chamber would constitute a great step in the progress of feminism, although not in the sense that the most ardent feminists would understand it. We are not granting woman the ballot, but assuring her a way to exercise her social influence to the profit of her country and the future of her race, and allowing her to keep for France her children."[109]

This was a far cry from feminist understandings of the problem. The populationist thrust behind the law of 1927 was clear to Odette Simon of the French Union for Women's Suffrage (UFSF), who sagely remarked that "the essential goal of this law is to increase as much as possible the number of French men and women."[110] Marcelle Kraemer-Bach, another leader of the UFSF, observed with cynicism that depopulation and not individual rights was the driving force behind the law's passage. The pressing need to create more French families led politicians to revise the Civil Code in favor of an independent nationality for married women and the *qualité de français* for their half-foreign children. In contrast, Kraemer-Bach praised the American Cable Act of 1922, which in her opinion had been inspired by a loftier goal: the liberal conviction of a shared humanity and the common set of rights which were said to emanate from it.[111] Only in the United States, she concluded, had independent nationality been granted in the spirit from which it was born: that every human being had the right to choose his or her nationality.[112]

Alice Berthet eloquently expressed the feminist position in the pages of *La Française*. She explained that because the virtual representation of women by their husbands was no longer suitable in the modern age, the law must be reformed to reflect the egalitarian promises of liberal Republican discourse. Women, like men, were entitled to liberties and rights, and should not only be subject to obligations. Independent nationality was therefore one of many rights to be claimed by French women as the Civil Code was gradually revised: "At the root of the question [of independent nationality] is the central idea of feminism: the recognition of the absolute, individual existence of woman as a juridical person [*personne morale*] and a citizen, with duties and rights equal to those of the rest of the human family, based on liberty and her conscience alone. Instead, secular laws conceived, elaborated, and imposed by men treat woman as a relative being. Both her material existence and her rights—up to and including that of her nationality—depend on men. Only her duties remain her own responsibility."[113]

Thus feminists once again placed their faith in the capacious language of French universalism, and argued that in accordance with this doctrine women must be permitted to retain their nationality in all the same circumstances as men.[114] In the end they won the battle, but not on their own terms. We have seen that for Berthet, the debate over independent nationality highlighted the "central idea of feminism": that women were individuals endowed with duties and rights equal to men, and that they too were citizens with a stake in the national body. For Jane Misme, founder and editor of *La Française*, the law on independent nationality was an attack on the idea of "marital supremacy," and thus one victory in a chain of reforms that began with the married women's property law in 1907 and culminated during the pre-Vichy period with the repudiation of legal incapacity in 1938.[115]

Instead, independent nationality was subsumed in the larger debate on French nationality that was to become the ensemble of the law of 1927, and cast as one further measure with the salutary effect of augmenting the French population. Because a depopulated France required all the men, women, and children it could muster, independent nationality served the critical purpose of retaining French women for the homeland. Sauteraud summed up the demographic motives behind the law, as well as the importance of the Republican mother's influence in the domestic sphere: "After having lost so many of its sons [in the war], the French nation must not become impoverished of its daughters as well. On the contrary, France must allow them to remain attached to their homeland, and by doing so, will favor the assimilation of their [foreign] husbands."[116] In this instance, the anti-individualism of pronatalist politics trumped the universalist promise of equal rights. Employing populationist rhetoric, politicians made a case for expanding the rights of women, if only to advance their vision of a rejuvenated France in which the household molded the citizenry. Feminists were able to find common ground with pronatalist politicians because each group argued one aspect of the contradictory rhetoric of Republicanism: while remaining true to the Republican idiom, feminists could logically lay claim to a "female individual" who was entitled to individual rights; while Republican politicians emphasized French women's reproductive obligations to the nation, and thereby reaffirmed gender complementarity.

Conclusion

GENDER, RACE, AND
REPUBLICAN EMBODIMENT

The case of independent nationality for married women is particularly pertinent to this story because it calls our attention to how, throughout the entire Third Republic, cultural sameness was not sufficient to bestow political citizenship upon French women, who remained disenfranchised until 1944. Moreover, until 1927 cultural sameness did not even insure French nationality: as we saw in chapter 5, French women who married foreigners were divested of that status. The effect was to disrupt the implied relationship of culture, nationality, and citizenship, which in turn precipitated a discursive and empirical crisis that could only be managed through reform of nationality law. Of course it would have been absurd to argue that French women were culturally different from French men; on the contrary, the doctrine of Republican motherhood described French women as guardians of tradition and repositories of French culture and mores. Thus Republican universalism called upon *biological* difference to naturalize a particularized and embodied identity, along with its corresponding logic of gender complementarity. As a result, it positioned women as differently sexed beings with differentiated bodies, and underscored the intimate labor of the domestic sphere.

As Joan Wallach Scott has famously argued, the history of French feminism has been dominated by an attempt to capitalize on the Republican language of universality and individual rights.[1] That is, feminists latched onto the emancipatory aspects of Republican discourse to make their case for women's equality. However, in the French Third Republic women were shackled by various forms of dependency: the formal inequality prescribed by the Napoleonic Civil Code, and their inability to exercise the right to vote. The idea of dependency was salient to both women and colonized subjects, for in an imperial France which also adhered to a gendered social taxonomy, anyone living without rights or in a perceived state of dependency was coded as "less than human or not yet properly human."[2] Because equality was contingent upon a sameness which gendered and racialized subjects could not persuasively embody, this not-quite-human status both justified and enabled the exclusion of women and colonized people from the universalist citizen body.

We have seen how feminists challenged women's dependent status by refusing female "enslavement" through prostitution, and how they called for equality under the law in their campaign for independent nationality. However, at crucial moments feminist demands were eclipsed by the equally compelling Republican logic of gender complementarity, reproductive obligations, and social—rather than political—citizenship. In this regard the destinies of French women and colonized subjects were linked, since both groups were described in terms of dependency. As subjects rather than citizens, people of color languished in a state of apprenticeship for civilized modernity. Like French women, they embodied the particularized difference necessary to Republican universalism.

The plight of racialized subjects returns us directly to the question of immigration. As we have seen throughout this book, within several disciplines and specialized forms of knowledge, racial hierarchy was a constitutive feature of immigration discourse in Republican France. According to this logic, European immigrants could be assimilated because they were *biologically* similar to French people, as both groups were classified as members of an essentialized and supranational vision of the "white race." But in pronatalist, productivist, medico-hygienic, and feminist discussions of immigration, white migrants were also deemed capable of *cultural* assimilation, or conforming to a unitary understanding of national values and competencies. For this reason Republican commentators fabricated an intergenerational narrative of France's revivified future, placing their hopes in the children and grandchildren of white foreigners to assist the native population in rebuilding the "French race." I have shown how social commentators widely agreed that by the second generation, the assimilation of Italians, Spaniards, and

Poles would be complete. Even for "more distant white populations," such as Eastern European Jews, Levantines, and sometimes even North African Berbers, immigration proponents believed that assimilation was ultimately possible, although it would require several generations.

This is quite different from the "endless temporal deferral" of citizenship rights for colonized subjects residing throughout Greater France.[3] If white foreigners were to be assimilated within a prescribed number of generations, immigration discourse explicitly and repeatedly referred to people of color as impossible to assimilate, and thus no concrete timeline for their integration was suggested. According to these accounts, colonized subjects could not be assimilated because they were not members of the white race. In keeping with an organicist understanding of the national body, they were coded as biologically distinct and particularizing elements, and race mixing with them could only lead to degeneration for the French nation. This radically essentialist reading of difference allowed French commentators to view foreigners of color as culturally distinct and incapable of acquiring the cultural competencies of national belonging. It was as if the quotidian gestures of Frenchness which European immigrants would gradually learn were somehow unintelligible to colonial subjects, despite the education and indoctrination that those subjects had received in the name of the civilizing mission. Here immigration discourse and imperial rhetoric converged with regard to the possibility of assimilating people of color into Greater France. By the interwar years colonial critics had conceded that African and Asian subjects could not be made French by merely adopting French language, customs, and values. For this reason, scholars have argued that in the 1920s and 1930s colonial policy abandoned the logic of *assimilation* in favor of *association*.[4] Association promoted indigenous cultures and institutions while encouraging colonized people to evolve according to their own framework. It overshadowed an earlier ideal of turning "natives" into Frenchmen, of assimilating bodies as well as territories, and holding out the promise of civic incorporation.

Immigration was therefore one component of a larger state project of constituting citizens and subjects, political identities which, I have argued, cannot be extracted from their gendered and racialized embodiments. This complicates a national narrative which from its genesis was framed with reference to a white male citizen. Nevertheless, I have emphasized that embodied others were an entity necessary to the elaboration of that narrative, rather than benighted elements awaiting universal inclusion in the Republican political form. For this reason, pronatalist, productivist, medico-hygienic, feminist, and juridical discourse focused on the bodies and bodily practices of French men and women, European and colonial subjects, and people of color residing within and beyond Greater France. At stake was not only the question of which sorts of bodies could be assimilated, but who was to perform the intimate labor of assimilation, and where this education would occur. Thus a French identity was something which could be biologically conveyed and also culturally acquired, and the tension between these two methods of transmission was part and parcel of the hybrid nature of Republican citizenship.

Shortly after the outbreak of the Second World War, Dr. René Martial, whose work on race and immigration we have considered in detail, published yet another article on the immigrant question in the popular literary magazine the *Mercure de France*. He wrote: "I have long insisted that at the outset immigration is an economic phenomenon: the pursuit of labor power. Shortly thereafter immigration also becomes a biological and psychological problem. In little time, this [latter] aspect becomes the primary concern because the continued presence of a massive number of foreigners in a given country tends to modify the race of its inhabitants."[5] Once again Martial argued that the labor power as well as the reproductive value of foreigners mattered when considering their suitability for life in France, and that because race was a mutable object subject to either degeneration or regeneration, it should be carefully considered by receiver nations of immigrants, such as France in the postwar period. Given Martial's strong opinions in the interwar years on *métissage*, social-hygiene reform, and the symbolism of French blood, it is unsurprising that he should have become one of the "racial experts" reporting to Vichy's General Commissariat for Jewish Questions, as well as director of the Commissariat's Institute of Anthroposociology.[6]

Martial's rather seamless transition between the Third Republic and the Vichy State leads us to a particularly contentious discussion within the historiography of modern France: to what degree did Vichy's anti-Jewish policies have their roots in the political culture of the previous Republican form?[7] While this book has focused on color-based racisms and only peripherally on the racialization of Jews in early-twentieth-century France, it documents the widespread and persistent use of racial language in immigration discourse during the Third Republic, and how the question of assimilability was debated with reference to European workers and colonial subjects. By combining universalizing and particularizing elements, proponents of immigration simultaneously called for integrating white European migrants and marking people of color as bioculturally different. Thus racialization and racism were familiar features of the Republican landscape, not aberrant ideologies which could only garner popular, institutional, and state support under Nazi occupation and Pétain's dictatorship.

The Vichy state affirmed other ostensibly natural hierarchies. In addition to placing whites above people of color, gentiles above Jews, and employers above workers, it most emphatically rearticulated patriarchal authority and suppressed fundamental rights for French women.[8] But rather than understand Vichy's hierarchical social order as a response to the perceived failures of Republican individualism, we must remember that these hierarchies were also a prominent feature of the Third Republic, as was the disapprobation that Republican critics had for those who refused its ideals of pronatalism, gender complementarity, and "appropriate" forms of racial mixing. While the promotion of race hygiene and salubrious reproductive practices was a primary focus of the Vichy state, these same concerns had been repeatedly expressed in immigration and imperial discourses in years prior to the Nazi occupation. Moreover, postwar family policies under the Fourth Republic (1946–58) were also informed by pronatalist demography, although family allowances and maternity leave for female citizens (who had received the right to vote in 1944) could not rebuild the French population without recourse to foreign immigration once again. Thus postwar policy makers returned to the Third Republic's demographic calculus, calling for the selection of foreign workers with reference to their productivity and their perceived assimilability.[9] Reproductive ideologies and practices remained indispensable to the French nation's future, as did the gendered and racialized identities which inhabited both public and intimate space.

NOTES

Embodiment and the Nation

1. Noiriel, *The French Melting Pot*, 5.
2. Noiriel, *Population, immigration, et identité nationale en France, 19ᵉ–20ᵉ siècle*, 53.
3. Stoler, *Carnal Knowledge and Imperial Power*, 7; Foucault, *The History of Sexuality*, 139–43. Especially salient work on intimacy, with varying understandings of the term, includes Lauren Berlant's formulation of the "intimate public sphere" in *The Queen of America Goes to Washington City*, chapter 1; Berlant, Introduction, 1–8; Boym, "Diasporic Intimacy"; Habermas, *The Structural Transformation of the Public Sphere*, 141–59; Stoler, *Carnal Knowledge and Imperial Power*, 1–21; Stoler, "Intimidations of Empire"; Summers, "Intimate Colonialism." Research which has specifically engaged the implications of intimacy as formulated by Stoler includes the various essays in her edited volume *Haunted by Empire*, as well as Spear, "Colonial Intimacies"; Perry, "The Autocracy of Love and the Legitimacy of Empire"; Pierce and Rao, eds., *Discipline and the Other Body*.
4. Useful works on domesticity include Chakrabarty, "The Difference-Deferral of a Colonial Modernity"; Chatterjee, "Colonialism, Nationalism, and Colonized Women"; Comaroff and Comaroff, "Homemade Hegemony," *Ethnography and the Historical Imagination*, 265–95; George, "Homes in the Empire, Empire in the Home"; Rafael, "Colonial Domesticity."
5. See also Agamben, *Homo Sacer*; Anderson, "States of Hygiene," 94–115.
6. See Cott, Afterword, in Stoler, ed., *Haunted by Empire*, 470.
7. I have borrowed this term as well from Ann Stoler, who has used it throughout her work.
8. Recent contributions to the study of race in modern France include Chapman and Frader, eds., *Race in France*; Ezra, *The Colonial Unconscious*; Hargreaves, *Immi-*

gration, "Race," and Ethnicity; MacMaster, *Colonial Migrants and Racism*; Peabody and Stovall, eds., *The Color of Liberty*; Silverman, *Deconstructing the Nation*; Wilder, *The French Imperial Nation-State*.

9. The paradigm of French universalism has been most thoroughly critiqued by historians of gender. See Landes, *Women and the Public Sphere in the Age of the French Revolution*; Fauré, *Democracy without Women*; Fraisse, *Reason's Muse*; Scott, *Only Paradoxes to Offer*; Scott, *Parité!* Critiques of French Republican universalism with regard to racial taxonomies are, in contrast, extremely rare. See the critical intervention of Wilder, *The French Imperial Nation-State*; and his "'Impenser' l'histoire de France."

10. Noiriel, *The French Melting Pot*; Noiriel, *Population, immigration, et identité nationale en France, 19ᵉ–20ᵉ siècle*; Horowitz and Noiriel, eds., *Immigrants in Two Democracies*; Brubaker, *Citizenship and Nationhood in France and Germany*; Lequin, ed., *Histoire des étrangers et de l'immigration en France*; Lequin, ed., *La mosaïque France*. Other informative works which neglect to address questions of gender and reproduction include Amar and Milza, *L'immigration en France au XXᵉ siècle*; Bonnet, *Les pouvoirs publics français et l'immigration dans l'entre-deux-guerres*; Kaspi, *Le Paris des étrangers*; Schor, *L'opinion publique française et les étrangers*.

11. Studies relying on oral histories are important exceptions. See Rouch, *"Comprar un prà"*; Breve, "Le rôle des femmes dans l'intégration des Italiens entre les deux guerres."

12. Heuer, *The Family and the Nation*; and the essays in Freedman and Tarr, eds., *Women, Immigration, and Identities in France*. Sociological work on immigration has more carefully analyzed questions of gender, but like historical scholarship, it tends to focus on the period after 1945.

13. McClintock, "Family Feuds," 62.

14. See for example Briggs, *Reproducing Empire*; Heng and Devan, "State Fatherhood"; Stevens, *Reproducing the State*; Roberts, *Civilization without Sexes*.

15. Roberts, *Civilization without Sexes*, 90.

16. Yuval-Davis and Anthias, eds., *Women-Nation-State*, 7. The authors list two other gendered engagements that I do not consider in a sustained manner in this work: the function of women as "symbolic signifiers of national difference," and women as active participants in national struggles.

17. Weinbaum, *Wayward Reproductions*, 37.

18. Ibid., 4.

19. See Grosz, *Volatile Bodies*.

20. This is of course a central argument of Foucault's *The History of Sexuality*. See also Domansky, "Militarization and Reproduction in World War One Germany";

Murard and Zylberman, "De l'hygiène comme introduction à la politique expérimentale."

21. Holt, "Foreword: The First New Nations."

22. Foucault, *The History of Sexuality*, 105.

23. This is a reflection of Foucault's observation that since the Classical Age, political power in the West has "assigned itself the task of administering life." See Foucault, *The History of Sexuality*, 139.

24. Parallel discussions of biopower that have influenced this study include Agamben, *Homo Sacer*; Anderson, "States of Hygiene"; Ong, "Making the Biopolitical Subject"; Rosemblatt, "Sexuality and Biopower in Chile and Latin America"; Stoler, *Race and the Education of Desire*.

25. While the biopolitics of colonial rule are an essential part of this story, my analysis necessarily focuses on European, African, and Asian immigration to the French metropole. Of course colonial and immigration discourses intersected in important ways, as subsequent chapters will demonstrate. For more on the biopolitics of imperialism see especially Pierce and Rao, eds., *Discipline and the Other Body*; Stoler, *Race and the Education of Desire*.

26. Canning, "The Body as Method?"

27. Scott, *Only Paradoxes to Offer*, 6.

28. Young, "Polity and Group Difference."

29. Stepan, "Race, Gender, Science, and Citizenship," 30.

30. Ibid., 29. See also Phillips, "Universal Pretensions in Political Thought"; Young, "Polity and Group Difference."

31. Scott, *Only Paradoxes to Offer*.

32. Wilder, *The French Imperial Nation-State*.

33. Ibid., 15.

34. See Silverman, *Deconstructing the Nation*; Scott, *Only Paradoxes to Offer*; Wilder, *The French Imperial Nation-State*.

35. Two otherwise useful studies that treat the pre-1945 period as though race were inconsequential are Hargreaves, *Immigration, "Race," and Ethnicity in Contemporary France*; and Silverman, *Deconstructing the Nation*. Tyler Stovall's work is an important exception to this general trend in the historiography. See "The Color Line behind the Lines"; "Colour-Blind France?"; "National Identity and Shifting Imperial Frontiers."

36. See especially Dubois, *A Colony of Citizens*; Fick, *The Making of Haiti*; Garraway, *The Libertine Colony*; Vaughan, *Creating the Creole Island*.

37. Massin, "Lutte des classes, lutte des races." See also Brubaker, *Citizenship and Nationhood in France and Germany*, 101; Weber, "Nos ancêtres les gaulois."

38. Goldberg, *Racist Culture*, 78; Mosse, *Toward the Final Solution*, 34.

39. Balibar, "Racism and Nationalism," 53.

40. Ibid., 43, emphasis in the original. See also Charles W. Mills's critique of liberal contract theory, which traces the formulation of a "transnational white polity, a virtual community of people linked by their citizenship in Europe at home and abroad, and constituted in opposition to their indigenous subjects." See *The Racial Contract*, 29.

41. Roediger, "Whiteness and Ethnicity in the History of 'White Ethnics' in the United States," 182. The literature on whiteness and United States immigration is fairly developed. See Allen, *The Invention of the White Race*; Brodkin, *How Jews Became White Folks and What That Says about Race in America*; Guglielmo and Salerno, eds., *Are Italians White?*; Guglielmo, *White on Arrival*; Ignatiev, *How the Irish Became White*; Jacobson, *Whiteness of a Different Color*; Roediger, *The Wages of Whiteness*.

42. The classic text is Higham, *Strangers in the Land*. See also Jacobson, *Whiteness of a Different Color*; Ngai, "The Architecture of Race in American Immigration Law."

43. Skidmore, *Black into White*, especially 136–44; Skidmore, "Racial Ideas and Social Policy in Brazil," especially 23–26.

44. Helg, "Race in Argentina and Cuba"; Ferrer, "Cuba, 1898."

45. Anderson, *The Cultivation of Whiteness*; Walker, *Anxious Nation*.

46. Mauco is only referring to western and European "Mediterraneans." See *Les étrangers en France*, 145.

47. Jacobson, *Whiteness of a Different Color*, 5; Mills, *The Racial Contract*, 80; Wallerstein, "The Ideological Tensions of Capitalism," 34.

48. Both French and English variants are derived from the Greek word *ethnos*, meaning people. According to the Robert dictionary, "*ethnique*" first came into use in 1882, "*ethnie*" in 1896. For an example of the difficulty of employing contemporary understandings of ethnicity in this context see Dr. René Martial, who writes of the "biological substratum" of which *ethnie* is composed. Martial, *La race française*, 14.

49. Birnbaum, *Jewish Destinies*, viii. See also the work of Catherine Collomp, who observes that "the very notion of ethnicity has no place in classic French political culture." See "Immigrants, Labor Markets, and the State," 42. I have translated the few examples of the word "*ethnique*" in the documents as "ethnographic" rather than "ethnic." All such translations are indicated in the text.

50. See especially Omi and Winant, *Racial Formation in the United States from the 1960s to the 1990s*, 14–23.

51. Camiscioli, "Race-Making and Race-Mixing in the Early Twentieth-Century Immigration Debate."

52. Stovall, "The Color Line behind the Lines," 743–44.

53. Kuhl, *The Nazi Connection*; Stepan, *"The Hour of Eugenics"*; Schneider, *Quality and Quantity*.

54. Lambert, *La France et les étrangers*, 96. See also Collomp, "Immigration, Labor Markets, and the State," 47; Noiriel, *Les origines républicaines de Vichy*; Rosenberg, "Albert Sarraut and Republican Racial Thought."

55. Pluyette, *La doctrine des races et la sélection de l'immigration en France*, 5.

56. Malik, *The Meaning of Race*, 35. See also Milza, "L'intégration des Italiens en France"; Silverman, *Deconstructing the Nation*, 81.

Chapter One: Immigration, Demography, and Pronatalism

1. Archives Nationales (hereafter AN), C7725, Proposition de loi relative au recrutement de la main d'œuvre étrangère et coloniale et au régime des étrangers en France: procès-verbal de la séance du 28 décembre 1915.

2. Secondary literature on the demographic crisis includes McLaren, *Sexuality and Social Order*, 1–27, 169–83; Nye, *Crime, Madness, and Politics in Modern France*, 121–70; Nye, *Masculinity and Male Codes of Honor in Modern France*, 72–97; Offen, "Depopulation, Nationalism, and Feminism in Fin-de-Siècle France," 648–76; Pederson, *Family, Dependence, and the Origins of the Welfare State*, especially 25–78; Roberts, *Civilization without Sexes*, 89–151; Spengler, *France Faces Depopulation*.

3. Here I disagree with Mary Louise Roberts and Andrés Horacio Reggiani, who claim that French pronatalism paid scant attention to the issue of foreign immigration. See Roberts, *Civilization without Sexes*, 103; Reggiani, "Procreating France," 752. Françoise Thébaud notes that the Alliance Nationale pour l'Accroissement de la Population Française assumed an "ambiguous" stance with regard to foreigners but does not explore its policy on immigration. See "Le mouvement nataliste dans la France de l'entre-deux-guerres."

4. Foucault, "Security, Territory, and Population," 67.

5. Foucault, "The Birth of Biopolitics," 73.

6. Foucault, *The History of Sexuality*, 105.

7. Cole, *The Power of Large Numbers*; Ipsen, *Dictating Demography*; Schneider, *Quality and Quantity*; Soloway, *Demography and Degeneration*.

8. Domansky, "Militarization and Reproduction in World War One Germany," 427–63.

9. Davin, "Imperialism and Motherhood"; Donzelot, *The Policing of Families*; Schafer, *Children in Moral Danger and the Problem of Government in Third Republic France*.

10. Pick, *Faces of Degeneration*.

11. Childers, *Families, Fathers, and the State in France*, 16.

12. Thébaud, "Le mouvement nataliste dans la France de l'entre-deux-guerres," 276.

13. Mayeur and Rebérieux, *The Third Republic from its Origins to the Great War*, 330.

14. Amar and Milza, *L'immigration en France au XXᵉ siècle*, 271.

15. Noiriel, *Population, immigration, et identité nationale en France, 19ᵉ–20ᵉ siècle*, 53.

16. Reynolds, *France between the Wars*, 25–26.

17. See Wilder, *The French Imperial Nation-State*.

18. On "civilization theory" and its proponents see Spengler, *France Faces Depopulation*, 162–68.

19. Leroy-Beaulieu, *La question de la population*.

20. Ibid., 237. On the shift away from Malthusianism see Charbit, *Du malthusianisme au populationnisme*.

21. Gianturco, "Le problème international de la population," 225–26.

22. Leroy-Beaulieu, *La question de la population*, 184. While providing a negative appraisal of democracy, the demographer Arsène Dumont also linked its emergence with the state of civilization. See *Dépopulation et civilisation*, 145–55.

23. Leroy-Beaulieu, "La question de la population et la civilisation," 871; Dumont, *Dépopulation et civilisation*, 106, 130, 238–51. Demographic maxims relating civilization and fecundity were relatively widespread in this period. For example, Gaetan Delauney claimed that "inferior species are more fertile than superior ones, and fertility diminishes as one moves upward through the steps of evolution." Similarly, his colleague Dr. Paul Jacoby compared the fertility of various French departments with regard to the level of civilization he claimed they had attained. See Cole, "'There Are Only Good Mothers,'" 665. Class and race were frequently conflated in demographic analyses of fecundity and civilization within France itself, thus casting French citizens from impoverished regions as "uncivilized." See Dumont, *Dépopulation et civilisation*, 241; Sicard de Plauzoles, "La lutte contre les maladies sociales," 284–89; Tournaire, *La plaie française*, 204–6. For an analysis of class, race, and demographic discourse see Winter, "The Fear of Population Decline in Western Europe," 186–87; Massin, "Lutte des classes, lutte des races," 127–43.

24. Bertillon, *La dépopulation de la France*, 130 (see also 128–37); Dumont, *Dépopulation et civilisation*, 80–88; Martial, *Traité de l'immigration et de la greffe interraciale*, 176–82; Sipperstein, *La grève des naissances en Europe et ses problèmes*, 101–28.

25. Dumont, *Dépopulation et civilisation*, 241.

26. Levine, *Prostitution, Race, and Politics*, 182. She writes: "The idea of empire as a web of lust and sexual intrigue rested on an idea of sexuality as a premodern phenomenon that modernity and rationality had learned to contain. The east's

problem was its failure to move beyond the primitivism of unchained nature, to contain sex within boundaries that made it productive and purposeful rather than merely sensual and pleasurable." See 180–81.

27. Prostitution will be addressed in chapter 4 and polygamy in chapter 5.

28. Passing mention is made of this point in Ogden and Huss, "Demography and Pronatalism in France in the 19th and 20th Centuries," 293.

29. Pluyette, *La doctrine des races et la sélection de l'immigration en France*, 140; Martial, *Traité de l'immigration et de la greffe inter-raciale*, 240–41.

30. Isaac, "Discours," Congrès National de la Natalité, *Compte rendu* (1922), 19.

31. Tournaire, *La plaie française*, 231.

32. Laffey, "Racism and Imperialism"; Massin, "Lutte des classes, lutte des races," 137; Rosenberg, "Albert Sarraut and Republican Racial Thought."

33. M.M., "Le Péril Blanc," *Relèvement social*, November 1929, 3.

34. Boverat, "La dénatalité, ses causes et les mesures à prendre pour l'enrayer," 4. See also Tournaire, *La plaie française*, 247.

35. Laffey, "Racism and Imperialism."

36. On the possibility of Asian imperialism see Leroy-Beaulieu, *Question de la population*, 153–70, 487; Maunier, *The Sociology of Colonies*, 35–36, 387; Tournaire, *La plaie française*, 246; Varlez, "Les problèmes de migration à la Conférence de la Havane de 1918," 11.

37. For more on Haury see Koos, "Engendering Reaction," 73–119.

38. Leroy-Beaulieu, *Question de la population*, 487. See also Gemaehling, *Vers la vie*, 22–23; Haury, *La vie ou la mort de la France*, 12; *Natalité: Organe de propagande de l'Alliance Nationale contre la Dépopulation* 27 (May 1939), 2.

39. Le Bras, "The Demographic Argument in France," 26–27.

40. Leroy-Beaulieu, *Question de la population*, 287.

41. Dumont, "Démographie des étrangers habitant en France," 425.

42. Le Conte, *Étude sur l'émigration italienne*, 388–99. Nevertheless, the Italians were sometimes likened to the Chinese because of their "docile obedience" and their willingness to accept low wages. See Gide and Lambert, "Les troubles d'Aigues-Mortes," 839–41, in which the Italians are referred to as the "Chinese of Europe," and Di Calboli, *L'Italie vagabonde*, 28. In the United States, however, where the racial stock of Italian immigrants was less valued, the Dillingham Commission's Report on Immigration warned of the "immense capacity of the Italian race to populate other parts of the earth," such as in Argentina and Brazil, where Italians now outnumbered the Spanish and Portuguese. See Jacobson, *Whiteness of a Different Color*, 80.

43. Offen, "Depopulation, Nationalism, and Feminism in Fin-de-siècle France."

44. Leroy-Beaulieu, *Question de la population*, 270–73.

45. Boverat, "La dénatalité, ses causes et les mesures à prendre pour l'enrayer," 4–5.

46. Childers, *Families, Fathers, and the State in France*, 77, 43; see also 26.

47. In Roberts, *Civilization without Sexes*, 111.

48. Troullier, "Immigration-Démographie," 314, emphasis in original.

49. See for example Duquesnoy, "Les mineurs polonais dans le bassin houiller du Nord," *Correspondance de l'École Normale Sociale* (June–August 1939), in AN, 6AS 36, Fonds Max Lazard; Guériot, "La politique de l'immigration," 433; Mauco, *Les étrangers en France*, 524.

50. "Immigration et naturalisation," *Revue de l'Alliance Nationale pour l'Accroissement de la Population Française* 134 (September 1923), 279.

51. Troullier, "Immigration-Démographie," 299. See also "Rapport de Charles Lambert, député du Rhône, sur la naturalisation des étrangers," Congrès National de la Natalité, *Compte rendu* (1927), 73.

52. On the Alliance and its trajectory in the 1930s see Koos, "Gender, Anti-individualism, and Nationalism," 699–723; Thébaud, "Le mouvement nataliste dans la France de l'entre-deux-guerres."

53. McLaren, *Sexuality and Social Order*, 173; Pederson, *Family, Dependence, and the Origins of the Welfare State*, 62–63.

54. Pederson, *Family, Dependence, and the Origins of the Welfare State*, 61.

55. Fernand Boverat, "Il faut à la France une politique d'immigration," *Revue de l'Alliance Nationale pour l'Accroissement de la Population Française* 129 (April 1923), 119. For a detailed discussion of Boverat's career see Koos, *Engendering Reaction*, 27–72. See also Talmy, *Histoire du mouvement familial en France*, vol. 2, 222–23.

56. Fernand Boverat, "Une politique de naturalisation," *Revue de l'Alliance Nationale pour l'Accroissement de la Population Française* 138 (January 1924), 49.

57. Isaac, "Discours," Congrès National de la Natalité, *Compte rendu* (1926), 13.

58. Fernand Boverat, "Comment faciliter la naturalisation de bons éléments français," Congrès National de la Natalité, *Compte rendu* (1925), 53.

59. Fernand Boverat, "Rapport sur la naturalisation," Congrès National de la Natalité, *Compte rendu* (1922), 58.

60. Albert Troullier, "42 millions d'Italiens," *Revue de l'Alliance Nationale pour l'Accroissement de la Population Française* 165 (April 1926), 102. See also Isaac, "Discours," Congrès National de la Natalité, *Compte Rendu* (1925), 20; Isaac, "Discours," Congrès National de la Natalité, *Compte Rendu* (1926), 13.

61. Boverat, "Il faut à la France une politique d'immigration," 119.

62. There is a long French tradition of "whitening" the Kabyles, hence distinguishing Berber-speaking North Africans from Arabs. See Lorcin, *Imperial Identities*.

63. Boverat, "Il faut à la France une politique d'immigration," 119–20. A similar taxonomy is put forth by Georges Rossignol in the pronatalist newspaper *Pour la*

Vie. While he marvels at the prolific Italians, Rossignol warns against encouraging the migration of people from "races that are difficult to assimilate, such as the Arabs, Chinese, and Blacks." See "Des enfants ou des étrangers, nous pouvons encore choisir," *Pour la Vie* 81 (January 1924).

64. Fernand Boverat, "Rapport général sur l'immigration et l'émigration étrangères dans le département: ses effets sur la nuptialité et la natalité," Conseil Superieur de la Natalité, *Rapports et vœux* (1936), 43.

65. For more on Duval-Arnould see Koos, *Engendering Reaction*, 149–92.

66. Louis Duval-Arnould, "Les problèmes de l'immigration étrangère en France," Semaines Sociales de France, *Compte rendu* (1926), 626.

67. Ibid., 627.

68. Mgr. Vanneufville, "La main-d'œuvre étrangère et les migrations ouvrières," Semaines Sociales de la France, *Compte rendu* (1920), 345.

69. One of the best critiques of Republican secularism is Auslander, "Bavarian Crucifixes and French Headscarves."

70. *L'Illustration* was a well-respected weekly with a predominantly middle-class readership. Its average circulation was about 200,000. See Schor, *L'opinion publique française et les étrangers*, 13–14.

71. Talmy, *Histoire du mouvement familial en France*, vol. 2, 220.

72. Naudeau, *La France se regarde.* For the social reformer Émile Pourésy's glowing review of Naudeau's book see *Relèvement social*, 1 January 1932, 1–2.

73. Naudeau, *La France se regarde*, 11, 116. For his appreciation of Bertillon, Leroy-Beaulieu, and Dumont see 442–43, 448–50.

74. Here especially Naudeau follows Dumont. See Cole, *The Power of Large Numbers*, 207.

75. Ibid., 197.

76. See Roberts, *Civilization without Sexes.*

77. According to Clifford Rosenberg, the phrase is originally attributed to General Mangin, who stated that "France is a country of one-hundred million inhabitants: forty million metropolitans, the rest natives and settlers in the colonies." See "Albert Sarraut and Republican Racial Thought," 103–4; and his *Policing Paris*, 110.

78. Naudeau, *La France se regarde*, 8.

79. Ibid., 68; see also 39, 66.

80. Ibid., 116.

81. Ibid., 66; see also 186.

82. Ibid., 54, 154–55, 333–34.

83. "Rapport sur l'immigration et l'émigration étrangères," Conseil Superieur de la Natalité, *Rapports et vœux* 6 (1936), 10.

84. Boverat, "Rapport général sur l'immigration et l'émigration étrangères dans le département," 42.

85. Isaac, "Discours," Congrès National de la Natalité, *Compte Rendu* (1926), 13.

86. For more on Mauco see Adler, *Jews and Gender in Liberation France*, 106–43; Roudinesco, "Georges Mauco (1899–1988)"; Weil, "Georges Mauco."

87. Mauco, *Les étrangers en France*, 184, 186.

88. Landes, *Women and the Public Sphere in the Age of the French Revolution*.

89. *L'Amitié Française*, 13 January 1919, in Schor, *L'opinion publique française et les étrangers*, 526.

90. Maurice Ajam, "La greffe étrangère," *La Dépêche*, 1 February 1929, in *Revue de l'Immigration* 10 (February 1929).

91. Mauco, *Les étrangers en France*, 532.

92. Naudeau, "Les dangers et les ressources de l'immigration," 392.

93. Boverat, "Rapport général sur l'immigration," 42.

94. Pederson, *Family, Dependence, and the Origins of the Welfare State*.

95. Talmy, *Histoire du mouvement familial en France*, vol. 1, 211–17.

96. "Rapport sur l'immigration et l'émigration étrangères," 12.

97. Boverat, "Le chômage et les immigrés," Rapport présenté à la section permanente du Conseil Superieur de la Natalité, 19 January 1931, suppl. to fasc. 1, 1931, 3.

98. Ibid., 1–2. See also Boverat, "Le chômage et les immigrés: ne refoulons pas les chefs de famille," *Revue de l'Alliance Nationale pour l'Accroissement de la Population Française* 223 (February 1931), 402–5.

99. Ibid., 3–4.

100. Ibid., 4–5.

101. "Comment naturaliser des pères de famille étrangère," *Natalité* 2 (May 1925).

102. This is a significant revision of the conclusion to which I came in an earlier version of this chapter. See Camiscioli, "Producing Citizens, Reproducing the 'French Race.'" On the pitfalls of understanding French Republicanism in terms of "failed universalism" (as I did in the article cited above), see Wilder, *The French Imperial Nation-State*.

103. Pollard, *Reign of Virtue*, 33, 40.

104. See also Adler, *Jews and Gender in Liberation France*; Noiriel, *Les origines républicaines de Vichy*.

Chapter Two: Labor Power and the Racial Economy

1. Guériot, "La politique de l'immigration," 419.

2. Ibid., 420.

3. Scholarship on this theme is abundant; some works that I have found particularly

helpful include Auslander, *Taste and Power*; Cross, *Immigrant Workers in Industrial France*; Downs, *Manufacturing Inequality*; Frader and Rose, "Introduction: Gender and the Reconstruction of European Working-Class History"; McClelland, "Masculinity and the 'Representative Artisan' in Britain"; Roediger, *The Wages of Whiteness*; Rose, "Gender at Work"; Scott, "Work Identities for Men and Women"; Takaki, *Iron Cages*.

4. The most important theorist of the liberal economic position on immigration was Paul Leroy-Beaulieu, director of the journal *L'Économiste français*. On the role of political economy in establishing immigration as a legitimate field of study see Noiriel, *The French Melting Pot*, 53–54. Opposition to the liberal economic position is expressed by Frézouls, *Les ouvriers étrangers en France devant les lois du travail et de la prévoyance sociale*; and Lugand, *L'immigration des ouvriers étrangers et les enseignements de la guerre*. Both sides of the debate are explained by Oualid in "Le droit migratoire."

5. See Wallerstein, "The Ideological Tensions of Capitalism," 29–36.

6. Cross, *Immigrant Workers*, 4–5; Moch, Introduction, 12. On the parallel of liberal economics and Republican politics see Kuisel, *Capitalism and the State in Modern France*, 1–5, 11.

7. Levasseur, "De l'émigration au 19ᵉ siècle," 400.

8. Ibid.

9. On economic productivism with regard to the colonial project see Warshaw, *Paul Leroy-Beaulieu and Established Liberalism in France*, 99–137.

10. See for example the argument of the protectionist Paul Frézouls, juxtaposing the "internationalism" of classical economics with the German school, "which reminds us that the world is divided into separate nations," and thus that a national and perhaps even nationalistic economy is the most likely means to insure the well-being of its subjects. *Les ouvriers étrangers en France devant les lois du travail et de la prévoyance sociale*, 38.

11. Kuisel, *Capitalism and the State in Modern France*, 7; see also Cross, *Immigrant Workers*, 5.

12. Nogaro and Weil, *La main-d'œuvre étrangère et coloniale pendant la guerre*, 114. See also Cross, *Immigrant Workers*, chapter 2.

13. Nogaro and Weil, *La main-d'œuvre étrangère et coloniale pendant la guerre*, 25.

14. On the racialization of wartime recruits see also Horne, "Immigrant Workers in France during World War I," 79–80; Dornel, "Les usages du racialisme"; Frader, "From Muscles to Nerves"; Lewis, "Une théorie raciale des valeurs?"; Stovall, "Colour-Blind France?"; Stovall, "The Color Line behind the Lines"; Stovall, "National Identity and Shifting Imperial Frontiers"; and the problematic article

by Vidalenc, "La main-d'œuvre étrangère en France et la Première Guerre Mondiale," in which the author uncritically adopts many of the racist assumptions of his sources.

15. Gianturco. "Le problème international de la population." For more on the role of the International Labor Office in regulating international migrations see Catalogne, *La politique de l'immigration en France depuis la guerre de 1914*, 8; Rodet, *L'immigration des travailleurs étrangers en France*, 45–80.

16. Mauco, *Les étrangers en France*, ii, 27, 32, 35. On the upward social mobility of French workers at this time see Noiriel, *Workers in French Society in the Nineteenth and Twentieth Centuries*, 97–100.

17. Mauco, *Les étrangers en France*, 509.

18. Oualid, "Le droit migratoire," 1–2.

19. Ibid., 2.

20. Ibid., 3.

21. Ibid., 3–5.

22. Martial, *Traité de l'immigration et de la greffe inter-raciale*, 31–48; Mauco, *Les étrangers en France*, 8–13. See also Lequin, *Histoire des étrangers et de l'immigration en France*, 321–33.

23. Schirmacher, *Spécialisation du travail à Paris*, 16–17.

24. Ibid., 150.

25. Mauco, *Les étrangers en France*, 40, 49.

26. Noiriel, *Workers in French Society in the Nineteenth and Twentieth Centuries*, 8.

27. Mauco, *Les étrangers en France*, 50.

28. Ibid., 14.

29. On the European work science see Rabinbach, *The Human Motor*. See also Frader, "From Muscles to Nerves." On the French response to American-inspired scientific management see Maier, "Between Taylorism and Technocracy."

30. Frader, "From Muscles to Nerves," 127.

31. The report was delivered in June 1909 to Georges Clemenceau, president of the Council of Ministers. See Rabinbach, *The Human Motor*, 185–86.

32. Amar, *L'organisation physiologique du travail*.

33. Rabinbach, *The Human Motor*, 183. On the gendered premises of Amar's work see Frader, "From Muscles to Nerves," 133–34.

34. Amar, *L'organisation physiologique du travail*, 205–6, emphasis in original.

35. Ibid., 219.

36. Ibid., 221.

37. Ibid., 220.

38. Ibid., 222.

39. Lorcin, *Imperial Identities*. See also Rosenberg, "Albert Sarraut and Republican Racial Thought."

40. Amar, *L'organisation physiologique du travail*, 222.

41. Cross, *Immigrant Workers*, 5; Kuisel, *Capitalism and the State in Modern France*, x.

42. Mauco, *Les étrangers en France*, 69.

43. Nogaro and Weil, *La main-d'œuvre étrangère et coloniale pendant la guerre*, 25.

44. Similarly, when the term "foreign workforce" (*main-d'œuvre étrangère*) was employed, it did not include nonwhite workers.

45. AN, 94AP 135, Note du SSE de l'Artillerie et des Munitions aux Directeurs des Établissements du Service des Poudres, 2 October 1916.

46. AN, 94 AP 130. During the war male and female workers were set in opposition in a very similar manner. See William Oualid, who wrote: "In masonry . . . it has been found that four women are required to do the work of three men." "The Effect of the War upon Labor in France," 160–61. See also Downs, *Manufacturing Inequality*.

47. 40AS 40. "Projet de circulaire et de questionnaire qui pourraient être envoyés aux principales associations industrielles et agricoles, en vue de déterminer sommairement l'importance des besoins de main-d'œuvre," 1916. No responses to the survey were located in the archives of the Comité Central des Houillères de France.

48. AN, 94AP 135, SSE, MOE. Note pour M. Simiand, 20 February 1914.

49. Nogaro and Weil, *La main-d'œuvre étrangère et coloniale pendant la guerre*, 2.

50. Stovall, "Colour-Blind France?," 41.

51. Stovall, "The Color Line behind the Lines," 745.

52. Stovall, "Love, Labor, and Race."

53. Nogaro and Weil, *La main-d'œuvre étrangère et coloniale pendant la guerre*, 26–27.

54. AN, 94AP 129, Résumé des contrôleurs régionaux de la main-d'œuvre militaire, January 1917.

55. AN, F14 11331, "Instructions relatives à l'emploi de la main-d'œuvre chinoise."

56. Ibid. A more favorable account of Chinese workers (which nevertheless notes their "weakness of character") appears in AN, 94AP 57.

57. Mauco, *Les étrangers en France*, 269.

58. AN, 94AP 120, Ministère de la Guerre, "Note pour le sous-secrétariat d'état au sujet des ouvriers annamites."

59. 40AS 40. Commission Administrative de l'Office Central de Placement, Procès-verbaux et des documents sur le placement et le recrutement de la main-d'œuvre, 1916–17. Note sur le recrutement de la main-d'œuvre coloniale et étrangère.

60. AN, 94AP 120, Ministère de la Guerre, "Note pour le sous-secrétariat d'état au sujet des ouvriers annamites." On the overlap of racialized and gendered attributes in French descriptions of factory labor see Frader, "From Muscles to Nerves."

61. Marius Moutlet, "Un gros problème: la main-d'œuvre exotique: ce qu'on fait, ce qu'on doit faire," *L'Humanité*, 7 February 1916, AN, 94AP 120. The classic account is Thompson, "Time, Work-Discipline, and Industrial Capitalism."

62. See also Rosenberg, *Policing Paris*, 123.

63. AN, 94AP 129, Résumé des contrôleurs régionaux de la main-d'œuvre militaire pour le mois de janvier 1917.

64. AN, 94AP 129, Résumé des contrôleurs régionaux de la main-d'œuvre militaire pour le mois de mars 1917.

65. AN, 94AP 135, Note from Le Gentil, sous-lieutenant, to the SSE de l'Artillerie et Munitions, 20 July 1916, "Rapports sur la main-d'œuvre portugaise en France." A favorable account of Portuguese labor is also provided in AN, 94AP 129, Résumé des contrôleurs régionaux de la main-d'œuvre militaire pour le mois de janvier 1917; and in Nogaro and Weil, *La main-d'œuvre étrangère et coloniale pendant la guerre*, 52, where their labor was reported as satisfactory as long as they were well supervised. Similarly, the Greeks were considered "extremely inferior" in the report of January 1917, while another labeled them "elements of first choice" because of their sobriety, intelligence, and morality. See AN, 94AP 135, Rapport de Henri Pernot, chargé de cours à la Sorbonne au sous-secrétariat de l'artillerie et des munitions sur une mission à Nantes relative à la main-d'œuvre grecque, 13–19 August 1916.

66. Mauco, *Les étrangers en France*, 71.

67. Lugand, *L'immigration des ouvriers étrangers et les enseignements de la guerre*, 57, 39 n. 2.

68. AN, F22 330. Bureau d'Études Économiques, procès-verbal no. 19, 17 May 1918. Traités du travail et politique de l'immigration.

69. AN, F22 330, Bureau d'Études Économiques, Exposé relatif aux clauses dans les traités au sujet de la main-d'œuvre, reported by Nogaro, 31 May 1918.

70. AN, 94AP 120, Ministère de l'Armement et des Fabrications de la Guerre, Direction de la Main-d'œuvre, "L'introduction de la main-d'œuvre étrangère pendant la guerre et la politique de l'immigration." This citation appears virtually unchanged in Bertrand Nogaro, "L'introduction de la main-d'œuvre étrangère pendant la guerre," *Revue de l'économie politique* 6 (October–December 1920), 719.

71. Catalogne, *La politique de l'immigration en France depuis la guerre de 1914*, 55.

72. Pairault, *L'immigration organisée et l'emploi de la main-d'œuvre étrangère en France*, 186.

73. AN, 40 AS 48, Enquête du Comité Général des Houillères de France concernant

l'emploi de la main-d'œuvre nord-africaine dans l'industrie et le commerce de la métropole, 15 November 1937.

74. AN, 40 AS 48, Enquête du Comité Général des Houillères de France.

75. Ray, *Les Marocains en France*, 25.

76. Mauco, *Les étrangers en France*, 272.

77. Ibid., 270.

78. Oualid, "The Occupational Distribution and Status of Foreign Workers in France," 161, 180. Oualid is willing to concede that the Spaniards and Portuguese are often exceptions to this rule; their output in French mines is satisfactory even though they "have little in common with the rest of central and western Europe."

79. The chart appears in Oualid, "The Occupational Distribution and Status of Foreign Workers in France," 182. This study is widely cited in the literature on foreign labor. See for example Mauco, *Les étrangers en France*, 270.

80. "Le Fait de l'Occupation Créatrice," *Revue de l'immigration* 3 (July 1928), 2.

81. Rosenberg, *Policing Paris*, 124–25.

Chapter Three: Hybridity and Its Discontents

1. In the interest of historical specificity, I employ the term "métissage" rather than "miscegenation," as it is often translated. "Miscegenation" was coined in the American South of the Jim Crow era, and in my opinion does not connote race mixing between whites, a notion critical to my argument. Moreover, in the French language the term "métissage" does not necessarily have a negative connotation, whereas "miscegenation" arguably does. For an explanation of the American invention of the word see Fredrickson, "Mulattoes and *Métis*: Attitudes toward Miscegenation in the United States and France since the Seventeenth Century." As is evident from the article's title, Fredrickson employs the term "miscegenation" in both the French and American cases. Thanks to Tom Holt for first pointing out to me the possible problems of this translation.

2. On ethnographic science see Stocking, *Race, Culture, and Evolution*. On the French eugenics movement see Schneider, *Quality and Quantity*. Pierre-André Taguieff traces the trajectory of eugenicist theory from late-nineteenth-century anthropology through the Second World War in "Eugénisme ou décadence?"

3. Here my analysis engages with that of Gary Wilder in *The French Imperial Nation-State*.

4. This is the argument of Rogers Brubaker in *Citizenship and Nationhood in France and Germany*. It is crucial to note Brubaker's awareness that both universalist and particularist views have coexisted throughout French and German history (see p. 2 of his book). However, he chooses not to focus on these nuances, elaborating instead on what becomes, in the course of his text, a sharp opposition between

these two forms of national belonging. For critiques of this dichotomous position see Silverman, *Deconstructing the Nation*, 19–27; Silverman, "Rights and Difference"; Noiriel, *The French Melting Pot*, 10–11; Weil, *Qu'est-ce qu'un français?*; and especially Wilder, *The French Imperial Nation-State*.

5. See Noiriel, *The French Melting Pot*, 17.

6. Saada, "Race and Sociological Reason in the Republic." Saada's book *Les enfants de la colonie* was published too late for me to substantively engage its arguments.

7. Blanckaert, "Of Monstrous Métis?," 43.

8. Mosse, *Toward the Final Solution*, 51–93; Saada, "Race and Sociological Reason in the Republic"; Taguieff, *The Force of Prejudice*, especially 213–14; White, *Children of the French Empire*, 93–123; Vergès, *Monsters and Revolutionaries*, especially 28–29; Yee, "*Métissage* in France."

9. Blanckaert, "Of Monstrous Métis," 47.

10. This is frequently, but not uniquely, the use of the term "mestizaje" in the Latin American context. See for example Skidmore, *Black into White*, especially 136–44; Helg, "Race in Argentina and Cuba, 1880–1930," 37–69.

11. Blanckaert, "Of Monstrous Métis," 48; Yee, "*Métissage* in France," 416.

12. See Stocking, *Race, Culture, and Evolution*, chapters 2–3.

13. Taguieff, *The Force of Prejudice*, 213–14. Broca's position on the fertility of the *métis* is more subtle than simply proclaiming their sterility. For a full account see Blanckaert, "Of Monstrous Métis."

14. Gobineau, *The Inequality of Human Races*. For useful commentary on salient parts of Gobineau's text see Todorov, *On Human Diversity*, 129–40.

15. Ann Laura Stoler has described this earlier tolerance of interracial sex in several colonial contexts. See "Carnal Knowledge and Imperial Power: Gender and Morality in the Making of Race," *Carnal Knowledge and Imperial Power*, 41–78. Alice Conklin has demonstrated the same leniency in French West Africa before the First World War in *A Mission to Civilize*. For work on métissage in the French Caribbean, the Indian Ocean, and the South Pacific, areas I do not consider directly in this chapter because of their eighteenth- and nineteenth-century focus, see Bullard, *Exile to Paradise*; Garraway, *The Libertine Colony*; Matsuda, *Empire of Love*; Vaughan, *Creating the Creole Island*.

16. Stoler, *Carnal Knowledge and Imperial Power*, 48. See also Conklin, *A Mission to Civilize*; White, *Children of the French Empire*.

17. Stoler, *Carnal Knowledge and Imperial Power*, 48; White, *Children of the French Empire*, 32.

18. See especially Maunier, *The Sociology of Colonies*, 126–27. See also Conklin, *A Mission to Civilize*, 169–70.

19. Stoler, "Rethinking Colonial Categories: European Communities and the Boundaries of Rule," *Carnal Knowledge and Imperial Power*, 22–40.

20. Martha Elizabeth Hodes has argued the same in the American context with regard to the antebellum South. See *White Women, Black Men*.

21. Conklin, *A Mission to Civilize*, 171–73; Saada, "Enfants de la colonie," 77–78; Stoler, *Carnal Knowledge and Imperial Power*, 67–70; Vergès, *Monsters and Revolutionaries*, 29–30, 102–3. Owen White provides a nuanced account of the colonial administration's view of mixed-race children in French West Africa, where they were alternately viewed as "indispensable auxiliaries or dangerous *déclassés*." See White, *Children of the French Empire*, 53.

22. The literary critics Elizabeth Ezra and Jennifer Yee have studied a number of positive accounts of métissage between whites and colonized people. However fascinating these counterexamples may be, this was not the dominant discourse on race mixing by the twentieth century. Ezra and Yee are nonetheless correct to highlight this mixophilic tendency within literary sources. See Ezra, *The Colonial Unconscious*, 36–46; Yee, "*Métissage* in France."

23. Conklin, "Redefining 'Frenchness'"; Stoler, "Sexual Affronts and Racial Frontiers."

24. Boulle, "Racial Purity or Legal Clarity?"; Aubert, "'The Blood of France.'"

25. Heuer, "The One Drop Rule in Reverse?"

26. Nogaro and Weil, *La main-d'œuvre étrangère pendant la guerre*, 25.

27. Stovall, "Love, Labor, and Race" and "The Color Line behind the Lines." For an interesting point of comparison see Bland, "White Women and Men of Colour."

28. AN, F22 539, "Rapport de Mme Avril de Sainte-Croix sur l'organisation de salles de repos dans les usines." See also Dornel, "Les usages du racialisme," 60; Downs, *Manufacturing Inequality*, 60; Stovall, "The Color Line behind the Lines," 747–48.

29. On popular unrest due to contact between French prostitutes and men of color see Horne, "Immigrant Workers in France during World War I," 80–81; Fletcher, "City, Nation, and Empire in Interwar Marseilles," 221. For violence provoked by interracial relationships with other working women see Stovall, "The Color Line behind the Lines."

30. Huber, Bunle, and Boverat, *La population de la France*, 223, 236.

31. Amar and Milza, *L'immigration en France au XXᵉ siècle*, 208.

32. Muñoz-Perez and Tribalat, "Mariages d'étrangers et mariages mixtes en France," 433.

33. E.C., "Mariages mixtes des Kabyles en France," 112.

34. Ray, *Les Marocains en France*, 198.

35. White, "Miscegenation and the Popular Imagination," 134. White also describes a

survey of the same year in *Eve* magazine, which asked its female readers whether they would marry a "man of color." Out of 2,040 replies 980 were affirmative, 1,060 negative. See 135–36.

36. René Martial, "Étrangers et métis," 527.

37. Clark, *Social Darwinism in France*; Gould, *The Mismeasure of Man*; Mazower, *Dark Continent*, 76–103; Mosse, *Toward the Final Solution*, 51–93.

38. Nye, *Crime, Madness, and Politics in Modern France*, xii; Nye, *Masculinity and Male Codes of Honor in Modern France*. See also Schneider, *Quality and Quantity*, 46.

39. See for example "Rapport de la Commission sur les Malades Étrangers dans les Hôpitaux," *Bulletin de l'Académie de Médecine*, 19 January 1926, 69; Dequidt and Forestier, "Les aspects sanitaires du problème de l'immigration en France," 1013; Martial, *Traité de l'immigration et de la greffe inter-raciale*.

40. Dequidt and Forestier, "Les aspects sanitaires du problème de l'immigration en France," 1013.

41. Cited in Schneider, *Quality and Quantity*, 237.

42. Two important exceptions are Schneider, *Quality and Quantity*; and Taguieff, *The Force of Predjudice*. Gérard Noiriel only briefly considers the organicist position before dismissing it as "marginal" because it lacked a "genuine institutional base" and "placed itself outside the problematic of Republicanism." See Noiriel, *The French Melting Pot*, 17.

43. Weber, *Peasants into Frenchmen*.

44. Conry, *L'introduction du darwinisme en France au XIXᵉ siècle*; Schneider, "Hérédité, sang, et opposition à l'immigration dans la France des années 30," 104.

45. This trajectory is carefully traced in Schneider, *Quality and Quantity*.

46. On Lapouge see Schneider, *Quality and Quantity*, 59–63, 236–39; Taguieff, "Eugénisme ou décadence?," 81–103. On the positivist response to Lapouge see Hecht, "The Solvency of Metaphysics."

47. White, *Children of the French Empire*, 96.

48. Schneider, *Quality and Quantity*, 237–38. George L. Mosse claims that after Gobineau, Lapouge was the most important racial theorist in modern France. See Mosse, *After the Final Solution*, 58.

49. For more on the parallels between France and America with regard to race and immigration see Camiscioli, "Race-Making and Race-Mixing in the Early Twentieth-Century Immigration Debate."

50. Georges Vacher de Lapouge, preface to the French edition of Grant, *Le déclin de la grande race*. Reference is made to this citation in Dequidt and Forestier, "Les aspects sanitaires du problème de l'immigration en France," 1016. On Lapouge's popularity in Brazil see Skidmore, *Black into White*, 52–53, 238–39 n. 39.

51. Dequidt and Forestier, "Les aspects sanitaires du problème de l'immigration en France," 1025–26.

52. Compte rendu de séance du 28 mai 1924, *Eugénique* 3, no. 6 (1924), 210. On the FES and the immigration question see Schneider, *Quality and Quantity*, 208–55.

53. Compte rendu de séance du 13 décembre 1922, *Eugénique* 3, no. 3 (1923), 87. This position is echoed by the FES treasurer and esteemed demographer Lucien March in "Natalité et Eugénique," *Eugénique* 2, no. 7 (1921), 244–45.

54. On the Société d'Anthropologie see Cohen, *The French Encounter with Africans*, 220, 232–34.

55. Compte rendu de séance du 23 mai 1923, *Eugénique* 3, no. 4 (1923), 134.

56. Apert, "Immigration et métissage," 1566.

57. For key elements of Richet's eugenics see Richet, "La séléction humaine."

58. Apert's statement regarding the beauty of mixed-race people is in keeping with literary notions of "la belle métisse." See Yee, "*Métissage* in France," 420–21; Ezra, *The Colonial Unconscious*, 36–43. Note that the category of the belle métisse is necessarily gendered feminine, although that linkage cannot be determined with certainty from Apert's text. The closest masculine analogue is the "Romantic *métis*." See Yee, "*Métissage* in France," 417.

59. Apert, "Immigration et métissage," 1566–67.

60. Apert, "Le problème des races," 157.

61. "Discussion de la Communication du Docteur Eugène Apert, 'Le problème des races,'" *Eugénique* 3, no. 5 (1924), 162; Troullier, "Immigration-Démographie," 300.

62. Apert, "Le problème des races," 155–56.

63. Apert, "Immigration et métissage," 1567.

64. Apert, "Le problème des races," 156.

65. Ibid., 157.

66. Apert, "Immigration et métissage," 1569.

67. Faivre, *Aspect médical et social du problème des étrangers en France*, 45.

68. Dequidt and Forestier, "Les aspects sanitaires du problème de l'immigration en France," 1003–4.

69. Pinon, *Les problèmes médicaux de l'immigration*, 50.

70. Martial, "Etrangers et métis," 515; Meylan, *Les mariages mixtes en Afrique du Nord*, 38.

71. Apert, "Le problème des races," 155; Apert, "Immigration et métissage," 1565; Bérillon, *Les caractères nationaux*, 6, 62.

72. Dequidt and Forestier, "Les aspects sanitaires du problème de l'immigration en France," 1003. For the proceedings of this conference see *Conférence international de l'émigration et de l'immigration*.

73. René Martial, *Vie et constance des races*, 244.

74. Martial, "Etrangers et métis," 517.

75. For additional information on Martial see Larbiou, "René Martial, 1873–1955"; Schneider, *Quality and Quantity*, 230–55.

76. Martial, "Etrangers et Métis," 515. For a detailed account of the mixedness of the French race see Barzun, *The French Race*.

77. Martial is copiously cited in medical texts on immigration. Only Albin Faivre directly objects to Martial's theories, particularly that of "race résultat." See *Aspect médical et social du problème des étrangers en France*, 51–52. Faivre nevertheless believes that the races are unequal, and that crossings between whites and non-whites produce outright degenerates, or at the very least "social misfits" who are not accepted by either race.

78. Bérillon alone writes of the "purity of the French race." See *Les caractères nationaux*, 62.

79. St-Germain, *La grande invasion*, 199.

80. Pinon, *Les problèmes médicaux de l'immigration*, 50.

81. Millet, *Trois millions d'étrangers en France*, 89. Henry Louis Gates Jr. would disagree with the binary drawn by Millet, as Gates argues that Taine's work confounded understandings of race as blood with race as culture. See "Writing Race and the Difference It Makes," 3.

82. Wilder, *The French Imperial Nation-State*.

83. Insofar as Storoge may be referring to those of African origin currently residing in the United States, this document conflates immigration with the legacy of slavery. This is a fairly common error in early-twentieth-century French texts.

84. Storoge, *L'hygiène sociale et les étrangers en France*, 62–63.

85. Bercovici, *Contrôle sanitaire des immigrants en France*, 2.

86. Ibid., 92.

87. "Rapport de la Commission sur les Malades Étrangers," 68.

88. Ibid., 69.

89. Ibid., 68–69.

90. Ibid., 68.

91. Ibid., 72. Here again slavery and immigration are conflated.

92. Pairault, "Immigration et race," 1.

93. Ibid., 1–2.

94. Ibid., 2–3.

95. Martial, "Étrangers et Métis," 515.

96. Ibid., 527.

97. Pinon, *Les problèmes médicaux de l'immigration*, 50.

98. Schneider, *Quality and Quantity*, xx.

1. See also Watson, "The Trade in Women," in which white slavery is described as an "empty category" into which French people deposited their fears of cultural change.

2. Corbin, *Women for Hire*, 275–98.

3. Ibid., 280.

4. William Monarchville, *La traite de blanches et le Congrès de Londres* (Paris: Comité Française de Participation au Congrès, 1900), 7–8, in Watson, "The Trade in Women," 10. I have slightly altered her translation.

5. See chapter 1 in this book, and Watson, "The Trade in Women," 8–11.

6. On the regulationist system see Corbin, *Women for Hire*; Miller, "The 'Romance of Regulation.'" On prostitution in the period before regulationism in France see Conner, "Public Virtue and Private Women."

7. Dr. Alexandre Jean-Baptiste Duchâtelet, *De la prostitution dans la ville de Paris* (Paris: J. B. Baillière, 1836); Dr. Louis Fiaux, *La femme, le mariage, et le divorce*, in Corbin, *Women for Hire*, 53.

8. See Scott, *Only Paradoxes to Offer*.

9. This observation nicely dovetails with Gary Wilder's argument regarding colonized people in the Republican order, who possessed nationality without citizenship. See *The French Imperial Nation-State*.

10. Marcelle Legrand-Falco, "Note documentaire sur la réglemention de la prostitution" (July 1936), *Vingt-sept ans contre l'esclavage des femmes: un combat contre la prostitution: conférences françaises de Madame Legrand-Falco rassemblées par Denise Pouillon-Falco*, vol. III, 408; "Un Assainissement qui s'impose contre la traite des femmes et contre la prostitution reglémentée," Archives Legrand-Falco, IV/7.

11. Marie Bonnevial, "La Ligue Française pour le Droit des Femmes," *Relèvement social*, 1 January 1899.

12. Cited by Offen in "Intrepid Crusader," 357.

13. Guy, "'White Slavery,' Citizenship, and Nationality in Argentina," 202. According to Guy, the white slave campaign was a response to the immigration of European women abroad and not to the question of licensed brothels. See "Medical Imperialism Gone Awry: The Campaign against Legalized Prostitution in Latin America" in her *White Slavery and Mothers Alive and Dead*, 23.

14. Archives Legrand-Falco, II/3.

15. Skrobanek, Boonpakdi, and Janthakeero define "trafficking in persons" as "all acts involved in the recruitment and transportation of a person within and across national borders for work or services by means of violence or threat of violence,

abuse of authority or dominant position, debt-bondage, deception, or other forms of coercion." See *The Traffic in Women*, III.

16. Gemaehling, "Le proxénétisme en France."

17. *L'Œuvre*, 24 May 1930.

18. Guy, *Sex and Danger in Buenos Aires*, 25.

19. Archives de la Préfecture de Police, BA 1689, "La Traite des Blanches," *L'Éclair*, 24 September 1904.

20. Of course the term "négrier" is etymologically related to "Negro" and thus already profoundly racialized.

21. A further change was enacted in 1949, when the United Nations ratified the Convention for the Suppression of Traffic in Persons and the Exploitation or Prostitution of Others. The goal was to employ gender-neutral language to recognize male, and conceivably transgendered, prostitutes and victims.

22. Report of M. A. DeGraaf, League of Nations, *Records on the International Conference on the Traffic in Women and Children*, Geneva, 30 June–5 July 1921, 55. Some anti-trade activists had previously called for this change in language; for example, as early as 1910 Ghénia Avril de Sainte-Croix suggested similar revisions to the delegates at the International Conference on the White Slave Trade held in Madrid. See Watson, "The Trade in Women," 115. Thanks to Karen Offen for pointing this out to me.

23. Archives Legrand-Falco, II/3, Marcelle Legrand-Falco, "La réglementation de la prostitution: ses origines: la traite des femmes et la Société des Nations" (undated [before 1939]), 18.

24. On the Ligue pour le Relèvement de la Moralité Publique see Annie Stora-Lamarre, *L'Enfer de la IIIe République*, 79–104.

25. Emile Pourésy, "La Barbarie Nationale," *Relèvement Social* 9 (November 1935), 1. See also Elisabeth Palinsky, "La prostitution et sa réglementation" (1933), in Archives Legrand-Falco, IV/1.

26. Corbin, *Women for Hire*, 285.

27. See especially Bristow, *Prostitution and Prejudice*.

28. Molly Watson rightly argues that French anti-Semitism facilitated the public's linking of white slavery to the Stavisky affair of 1934, during which the popular opinion was that the financial scams of the naturalized Ukrainian Jew Alexandre Stavisky were indicative of Jewish disloyalty to the nation. According to this anti-Semitic logic, just as Jews would exploit the nation politically and economically, so too would they exploit its women sexually. See "The Trade in Women," 157–60.

29. Gemaehling, "Le proxénétisme en France," 17. For more on Zwy Migdal see Guy,

Sex and Danger in Buenos Aires, 120–25, 128–29; Watson, "The Trade in Women," 166–70.

30. Archives Legrand-Falco, 11/6, discourse of Paul Gemaehling, recorded in notes from meeting of the Union Temporaire contre la Prostitution Réglementée, 6 March 1934.

31. "Les traficants de chair blanche," *Relèvement social* 6 (15 March 1910), 3.

32. Archives Legrand-Falco, 1/3, draft of petition to the Senate by the Union Temporaire contre la Prostitution Réglementée (1937). The classic book on Buenos Aires is Guy, *Sex and Danger in Buenos Aires*.

33. Londres, *Le chemin de Buenos-Aires*, 29. For more on Londres see Assouline, *Albert Londres*; Mosset, *Albert Londres ou l'aventure du grand reportage*; Watson, "The Trade in Women," 166–75.

34. For one, it is likely that he meant to write "franchuta," rather than "franchucha," as the latter expression does not appear to exist in the Spanish language, and the former would accurately convey his meaning.

35. Guy, *Sex and Danger in Buenos Aires*, 23.

36. A number of these cards can be found in AN, F7 14859, F7 14843. On the "casas francescas" see Londres, *Le chemin de Buenos-Aires*, 92.

37. AN F7 14858. Rapport du Capitaine Gouspy, attaché militaire sur la traite des Françaises en Argentine et en Uruguay, considérée comme élément de contre-propagande, 20 April 1919.

38. Guy, *Sex and Danger in Buenos Aires*, 34. On French influence see 78, 80.

39. Archives Legrand-Falco, 11/3, Isadore Maus, *Édition du Comité National Belge de Défense National Belge contre la Traite des Femmes et Enfants* (Bruxelles, n.d.), 5. Of course these figures would only take into account registered prostitutes and not women working illegally outside licensed brothels, many of whom were not European. On "francesas" in Rio see Caulfield, *In Defense of Honor*, 58, 69; on Mexico see Bliss, *Compromised Positions*, 143.

40. Londres, *Le Chemin de Buenos-Aires*, 126, 180.

41. Emile Pourésy, "Le Congrès International contre la Traite des Blanches," *Relèvement social* 22 (15 November 1910), 2.

42. On the white slave debate in other contexts see Bristow, *Prostitution and Prejudice*; Guy, *Sex and Danger in Buenos Aires*; Levine, *Prostitution, Race, and Politics*, 245–50.

43. On regulated prostitution based on the "French system" abroad see Bliss, *Compromised Positions*; Engelstein, *The Keys to Happiness*; Guy, *Sex and Danger in Buenos Aires*; Henriot, *Prostitution and Sexuality in Shanghai*; Hershatter, *Dangerous Pleasures*; Svanström, *Policing Public Women*; Taraud, *La prostitution coloniale*.

44. Alloula, *The Colonial Harem*; Clancy-Smith, "Islam, Gender, and Identities in the Making of French Algeria"; Taraud, *Mauresques*.

45. Champly, *Sur le chemin de Changhaï*, 93.

46. Ibid., 27.

47. Ibid., 75–76.

48. AN, F7 14856, letter from the French chargé d'affaires in Central America, 24 June 1925.

49. Archives Legrand-Falco, 11/6, discourse of Maria Vérone, recorded in notes from meeting of the Union Temporaire contre la Prostitution Réglementée, 6 March 1934.

50. Union Temporaire contre la Prostitution Réglementée, *Bulletin Annuel*, 1936, 54.

51. On nationalism and respectability see Mosse, *Nationalism and Sexuality*.

52. Archives Legrand-Falco, 11/6, discourse of Paul Gemaehling, recorded in notes from meeting of the Union Temporaire contre la Prostitution Réglementée, 6 March 1934.

53. On the implications of viewing prostitution as a "matter of personal choice and a form of work" see Doezema, "Forced to Choose." Revisionist feminist readings of prostitution and the "traffic in women" are responding most notably to the work of Barry, *Female Sexual Slavery* and *The Prostitution of Sexuality*.

54. Corbin, *Women for Hire*, 285; Walkowitz, *Prostitution and Victorian Society*, 247.

55. On the debate over whether the sex worker contracts out her body or her labor time, see especially Pateman, *The Sexual Contract*, 189–218; Stanley, *From Bondage to Contract*, 218–63. For Nancy Fraser's critique of Pateman see "Beyond the Master/Subject Model."

56. Marjan Wijers, "Keep Your Women Home: European Policies on Trafficking in Women," cited in Jo Doezema, "Loose Women or Lost Women," 40.

57. Kamala Kempadoo argues that "prostitution appears to be one of the last sites of gender relations to be interrogated though a critical feminist lens that assumes that women are both active subjects and subjects of domination." See "Introduction: Globalizing Sex Workers" in *Global Sex Workers*, ed. Kempadoo and Doezema, 9. Similarly, Jo Doezema makes the provocative point that the dichotomy between forced and voluntary prostitution serves to "reproduce the whore/madonna division within the category 'prostitute.'" See "Forced to Choose," *Global Sex Workers*, ed. Kempadoo and Doezema, 46–47. See also, in the same volume, Murray, "Debt-Bondage and Trafficking," 51–64. Cf. the argument of Hall and Ryan in *Sex Tourism*, 50.

58. AN, F7 14854, Dossier Traite des Blanches, Circulaires, 1916–1940.

59. "La présidente du Conseil National des Femmes à la Société des Nations: com-

mission consultative sur la traite des femmes et des enfants," *L'Abolitionniste* 23–24 (15 July–15 October 1921), 11–12.

60. Obed Smith, "Employment Abroad, and the Protection of Women Emigrants," League of Nations, *Records on the International Conference on the Traffic in Women and Children*, Geneva, 30 June–5 July 1921, 44.

61. Archives Legrand-Falco, IV/7.

62. AN, F7 14857, dossier Gabriel Sicard, flyer dated 1936.

63. Cited in Watson, "The Trade in Women," 53 n. 130.

64. See also ibid., 33.

65. On prostitution and the French Army see Rhoades, *"No Safe Women."*

66. Literally "abattage" refers to the slaughter of animals or the felling of trees.

67. Corbin, *Women for Hire*, 338–39.

68. Ibid., 338.

69. Archives de la Préfecture de Police, BI 44, dossier Fernande Kolb.

70. Briggs, *Reproducing Empire*, 26.

71. Archives Legrand-Falco, II/4A, report of Lévy-Bing to Ministry of Public Health, Paris, 30 September 1935. The complete Lévy-Bing report is reprinted in *La prophylaxie antivénérienne* 3 (March 1937), 168–205.

72. Archives de la Préfecture de Police, BI 43, dossier Augustine Keller.

73. Report of Lévy-Bing to Ministry of Public Health in *La prophylaxie antivénérienne* 3 (March 1937), 172.

74. Archives Legrand-Falco, II/4A, report of Lévy-Bing to Ministry of Public Health, Vincenne, Ivry, Drancy, St-Denis, 15 October 1935.

75. Archives de la Préfecture de Police, BMI 43, dossier Josephine Blais.

76. Archives de la Préfecture de Police, BMI 32, dossier Marie Oftinger, letter from président du conseil, Ministère de l'Intérieur, to the prefect of the Police Hygiène, 4ᵉ Bureau, 3 July 1931.

77. Emile Pourésy, "Paris veut faire parler de lui," *Relèvement social: édition abolitionniste* 6 (15 June 1930), 1.

78. Archives de la Préfecture de Police, BA 1689, 7 February 1931, report of Police Judiciaire on the meeting on 6 February 1931 of the Union Temporaire contre la Prostitution Réglementée.

79. Archives de la Préfecture de Police, BMI 32, dossier Marie Oftinger, letter from Brigadier Chef Couturier to the Prefect of Police, 15 July 1931.

80. Archives de la Préfecture de Police, BMI 32, dossier Marie Oftinger, letter from Brigadier Chef Couturier to the Prefect of Police, 14 November 1930.

81. Archives de la Préfecture de Police, BMI 32, dossier Marie Oftinger, letter from Prefect of Police Chiappe to the Conseiller of Grenelle, "À propos du lupinar de la rue Frémicourt."

82. Rhoades, *"No Safe Women,"* 5.

83. Ibid., 79.

84. Service Historique de l'Armée de la Terre, 7N 1022, supplement, dossier 2, copy of letter transmitted to the Commander General of the 13th Infantry. Besançon, 28 December 1936.

85. Service Historique de l'Armée de la Terre, 7N 1022, supplement, dossier 2, "Note au sujet des maisons de tolérances et BMC pour les troupes nord-africaines." État-Major de l'Armée, Section Outre-Mer, 1935.

86. Stoler, *Race and the Education of Desire*, 129 n. 96.

87. Service Historique de l'Armée de la Terre, 7N 1022, supplement, dossier 2, "Note au sujet des maisons de tolérances et BMC pour les troupes nord-africaines." État-Major de l'Armée, Section Outre-Mer, 1935. See also the note of 6 June 1935 of the Section Outre-Mer.

88. Service Historique de l'Armée de la Terre, 7N 1022, supplement, dossier 2, note of 6 June 1935 of the Section Outre-Mer.

89. Service Historique de l'Armée de la Terre, 7N 1022, supplement, dossier 3, "Note pour les 1er et 3e Bureaux de l'EMA," 15 March 1935.

90. Service Historique de l'Armée de la Terre, 7N 1022, supplement, dossier 2, letter of Colonel Massoni to the Commissaire Central de l'Hôtel de Ville of Belfort, 22 December 1936.

91. Service Historique de l'Armée de la Terre, 7N 1022, supplement, dossier 3, "Note sur la surveillance de l'état d'esprit des travailleurs indigènes," 18 September 1935.

92. Service Historique de l'Armée de la Terre, 7N 1022, supplement, dossier 3, "Note relative à la surveillance de l'état d'esprit des militaires nord-africains," 1935.

93. Service Historique de l'Armée de la Terre, 7N 1022, supplement, dossier 1, letter to minister of war, EMA-SOM, 13 June 1936.

94. Service Historique de l'Armée de la Terre, 27N 65, dossier 1, "Note pour le commendement au sujet de l'installation des maisons de tolérances pour les soldats indigènes," 3 April 1940.

95. Service Historique de l'Armée de la Terre, 7N 1022, supplement, dossier 1, "Rapport du Chef de Bataille Dejouas au sujet de sa visite au 15e RTA à Périgueux et Bergerac, 3 June 1936."

96. Société des Nations, *Actes de la Conférence Diplomatique Relative à la Répression de la Traite des Femmes Majeures* (Geneva, 1933).

97. On the army's somewhat delayed understanding of the conflict see Service Historique de l'Armée de la Terre, 7N1022, supplement, correspondance générale from président du conseil, Ministère de l'Interieur, to minister of war, 3rd Bureau.

98. Here I am engaging with an argument made by Antoinette Burton in "From Child Bride to 'Hindoo Lady,'" 1145.

99. Paul Gemaehling, "Que devons-nous attendre de la nouvelle convention internationale relative à la traite de femmes?," *L'Abolitionniste*, 15 January 1934.

100. "Le prestige pour la femme blanche," *L'Abolitionniste*, October 1936, 3.

101. Ibid.

102. "Mœurs et Morale Sexuelle," *L'Abolitionniste*, July 1919, 5.

103. Emile Pourésy, "Les BMC," *L'Abolitionniste*, March 1936, 3.

104. AN, F60 603, fascicule de l'Union Temporaire, 25 March 1936.

105. Bibliothèque Marguerite Durand, dossier 351 PRO: Union Temporaire, notes from meeting of Union Temporaire contre la Prostitution Réglementée, 25 March 1935.

106. Service Historique de l'Armée de la Terre, 3H2478/D4, letter of Lieutenant Colonel Parlance to commanding general of the Goums Marocains, 1 June 1945; letter from General Guillaume to M. le Directeur des Affaires Politiques in Rabat, n.d. [probably 1945].

107. Service Historique de l'Armée de la Terre, 3H2561/D4, 1er Goum Marocain: Notes concernant le BMC, 1937 et 1946; Capitain Fouchet, "Consignes pour les BMC de la place," 1 January 1937; 3H2684/7; Chef de Bataillon Guerin, "Consignes pour le BMC," 3 January 1949.

108. Service Historique de l'Armée de la Terre, 7N 1022, supplement, dossier 2, letter from Lieutenant Colonel Clerc to General Comdt of the 11th Regiment, 18 November 1936.

109. Archives Legrand-Falco, V/4, "Rapport du secrétariat de la Fédération Abolitionniste: l'actuel rapport part du congrès de Paris," May 1937.

110. Miller, "The 'Romance of Regulation,'" 368.

111. Bibliothèque Marguerite Durand, dossier 351 PRO: Union Temporaire, notes from meeting of the Union Temporaire contre la Prostitution Réglementée, 25 March 1935.

112. Hershatter, *Dangerous Pleasures*, 283–84.

113. Report of Dr. Colombiani and Dr. Lépinay, *La prophylaxie antivénérienne*, July–August 1934, 360.

114. Taraud, *La prostitution coloniale*, 67, 108–9. See also Wright, *The Politics of Design in French Colonial Urbanism*.

115. Bibliothèque Marguerite Durand, dossier 351 PRO: Union Temporaire, Théodore Monod on the reserved quarters in Meknès, in notes from meeting of the Union Temporaire contre la Prostitution Réglementée, 3 March 1933.

116. Taraud, *La prostitution coloniale*, 112.

117. Miller, "The 'Romance of Regulation,'" 372.

118. Cited in Taraud, *La prostitution coloniale*, 289.

119. For the regulationist position see the discourse of Gervais, Union Internationale Contre le Péril Vénérien, *Assemblée Générale, Texte des Rapports et Compte Rendu des Débats* (1938), 32; and, in the same volume, Maurice Raynaud, L. Colonieu, and E. Hadida, "L'organisation de la lutte antivénérienne en Algérie," 92–94. Similar debates concerned whether homosexuality and pederasty were imported by Europeans or already present in colonial societies. See Aldrich, *Colonialism and Homosexuality*, 14–15.

120. Émile Pourésy, "Civilisation décadente," *Relèvement social* 1 (January 1928), 1.

121. Emile Pourésy, "Singulière Civilisation," *L'Abolitionniste*, 15 February 1934.

122. Archives de la Préfecture de Police, BA/1689, transcript of meeting of the Union Temporaire, 6 February 1931.

123. "Le quartier réservé de Marrakech," *L'Abolitionniste* 1–2 (15 January 1933), 4.

124. Emile Pourésy, "Civilisation décadente," *Relèvement social* 1 (January 1928), 1.

125. Ibid.

126. "Nous descendons la pente," *L'Abolitionniste* 3 (15 March 1933), 33.

127. "Civilisation: l'ésclavage blanche au Tonkin," *Relèvement social: édition abolitionniste* 3 (15 March 1930), 2.

128. Paul Gemaehling, "Que devons-nous attendre de la nouvelle convention internationale relative à la traite des femmes?," *L'Abolitionniste*, 15 January 1934.

129. This postcard instructs the Frenchman that in the colonial setting, where the white woman (or "thrush") is scarce, one must make do with the less delectable meat of the woman of color (or "blackbird"). The full expression in French is *Faute des grives, on mange des merles.*

130. Stoler, *Carnal Knowledge and Imperial Power*, 75–76.

131. Conklin, "Redefining "Frenchness"; Stoler, "Sexual Affronts and Racial Frontiers."

132. Canning, *Gender History in Practice*, 33.

Chapter Five: Intermarriage, Nationality, Rights

1. In Weil, *Qu'est-ce qu'un français?*, 215.

2. Muñoz-Perez and Tribalat, "Mariages d'étrangers," 454.

3. Weil, *Qu'est-ce qu'un français?*, 218.

4. The most thorough treatment of the Code through a gendered lens is Heuer, *The Family and the Nation.*

5. I first compared the pronatalist and feminist positions on independent nationality in my "Intermarriage, Independent Nationality, and the Individual Rights of French Women." However, I have since revised my original conclusions.

6. *La Française* was founded by Jane Misme in 1906. While it was originally conceived as a general feminist publication linking the various republican factions of the movement, it became the official mouthpiece of the moderate Conseil National des Femmes Françaises, an umbrella group for a broad array of women's associations. By 1926, however, the newspaper was turned over to the CNFF's affiliate, the Union Française pour le Suffrage des Femmes. See Hause with Kenney, *Women's Suffrage and Social Politics in the Third Republic*, 104–5, 109–12; Smith, *Feminism in the Third Republic*, 16–17.

7. In contrast, Catholic and socialist feminists were generally absent from this debate. Because Catholic feminists were typically uncritical of the family's established hierarchy, their position on the Code's reform was far more ambivalent. As for socialist feminists, because they believed that revolution would precede female emancipation, the equal status of husbands and wives before the law was not of immediate concern. On Catholic feminists see Hause with Kenney, *Women's Suffrage and Social Politics in the Third Republic*, 166–68; Smith, *Feminism and the Third Republic*, 46–49, 184–93. On the failed alliance of feminism and socialism see Sowerwine, *Sisters or Citizens?*

8. On coverture—or the notion that a married woman's civil identity was "covered" by her husband's—see Kerber, "The Meanings of Citizenship."

9. Jane Misme, "La nationalité de la femme mariée: il faut réformer la loi," *La Française*, 18 November 1916.

10. The modern tendency for law to treat family members as separate and independent individuals is traced by Glendon, *The Transformation of Family Law*. More on the legal position of women under the Code can be found in Lewis, "The Legal Status of Women in Nineteenth-Century France"; McMillan, *Housewife or Harlot*, 25–28; Moses, *French Feminism in the Nineteenth Century*, 18–20. For an account of the campaign to revise the Code's stance on married women in the interwar years see Smith, *Feminism in the Third Republic*, 163–211.

11. Glendon, *The Transformation of Family Law*, 86–90.

12. According to Carole Pateman, the premise of Article 213 is an especially important indication of the one-sidedness of the marriage contract. See *The Sexual Contract*.

13. Glendon, *The Transformation of Family Law*, 89.

14. Hause with Kenney, *Women's Suffrage and Social Politics in the Third Republic*, 23.

15. Neyrand and M'sili, *Mariages mixtes et nationalité française*, 23.

16. Hause with Kenney, *Women's Suffrage and Social Politics in the Third Republic*, 23.

17. Eugène Audinet, "Du conflit entre les lois personelles des époux lorsque la

femme, française ou étrangère, conserve sa nationalité primitive," *Journal du droit international privé* 57 (1930), 319; Naccary, *La nationalité de la femme mariée dans les principaux pays*, 8–9; Sauteraud, "Du maintien de la nationalité de la femme française qui épouse un étranger," 199; Trinh, *De l'influence du mariage sur la nationalité de la femme mariée*, 4.

18. Trinh, *De l'influence du mariage sur la nationalité de la femme mariée*, 4. See Ephesians 5:22 and Matthew 19:5–6.

19. Çauwès, *Des rapports du mariage avec la nationalité*, 2–3; Naccary, *La nationalité de la femme mariée dans les principaux pays*, 8–9; Pelletier, *La nationalité de la femme mariée*, 9.

20. Naccary, *La nationalité de la femme mariée dans les principaux pays*, 19; Trinh, *De l'influence du mariage sur la nationalité de la femme mariée*, 12. While the Code dictated that the marital domicile was determined by the husband, unlike the Prussian Code of 1794 and the German Code of 1896 it never required a woman to change her name after marrying. See Glendon, *The Transformation of Family Law*, 104.

21. Naccary, *La nationalité de la femme mariée dans les principaux pays*, 7–8; Stoenesco, *La nationalité ne s'impose pas*, 1–16.

22. For a detailed list of countries which expatriated women upon marriage to a foreigner see Flournoy and Hudson, eds., *A Collection of Nationality Laws of Various Countries as Contained in Constitutions, Statutes, and Treaties*.

23. Augustine-Adams, "'With Notice of the Consequences'"; Bredbenner, *A Nationality of Her Own*; Cott, "Marriage and Women's Citizenship in the United States"; Gardner, *The Qualities of a Citizen*; Kerber, *No Constitutional Right to Be Ladies*, 33–46; Sapiro, "Women, Citizenship, and Nationality."

24. Baldwin, "Subject to Empire"; Heuer, *The Family and the Nation*, especially chapter 7; Kirshner, "Mulier alibi nupta," 147–75; Kirshner, "Women Married Elsewhere," 377–429; Studer, "Citizenship as Contingent National Belonging."

25. On the Dutch Indies see Ann Laura Stoler, "Sexual Affronts and Racial Frontiers: Cultural Competence and the Dangers of *Métissage*" in her *Carnal Knowledge and Imperial Power*, especially 101–6. Lora Wildenthal treats this question in the German colonial context in *German Women for Empire*.

26. For example, this was the case in parts of Latin America. See Augustine-Adams, "Constructing Mexico" and "'She Consents Implicitly.'"

27. League of Nations, *Nationality of Women: Report by the Secretary General*, V. 7 (Geneva: League of Nations Publications, 1931), 9.

28. *Journal officiel: lois et décrets*, 14 August 1927, 8697.

29. Calbairac, *La nationalité de la femme mariée*, 14. After the law's passage Calbairac published an updated version of this work entitled *Traité de la nationalité de la*

femme mariée. Unlike other male jurists, Calbairac unambiguously supported independent nationality and expressed admiration for the international feminist movement's efforts toward reform.

30. Naccary, *La nationalité de la femme mariée dans les principaux pays*, 20.

31. Unmarried and separated women had received full legal capacity in 1893.

32. Bredbenner, *A Nationality of Her Own*, 80–82, 87, 111; Cott, "Marriage and Women's Citizenship," 1464.

33. Scott, *Only Paradoxes to Offer*.

34. The classic text on the applicability of contract theory to women is Pateman, *The Sexual Contract*.

35. Pateman, "Women and Consent," 71–89.

36. For a discussion of some of these issues see Phillips, *Engendering Democracy*, 23–59.

37. The call for independent nationality appeared on the feminist program drafted in 1869 by Léon Richer, co-founder of the Ligue Française pour le Droit des Femmes. See Smith, *Feminism in the Third Republic*, 180.

38. Smith, *Feminism and the Third Republic*, 168–69.

39. Jean Champcommunal, "Un conflit de lois à l'ordre du jour," 3–5. Cf. Savatier, "Puissance maritale," in which he makes the common counterargument that that the Civil Code is fundamentally based on reciprocity and therefore does not in any way subordinate women. However, according to Savatier this does not obviate the husband's responsibility for the couple's "common interests."

40. Kapralik, *La nationalité de la femme mariée*, 60.

41. Calbairac, *La nationalité de la femme mariée*, 244; Trinh, *De l'influence du mariage sur la nationalité de la femme mariée*, 28–29.

42. *Journal officiel: documents parlementaires: Chambre*, séance du 18 février 1919, annexe no. 5716, 1935.

43. "Les françaises veulent rester françaises," *La Française*, 5 May 1923.

44. Pelletier, *La nationalité de la femme mariée*, 27–31; Savatier, "Puissance maritale," 226.

45. Savatier, "Puissance maritale," 226.

46. Ibid., 219–20.

47. The classic text is Weiss, *Traité théorique et pratique de droit international privé*, in which it is argued that nationality is a contractual bond uniting the state to each of its members. Weiss, along with several other prominent jurisconsults, eventually backed reform. See Sauteraud, "Du maintien de la nationalité de la femme française qui épouse un étranger," 203.

48. This was the argument of the law professor Eugène Audinet, as cited in Stoenesco, *La nationalité ne s'impose pas*, 4–5.

49. Calbairac, *La nationalité de la femme mariée*, 243; Suzanne Grinberg, "Le mariage ne doit imposer à la femme la nationalité du mari: de la nationalité de la femme mariée," *La Française*, 20 April 1916; Naccary, *La nationalité de la femme dans les principaux pays*, 120; Sauteraud, "Du maintien de la nationalité de la femme de la femme française qui épouse un étranger," 199, and "Le changement de la nationalité de la femme française qui épouse un étranger," *La française*, 25 January 1919. These texts are informed by Weiss, *Traité théorique et pratique de droit international privé*.

50. The "presumed consent" of French women has a fascinating parallel in the "enforced consent" of colonial subjects. See Gary Wilder, *The French Imperial Nation-State*, 13.

51. "Presumed consent" is hence another instance — like Rousseau's "silent consent" and the supposition that "no really means yes" — in which a woman's volition is assumed, distorted, or ventriloquized. The purported difficulty of evaluating consent in rape trials is one of the clearest examples of this problem. See Pateman, "Women and Consent"; and Estrich, "Rape," 163–67, 175–79, 181.

52. Augustine-Adams, " 'She Consents Implicitly,' " 20–21.

53. Grinberg, "Le mariage ne doit pas imposer à la femme."

54. Sauteraud, "Le changement de la nationalité de la femme française qui épouse un étranger."

55. Pelletier, *La nationalité de la femme mariée*, 9.

56. Oualid, *L'immigration ouvrière en France*, 60; Pelletier, *La nationalité de la femme mariée*, 10, 32; Picot, *La réforme de la loi française sur la nationalité*, 20; Sauteraud, "Du maintien de la nationalité de la femme française qui épouse un étranger," 198; Trinh, *De l'influence du mariage sur la nationalité de la femme mariée*, 4–5.

57. Trinh, *De l'influence du mariage sur la nationalité de la femme mariée*, 4.

58. *Journal officiel: documents parlementaires: Sénat*, séance du 17 janvier 1918, annexe no. 18, p. 15.

59. Marcel Sauteraud, "Le changement de la nationalité en France par le mariage (suite)," *La Française*, 1 February 1919.

60. Sauteraud, "Du maintien de la nationalité de la femme française qui épouse un étranger," 198.

61. On the vast body of literature praising French women during the Great War see Thébaud, *La femme au temps de la guerre de 14*.

62. Sauteraud, "Le changement de la nationalité en France par le mariage (suite)."

63. *Journal officiel: documents parlementaires: Chambre*, annexe no. 7303, 1920, 565.

64. "La nationalité de la femme française," *La Française*, 2 April 1927.

65. "La triste situation de la femme mariée à un étranger," *Le Matin*, 14 February 1927, in Bibliothèque Marguerite Durand, dossier "Nationalité, 1902–40."

66. Bibliothèque Marguerite Durand, dossier "Nationalité, 1902–40."

67. See especially Roberts, *Civilization without Sexes*.

68. Sauteraud, "Du maintien de la nationalité de la femme française qui épouse un étranger," 198–99.

69. Maria Vérone, "Les Françaises paieront-elles la taxe sur les étrangers?," *L'Œuvre*, 26 October 1926.

70. *L'Œuvre*, 4 June 1922. See also Maria Vérone, "Le danger d'épouser un étranger," *L'Œuvre*, 22 March 1923.

71. Odette Simon, "La femme et la loi: la nationalité de la femme mariée," *La Française*, 18 September 1926.

72. "La fausse situation de la femme mariée à un étranger: une grave menace pour la natalité," *Minerva*, 30 January 1927, in Bibliothèque Marguerite Durand, dossier "Nationalité, 1902–40."

73. Grinberg, "Le mariage ne doit pas imposer à la femme," *La Française*, 20 April 1916.

74. "La triste situation de la femme mariée à un étranger."

75. Landes, *Women and the Public Sphere in the Age of the French Revolution*, 138.

76. *Journal officiel: documents parlémentaires: Sénat*, séance du 30 juillet 1918, annexe no. 4904, 2143.

77. Oualid, *L'immigration ouvrière en France*, 60.

78. Eugène Audinet, "L'effet du mariage sur la nationalité de la femme," *Journal du droit international privé* 47 (1920), 24.

79. "La nationalité de la femme mariée," *La Française*, 26 December 1925.

80. Amar and Milza, *L'immigration en France au XXᵉ siècle*, 207–10; Streiff-Fenart, *Les couples franco-maghrébins en France*, 8–11. The frequently cited survey from 1951 of the Institut National d'Études Démographiques, which was to gauge the integration and upward social mobility of Italian and Polish immigrants in France, considered intermarriage a crucial variable for study. See Girard and Stoetzel, *Français et immigrés*.

81. Amar and Milza, *L'immigration en France au XXᵉ siècle*, 209.

82. Eugène Audinet, "L'effet du mariage sur la nationalité de la femme," *Journal du droit international privé* 47 (1920), 23.

83. Kapralik, *La nationalité de la femme mariée*, 37; Pelletier, *La nationalité de la femme mariée*, 78–79.

84. Kapralik, *La nationalité de la femme mariée*, 37.

85. Sauteraud, "Du maintien de la nationalité de la femme française qui épouse un étranger," 197; and "Le changement de la nationalité en France de la femme française qui épouse un étranger."

86. On the choice of a marriage partner as an exercise of individual liberty see Çau-

wès, *Des rapports du mariage avec la nationalité*, 2; Trinh, *De l'influence du mariage sur la nationalité de la femme mariée*, 38. In fact the "right to marry" is not part of the French Constitution, although it has been invoked in several international conventions of the twentieth century, including the Universal Declaration of Human Rights of 1948 (article 16–1). Not until 1968 was the "right to marry" proclaimed by the French Court of Cassation, the highest court responsible for matters of private law. The groundwork for this decision was provided by a Paris Court of Appeals decision in 1963, in which an Air France flight attendant sought damages for wrongful termination after being dismissed from her position for marrying. Air France's termination of her contract was judged a violation of the "right to work" and the "right to marry." See Glendon, *The Transformation of Family Law*, 76–77.

87. Maria Vérone, "Dans les colonies: mariages mixtes," *L'Œuvre*, 10 February 1926. See also Trinh, *L'influence du mariage sur la nationalité de la femme mariée*, 38.

88. This did not deter some members of the French medical community from considering polygamy in the metropole as a drastic solution for the demographic crisis. See Roberts, *Civilization without Sexes*, 155. Their contribution was marginal to the debate, however.

89. The association of polygamy and ineligibility for citizenship occurred in other democratic contexts. For example, in the revisions of United States immigration procedures in 1891, polygamists were classed with anarchists, the insane, and felons as undesirables. See Cott, *Public Vows*, 139.

90. Alice Berthet, "La française doit rester française, même mariée à un étranger: la nationalité: droit moral," *La Française*, 25 January 1919.

91. Legrand-Falco, "Les états généraux du féminisme à l'Exposition Coloniale."

92. Vérone, "Dans les colonies."

93. Trinh, *L'influence du mariage sur la nationalité de la femme mariée*, 40.

94. Ibid., 38–39.

95. Note from the Ministry of Interior, 2 October 1919, reprinted in "Mariage entre Chinois et Françaises en France . . . Inconvénients," *Journal du droit international privé*, 1920, 365–67. Trinh's assessment of Franco-Chinese marriages is largely informed by this document.

96. Calbairac, *La nationalité de la femme mariée*, 11.

97. Vérone, "Dans les colonies." See also Vérone's "Blanches et noirs," *L'Œuvre*, 28 August 1924; and "Les mariages mixtes en Algérie," *L'Œuvre*, October 1925.

98. Sauteraud, "Le changement de la nationalité de la femme française qui épouse un étranger."

99. Lewis, "The Legal Status of Women in Nineteenth-Century France," 184–85.

100. Independent nationality did not resolve the problem of divorce. Audinet points out that if a French woman retaining her nationality exercises her right to divorce, but the laws of her spouse's country do not permit it, a marriage dissolved by one party will still exist for the other. See "L'effet du mariage sur la nationalité de la femme," 23. Jurists therefore advocated that a uniform approach to the dissolution of marriages between spouses of different nationalities be adopted at the level of international law. See the solutions proposed by Champcommunal, "Un conflit de lois à l'ordre du jour."

101. For statistics on mixed marriages between French nationals and foreigners see Muñoz-Perez and Tribalat, "Mariages d'étrangers et mariages mixtes en France," 433. On the legal problems that divorce poses to Franco-Italian couples see Naccary, *La nationalité de la femme mariée dans les principaux pays*, 92–94; Picot, *La réforme de la loi française sur la nationalité*, 121–22. See also Maria Vérone, "Divorce et Nationalité," *L'Œuvre*, 20 July 1922; "La nationalité de la femme," *L'Œuvre*, 18 July 1931.

102. With regard to the repudiation of the French wife in accordance with Muslim law, see the decision Mignot v. Abdelaziz Sfar, Tunis, 10 June 1908, in *Journal du droit international privé*, 1909, 1075–78; Moussa v. Moussa, 28 April 1925, Paris, in *Journal du droit international privé*, 1926, 406–7. On divorce between a French woman of Jewish origin and a Tunisian Jewish man see the decision of Lévy v. Taïeb, 11 December 1907, Tunis, in *Journal du droit international privé*, 1908, 1159–61. A comprehensive account of the legal ramifications of marriages between North Africans and Europeans is provided by Meylan, *Les mariages mixtes en Afrique du Nord*.

103. Sauteraud, "Du maintien de la nationalité de la femme française qui épouse un étranger," 203. See also *Journal officiel: documents parlementaires: Sénat*, annexe no. 18, 1918, 15.

104. *Journal officiel: documents parlementaires: Sénat*, séance du 10 février 1916, annexe no. 35, 81.

105. *Journal officiel: documents parlementaires: Sénat*, séance du 30 juillet 1918, annexe no. 4904, 2144.

106. *Journal officiel: débats parlementaires: Chambre*, "Discussion du projet de loi sur la nationalité," première séance du 31 mars 1927, 1101.

107. See for example Danel, "La loi sur la nationalité et la famille," 154–55; Risler, "Les résultats de la nouvelle loi sur la nationalité," 90–92; "Une loi sur la nationalité."

108. "A la Chambre des Députés: la nationalité de la femme mariée," *La Française*, 19 February 1927.

109. *Journal officiel: débats parlementaires: Chambre,* première séance du 31 mars 1927, 1102; see also the commentary by Marcelle Kraemer-Bach, "La nationalité de la femme mariée," *La Française,* 7 May 1927.

110. Odette Simon, "Une grande victoire: la nationalité de la femme mariée," *La Française,* 27 August 1927.

111. The American Cable Act was more egalitarian in theory than in practice. Only with the signing of a Pan-American Union Treaty in 1934 were all gender-based double standards purged from American nationality laws. See Bredbenner, *A Nationality of Her Own.*

112. Marcelle Kraemer-Bach, "La nationalité de la femme mariée," *La Française,* 7 May 1927.

113. Berthet, "La française doit rester française, même mariée à un étranger."

114. This is one element of the feminist odyssey described by Scott in *Only Paradoxes to Offer.*

115. Misme, "La nationalité de la femme mariée."

116. Sauteraud, "Du maintien de la nationalité de la femme française qui épouse un étranger," 203–4.

Gender, Race, and Republican Embodiment

1. Scott, *Only Paradoxes to Offer.*

2. Wilder, "Thinking Through Race."

3. Wilder, *The French Imperial Nation-State.*

4. Betts, *Assimilation and Association in French Colonial Theory*; Lewis, "One Hundred Million Frenchmen."

5. Martial, "Étrangers et métis," 513.

6. The Institute of Anthroposociology was created in 1942 and headed by Claude Vacher de Lapouge, son of the racial theorist Georges Vacher de Lapouge.

7. Marrus and Paxton, *Vichy France and the Jews*; Noiriel, *Les origines républicaines de Vichy*; Paxton, "Gérard Noiriel's Third Republic."

8. Pollard, *Reign of Virtue.*

9. Adler, *Jews and Gender in Liberation France.*

BIBLIOGRAPHY

Archives

Archives du Département de la Seine
   DE 1: Fonds Bucaille
Archives Legrand-Falco
Archives de la Préfecture de Police
   BI 44, BMI 43: Brigade des Mœurs
Archives Nationales
   C7725. Projets du loi, Chambre des Deputés
   F7 12652; F7 14663; F7 14843; F7 14853–14860. Police Générale
   F14 11331. Ministère des Travaux Publiques
   F22 330, 565. Ministère du Travail
   F60 603. Président du Conseil
   94AP 120, 129, 130, 135, 348. Fonds Albert Thomas
   6AS 26–28, 31, 32. Fonds Max Lazard
   40AS 40, 48. Comité Central des Houillières de France
Bibliothèque Historique de la Ville de Paris
   Fonds Bouglé. Box 6/ve: articles written by Maria Vérone
Bibliothèque Marguerite Durand
   Dossiers: Fédération Abolitionniste, Natalité, Nationalité, Nationalité de la Femme
   Mariée, Œuvre Libératrice, Union Temporaire
Service Historique de l'Armée de Terre
   2N 192; 7N(2) 1022; 9N(2) 968; 27 N 65

Official Records

Journal Officiel (individual documents cited in notes)

Records of Organizations

Congrès National de la Natalité, *Comptes rendus*
Conseil Supérieur de la Natalité, *Rapports et vœux*
Semaines Sociales de France, *Comptes rendus*
Société Française d'Eugénique, *Comptes rendus*

Newspapers and Journals

L'Abolitionniste
Eugénique
La Française
Journal de droit international privé
L'Œuvre
Pour la vie
La prophylaxie antivénérienne
Le relèvement social
Revue de l'Alliance Nationale pour l'Accroissement de la Population Française
Revue de l'immigration

Books, Articles, and Essays

Amar, Jules. *L'organisation physiologique du travail*. Paris: H. Dunod et E. Pinat, 1917.

Apert, Eugène. "Immigration et métissage: leur influence sur la santé de la nation." *Presse médicale* 75 (19 September 1923), 1565–69.

———. "Le problème des races et de l'immigration en France." *Eugénique* 3, no. 5 (1924), 149–67.

Association Israélite pour la Protection de la Jeune Fille. *La traite des femmes*. Paris, n.d.

Audinet, Eugène. "Du conflit entre les lois personelles des époux lorsque la femme, française ou étrangère, conserve sa nationalité primitive." *Journal de droit international privé* 57 (1930), 319–32.

———. "L'effet du mariage sur la nationalité de la femme." *Journal de droit international privé* 47 (1920), 17–25.

———. "Les heimatloses et leur condition juridique." *Journal de droit international privé* 52 (1925), 882–97.

Bercovici, Jean. *Contrôle sanitaire des immigrants en France*. Paris: Ernest Sagot, 1926.

Bérillon, Edgar. *Les caractères nationaux: leurs facteurs biologiques et psychologiques*. Paris: A. Legrand, 1920.

Bertillon, Jacques. *La dépopulation de la France: ses conséquences, ses causes: mesures à prendre pour la combattre.* Paris: Alcan, 1911.

Boverat, Fernand. "La dénatalité, ses dangers et les mesures à prendre pour l'enrayer." *Le musée social* 1 (January 1936), 1–14.

Bureau, Paul. *L'indiscipline des mœurs: étude de science sociale.* Paris: Blood et Gay, 1921.

Calbairac, Gaston. *La nationalité de la femme mariée.* Paris: Sirey, 1926.

———. *Traité de la nationalité de la femme mariée.* Paris: Sirey, 1929.

Carnot, Paul. "Puisqu'il y a un excédent de deux millions de femmes pourquoi ne pas importer des maris?" *Le Matin,* 29 July 1920.

Catalogne, Édouard. *La politique de l'immigration en France depuis la guerre de 1914.* Paris: André Tournon, 1925.

Çauwès, Albert. *Des rapports du mariage avec la nationalité.* Paris: Société du Recueil Général des Lois et des Arrêts, 1900.

Champcommunal, Jean. "Un conflit de lois à l'ordre du jour: le ménage à nationalités différentes." *Journal de droit international privé* 24 (1929), 1–25.

Champly, Henry. *Sur le chemin de Changhaï: la traite des blanches en Asie.* Paris: Jules Tallendier, 1933.

Chaptal, Emmanuel. "Le problème de l'immigration peut-il être résolu sans le concours des forces spirituelles?" *Revue de l'immigration* 35 (April 1931), 1–3.

Chromecki, Thadée. *Le problème de l'émigration polonaise et la France.* Paris: Presses Modernes, 1929.

Conférence international de l'émigration et de l'immigration. Rome, 15–31 May 1924. Rome: Commissariat Général Italien de l'Émigration, 1924–25.

Danel, Jean. "La loi sur la nationalité et la famille." *La vie intellectuelle,* January 1929, 154–55.

Dequidt, Georges, and Georges Forestier. "Les aspects sanitaires du problème de l'immigration en France." *Revue d'hygiène,* December 1926, 999–1049.

Di Calboli, Paulucci. *L'Italie vagabonde.* Paris: A. Davis, 1895.

———. *Larmes et sourires de l'émigration italienne.* Paris: Juven, 1909.

Dreyfus, Robert. "Les conflits de nationalités et la loi sur la nationalité du 10 août 1927." *Journal de droit international privé* 54 (1930), 928–52.

Duhamel, Jean. "Libres propos sur l'assimilation." *Revue de l'immigration* 9 (January 1929), 1–5.

Dumont, Arsène. "Démographie des étrangers habitant en France." *Bulletin de la Société d'anthropologie de France,* 1894.

———. *Dépopulation et civilisation: étude démographique.* Paris: Lecrosnier et Babé, 1890.

E. C. "Mariages mixtes des Kabyles en France." *France méditerranéenne et africaine: bulletin d'études économiques et sociales* 1 (1938), 100–117.

Faivre, Albin. *Aspect médical et social du problème des étrangers en France.* Paris: Vigot Frères, 1939.

Fender, Émile. *La crise du batiment dans la région parisienne.* Paris: Recueil, 1935.

Flournoy, Richard W., Jr., and Manley O. Hudson, eds. *A Collection of Nationality Laws of Various Countries as Contained in Constitutions, Statutes, and Treaties.* New York: Oxford University Press, 1929.

Fonville, Robert. *De la condition en France et dans les colonies françaises des indigènes des protectorats français.* Paris: Chauny et Quinsac, 1924.

Frézouls, Paul. *Les ouvriers étrangers en France devant les lois du travail et de la prévoyance sociale.* Montpellier: Gustave Firmin, 1909.

Gemaehling, Paul. "Le proxénétisme en France: son organisation, les moyens de le combattre." *Les Scandales de la Prostitution Réglementée.* Paris: Union Temporaire, n.d.

———. *Vers la vie: la décroissance de la natalité et l'avenir de la France.* Bordeaux: Comité Français pour le Relèvement de la Natalité, 1913.

Gianturco, Mario. "Le problème international de la population." *Revue politique et parlementaire* 426 (10 May 1930), 225–44.

Gide, André, and Charles Lambert. "Les troubles d'Aigues-Mortes." *Revue de l'économie politique*, September–October 1893, 839–41.

Gobineau, Arthur de. *The Inequality of Human Races.* New York: Howard Fertig, 1999.

Grant, Madison. *Le déclin de la grande race.* Paris: Playot, 1926; orig. pubd as *The Passing of the Great Race; or, The Racial Basis of European History* (New York: C. Scribner, 1916).

Guériot, Paul. "La politique de l'immigration." *Revue politique et parlementaire*, June 1924, 419–35.

Haury, Paul. *La vie ou la mort de la France.* Paris: Vuibert, 1923.

Kapralik, Edgar. *La nationalité de la femme mariée.* Paris: Presses Universitaires de France, 1925.

Kleczkowski, Georges. "De Goryniak à Gaurignac ou les étapes d'une assimilation." *Revue de l'immigration* 44 (April–June 1932), 1–8.

Lambert, Charles. *La France et les étrangers: dépopulation, immigration, naturalisation.* Paris: Delagrave, 1928.

League of Nations. *Nationality of Women: Report by the Secretary General*, vol. 7. Geneva: League of Nations, 1931.

Le Conte, René. *Étude sur l'émigration italienne.* Paris: A. Michalon, 1908.

Legrand-Falco, Marcelle. "Les états généraux du féminisme à l'Exposition Coloniale." *La Volonté*, 3 April 1931.

Leroy-Beaulieu, Paul. *La question de la population*. Paris: Félix Alcan, 1913.

———. "La question de la population et la civilisation." *Revue des deux mondes*, 15 October 1897.

Levasseur, Émile. "De l'émigration au 19ᵉ siècle." *Historical Aspects of the Immigration Problem: Select Documents*, ed. Edith Abbott. Chicago: University of Chicago Press, 1926.

"Une loi sur la nationalité." *La réforme sociale*, April 1927, 187–89.

Londres, Albert. *Le chemin de Buenos-Aires*. Paris: Arléa, 1998 [1927].

Lugand, Joseph. *L'immigration des ouvriers étrangers et les enseignements de la guerre*. Paris: Imprimeries Réunies, 1919.

Martial, René. "Étrangers et métis." *Mercure de France* 990 (September–October 1939).

———. "L'examen sanitaire des immigrants à la frontière et leur logement dans le pays." *Revue d'hygiène*, December 1926, 1050–92.

———. *La race française*. Paris: Mercure de France, 1934.

———. *Traité de l'immigration et de la greffe inter-raciale*. Cuesmes-lez-Mons, Belgium: Imprimerie Fédérale, 1931.

———. *Vie et constance des races: leçons d'anthropo-biologie professées à la faculté de médecine de Paris*. Paris: Mercure de France, 1939.

Mauco, Georges. *Les étrangers en France: leur rôle dans l'activité économique*. Paris: Armand Colin, 1932.

Maunier, René. *The Sociology of Colonies: An Introduction to the Study of Race Contact*, vol. 1, trans. E. O. Lorimer. London, Routledge, 1949 [1931].

Meylan, Michel. *Les mariages mixtes en Afrique du Nord*. Paris: Sirey, 1934.

Millet, Raymond. *Trois millions d'étrangers en France: les indésirables, les bienvenus*. Paris: Médicis, 1938.

Naccary, Carmen. *La nationalité de la femme mariée dans les principaux pays*. Geneva: Atar, 1925.

Naudeau, Ludovic. "Les dangers et les ressources de l'immigration." *L'Illustration* 1 (November 1924), 390–92.

———. *La France se regarde: le problème de la natalité*. Paris: Hachette, 1931.

Nogaro, Bertrand, and Lucien Weil. *La main-d'œuvre étrangère et coloniale pendant la guerre*. Paris: Presses Universitaires de France, 1933.

Oualid, William. "Le droit migratoire." *Revue de l'immigration* 27 (July 1930), 1–5.

———. *L'immigration ouvrière en France*. Paris: S.A.P.E., 1927.

———. "The Effect of the War upon Labour in France." *Effects of the War upon French Economic Life*, ed. Charles Gide. Oxford: Clarendon, 1923.

———. "The Occupational Distribution and Status of Foreign Workers in France." *International Labor Review* 20, no. 2 (August 1929), 161–84.

Ourgaut, Charles. *La surveillance des étrangers en France.* Toulouse: Imprimerie du Sud-Ouest, 1937.

Pairault, André. "Immigration et race." *Revue de l'immigration* 25 (May 1930), 1–3.

———. *L'immigration organisée et l'emploi de la main-d'œuvre étrangère en France.* Paris: Presses Universitaires de France, 1926.

Paon, Marcel. *L'immigration en France.* Paris: Payot, 1926.

Pasquet, Louis. *Immigration et main d'œuvre étrangère en France.* Paris: Rieder, 1927.

Pelletier, François. *La nationalité de la femme mariée.* Dijon: F. Massebeuf, 1925.

Perrin, Jean. *La main-d'œuvre étrangère dans les enterprises du batiment et des travaux publiques en France.* Paris: Presses Universitaires de France, 1925.

Pichon, Ernest-François. *Les maladies vénériennes aux colonies: leur prophylaxie dans l'armée coloniale.* Thesis, Faculté de Bordeaux, 1905.

Picot, André. *La réforme de la loi française sur la nationalité.* Paris: Picart, 1928.

Pinon, Louis-Laurent. *Les problèmes médicaux de l'immigration.* Paris: Faculté de l'Ecole de Médecine de Paris, 1938.

Pluyette, Jean. *La doctrine des races et la sélection de l'immigration en France.* Paris: Pierre Bossuet, 1930.

Rabinowicz, Léon. *Le problème de la population en France.* Paris: Marcel Rivière, 1919.

Raphael, Paul. "De quelques objections contre la politique des naturalisations." *Revue de l'immigration* 29 (October 1930), 1–8.

Ray, Joanny. *Les Marocains en France.* Paris: Sirey, 1938.

Renan, Ernst. *Œuvres complètes*, vol. 1. Paris: Calmann-Lévy, 1947.

Richet, Charles. "La sélection humaine." *Eugénique* 3, no. 1 (1922), 1–26.

Risler, Georges. "Les résultats de la nouvelle loi sur la nationalité." *Musée social,* March 1928, 90–93.

Rodet, Yves. *L'immigration des travailleurs étrangers en France.* Paris: Imprimerie de Montparnasse, 1924.

Rousseau, Jean-Jacques. *Politics and the Arts*, trans. Allan Bloom. Ithaca: Cornell University Press, 1968.

St-Germain, Jacques. *La grande invasion.* Paris: Flammarion, 1939.

Sauteraud, Marcel. "Du maintien de la nationalité de la femme française qui épouse un étranger." *Revue politique et parlementaire,* 10 November 1919, 196–205.

Savatier, René. "Puissance maritale." *Revue critique de législation et de jurisprudence,* 1936, 206–27.

Schirmacher, Käthe. *La spécialisation du travail à Paris.* Paris: Arthur Rousseau, 1908.

Sicard de Plauzoles. "La lutte contre les maladies sociales: la dégénérescence de l'homme, ses causes, et sa prophylaxie." *Prophylaxie antivénérienne* 6 (June 1938), 284–89.

Sipperstein, Frédéric. *La grève des naissances en Europe et ses problèmes*. Paris: Librairie Sociale et Économique, 1939.

Société des Nations. *Actes de la Conférence Diplomatique Relative à la Répression de la Traite des Femmes Majeures*. Geneva, 1933.

Stoenesco, Jean. *La nationalité ne s'impose pas*. Paris: Ernest Sagot, 1922.

Storoge, Victor. *L'hygiène sociale et les étrangers en France*. Paris: Marcel Vigne, 1926.

Tournaire, Albert. *La plaie française*. Paris: Librairie-Bibliothèque Auguste-Comte, 1922.

Trinh, Dinh Thao. *De l'influence du mariage sur la nationalité de la femme mariée*. Aix-en-Provence: Paul Roubaud, 1929.

Troullier, Albert. "Immigration-Démographie." *Économie nouvelle*, June 1928, 297–315.

Varlez, Louis. "Les problèmes de migration à la Conférence de la Havane de 1918." *Revue international du travail* 19, no. 1 (January 1919), 1–19.

Waltz, André. *Le problème de la population française: natalité, mortalité, immigration*. Paris: Société d'Études et d'Informations Économiques, 1924.

Weiss, André. *Traité théorique et pratique de droit international privé*. Paris: Sirey, 1907.

Wlocevski, Stéphane. *L'installation des Italiens en France*. Paris: Felix Alcan, 1934.

Selected Secondary Works

Accampo, Elinor, Rachel G. Fuchs, and Mary Lynn Stewart, eds. *Gender and the Politics of Social Reform in France, 1870–1914*. Baltimore: Johns Hopkins University Press, 1995.

Adler, Karen H. *Jews and Gender in Liberation France*. Cambridge: Cambridge University Press, 2003.

Agamben, Giorgio. *Homo Sacer: Sovereign Power and Bare Life*, trans. Daniel Heller-Roazen. Stanford: Stanford University Press, 1998.

Aldrich, Robert. *Colonialism and Homosexuality*. London: Routledge, 2003.

Allen, Theodore W. *The Invention of the White Race: The Origin of Racial Oppression in Anglo-America*. New York: Verso, 1994.

Alloula, Malek. *The Colonial Harem*, trans. Myrna Godzich and Wald Godzich. Minnesota: University of Minnesota Press, 1986.

Amar, Marianne, and Pierre Milza. *L'immigration en France au XXe siècle*. Paris: Armand Colin, 1990.

Anderson, Warwick. *The Cultivation of Whiteness: Science, Health, and Racial Diversity in Australia*. New York: Basic Books, 2003.

———. "States of Hygiene: Race 'Improvement' and Biomedical Citizenship in Australia and the Colonial Philippines." *Haunted by Empire: Geographies of Intimacy in North American History*, ed. Ann Laura Stoler. Durham: Duke University Press, 2006.

Assouline, Pierre. *Albert Londres: vie et mort d'un grand reporter, 1884–1932*. Paris: Balland, 1989.

Aubert, Guillame. "'The Blood of France': Race and Purity of Blood in the French Atlantic World." *William and Mary Quarterly* 61, no. 3 (2004), 439–78.

Augustine-Adams, Kif. "Constructing Mexico: Marriage, Law, and Women's Dependent Citizenship in the Late-Nineteenth and Early-Twentieth Centuries." *Gender and History* 18, no. 1 (April 2006), 20–34.

———. "'She Consents Implicitly': Women's Citizenship, Marriage, and Liberal Political Thought in Late Nineteenth and Early Twentieth-Century Argentina." *Journal of Women's History* 13, no. 4 (2002), 8–30.

———. "'With Notice of the Consequences': Liberal Political Theory, Marriage, and Women's Citizenship in the United States." *Citizenship Studies* 6, no. 1 (2002), 5–20.

Auslander, Leora. "Bavarian Crucifixes and French Headscarves: Religious Signs and the Postmodern European State." *Cultural Dynamics* 12, no. 3 (2000), 283–309.

———. *Taste and Power: Furnishing Modern France*. Berkeley: University of California Press, 1996.

Baldwin, Page. "Subject to Empire: Married Women and the British Nationality and Status of Aliens Act." *Journal of British Studies* 40, no. 4 (2001), 522–56.

Balibar, Étienne. "Racism and Nationalism." *Race, Nation, Class: Ambiguous Identities*, ed. Étienne Balibar and Immanuel Wallerstein, trans. Chris Turner. London: Verso, 1991.

Barbara, Augustin. *Les couples mixtes*. Paris: Bayard, 1993.

Baron, Ava. "Gender and Labor History: Learning from the Past, Looking to the Future." *Work Engendered: Toward a New History of American Labor*, ed. Ava Baron. Ithaca: Cornell University Press, 1991.

Barry, Kathleen. *Female Sexual Slavery*. New York: New York University Press, 1984.

———. *The Prostitution of Sexuality: The Global Exploitation of Women*. New York: New York University Press, 1995.

Barzun, Jacques. *The French Race*. Port Washington, N.Y.: Kennikat, 1966 [1932].

Bederman, Gail. *Manliness and Civilization: A Cultural History of Gender and Race in the United States, 1880–1917*. Chicago: University of Chicago Press, 1995.

Berlant, Lauren. Introduction. *Intimacy*. Chicago: University of Chicago Press, 2000.

————. *The Queen of America Goes to Washington City: Essays on Sex and Citizenship*. Durham: Duke University Press, 1997.

Berlière, Jean-Marc. *La police des mœurs sous la IIIe République*. Paris: Le Seuil, 1992.

Betts, Raymond F. *Assimilation and Association in French Colonial Theory, 1890–1914*. New York: Columbia University Press, 1961.

Birnbaum, Pierre. *Jewish Destinies: Citizenship, State, and Community in Modern France*, trans. Arthur Goldhammer. New York: Hill and Wang, 1995.

Bjork, Robert Marshall. "The Italian Immigration into France, 1870–1954." PhD diss., Syracuse University, 1955.

Black, Naomi. *Social Feminism*. Ithaca: Cornell University Press, 1989.

Blanckaert, Claude. "Of Monstrous Métis? Hybridity, Fear of Miscegenation, and Patriotism from Buffon to Paul Broca." *The Color of Liberty: Histories of Race in France*, ed. Sue Peabody and Tyler Stovall. Durham: Duke University Press, 2003.

Bland, Lucy. "White Women and Men of Colour: Miscegenation Fears in Britain after the Great War." *Gender and History* 17, no. 1 (April 2005), 29–61.

Bliss, Katherine Elaine. *Compromised Positions: Prostitution, Public Health, and Gender Politics in Revolutionary Mexico City*. University Park: Pennsylvania University Press, 2001.

Blum, Carol. *Strength in Numbers: Population, Reproduction, and Power in Eighteenth-Century France*. Baltimore: Johns Hopkins University Press, 2002.

Bonnet, Jean-Charles. *Les pouvoirs publics français et l'immigration dans l'entre-deux-guerres*. Lyon: Centre d'Histoire Économique et Sociale de la Région Lyonnaise, 1976.

Boulle, Pierre H. "Racial Purity or Legal Clarity? The Status of Black Residents in Eighteenth-Century France." *Journal of the Historical Society* 6, no. 1 (2006), 19–46.

Boym, Svetlana. "Diasporic Intimacy: Ilya Kabokov's Installations and Immigrant Homes." *Critical Inquiry* 24 (winter 1998), 498–524.

Bredbenner, Candice Lewis. *A Nationality of Her Own: Women, Marriage, and the Law of Citizenship*. Berkeley: University of California Press, 1998.

Breve, Marie-France. "Le rôle des femmes dans l'intégration des Italiens entre les deux guerres: une étude de cas." *L'immigration italienne en France dans les années 20: actes du colloque franco-italien, Paris 15–17 octobre 1987*. Paris: CEDEI, 1988.

Briggs, Laura. *Reproducing Empire: Race, Sex, Science, and U.S. Imperialism in Puerto Rico*. Berkeley: University of California Press, 2002.

Bristow, Edward J. *Prostitution and Prejudice: The Jewish Fight against White Slavery, 1870–1939*. New York: Schocken, 1983.

Brodkin, Karen. *How Jews Became White Folks and What That Says about Race in America*. New Brunswick: Rutgers University Press, 1998.

Brubaker, Rogers. *Citizenship and Nationhood in France and Germany*. Cambridge: Harvard University Press, 1992.

Bullard, Alice. *Exile to Paradise: Savagery and Civilization in the South Pacific, 1790–1900*. Stanford: Stanford University Press, 2000.

Burton, Antoinette. "From Child Bride to 'Hindoo Lady': Rukhmabai and the Debate on Sexual Respectability in Imperial Britain." *American Historical Review* 103, no. 4 (October 1998), 1119–46.

———. "Who Needs the Nation? Interrogating 'British' History." *Journal of Historical Sociology* 10, no. 3 (September 1997), 227–48.

Camiscioli, Elisa. "Intermarriage, Independent Nationality, and the Individual Rights of French Women: The Law of 10 August 1927." *French Culture, Politics, and Society* 17, nos. 3–4 (summer–fall 1999), 52–74.

———. "Producing Citizens, Reproducing the 'French Race': Immigration, Demography, and Pronatalism in Early Twentieth-Century France." *Gender and History* 13, no. 3 (fall 2001), 593–621.

———. "Race-Making and Race-Mixing in the Early Twentieth-Century Immigration Debate." *Transnational Spaces and Identities in the Francophone World*, ed. Hafid Gafaïti, Patricia Lorcin, and David Troyansky. Lincoln: University of Nebraska Press, 2009.

Canning, Kathleen. "The Body as Method? Reflections on the Place of the Body in Gender History." *Gender and History* 11, no. 3 (November 1999), 499–513.

———. *Gender History in Practice: Historical Perspectives on Bodies, Class, and Citizenship*. Ithaca: Cornell University Press, 2006.

Caulfield, Sueann. *In Defense of Honor: Sexual Morality, Modernity, and Nation in Early Twentieth-Century Brazil*. Durham: Duke University Press, 2000.

Chakrabarty, Dipesh. "The Difference-Deferral of a Colonial Modernity: Public Debates on Domesticity in British Bengal." *Tensions of Empire: Colonial Cultures in a Bourgeois World*, ed. Frederick Cooper and Ann Laura Stoler. Berkeley: University of California Press, 1997.

Chapman, Herrick, and Laura L. Frader, eds. *Race in France: Interdisciplinary Perspectives on the Politics of Difference*. New York: Berghahn, 2004.

Charbit, Yves. *Du malthusianisme au populationnisme: les économistes français et la population, 1840–1870*. Paris: Presses Universitaires de France, 1981.

Charnay, Jean-Paul. *La vie musulmane en Algérie d'après la jurisprudence de la première moitié du XXe siècle*. Paris: Presses Universitaires de France, 1991.

Chatterjee, Partha. "Colonialism, Nationalism, and Colonized Women: The Contest in India." *American Ethnologist* 16, no. 4 (November 1989), 622–33.

Childers, Kristen Stromberg. *Fathers, Families, and the State in France, 1914–1945.* Ithaca: Cornell University Press, 2003.

Clancy-Smith, Julia. "Islam, Gender, and Identities in the Making of French Algeria, 1830–1962." *Domesticating the Empire: Race, Gender, and Family Life in French and Dutch Colonialism,* ed. Julia Clancy-Smith and Frances Gouda. Charlottesville: University Press of Virginia, 1998.

Clark, Linda L. *Social Darwinism in France.* University: University of Alabama Press, 1984.

Cohen, William B. *The French Encounter with Africans: White Response to Blacks, 1530–1880.* Bloomington: Indiana University Press, 2003.

Cole, Joshua H. *The Power of Large Numbers: Population, Politics, and Gender in Nineteenth-Century France.* Ithaca: Cornell University Press, 2000.

———. "'There Are Only Good Mothers': The Ideological Work of Women's Fertility in France before World War I." *French Historical Studies* 19, no. 3 (spring 1996), 639–72.

Collomp, Catherine. "Immigrants, Labor Markets, and the State: A Comparative Approach: France and the United States, 1880–1930." *Journal of American History* 86, no. 1 (June 1999), 42.

Comaroff, Jean, and John L. Comaroff. *Ethnography and the Historical Imagination.* Boulder: Westview, 1992.

Conklin, Alice L. *A Mission to Civilize: The Republican Idea of Empire in France and West Africa, 1895–1930.* Stanford: Stanford University Press, 1997.

———. "Redefining 'Frenchness': Citizenship, Race Regeneration, and Imperial Motherhood in France and West Africa, 1914–1940." *Domesticating the Empire: Race, Gender, and Family Life in French and Dutch Colonialism,* ed. Julia Clancy-Smith and Frances Gouda. Charlottesville: University Press of Virginia, 1998.

Conner, Susan. "Public Virtue and Private Women: Prostitution in Revolutionary Paris, 1793–1794." *Eighteenth-Century Studies* 28, no. 2 (1994–95), 221–40.

Conry, Yvette. *L'introduction du darwinisme en France au XIXᵉ siècle.* Paris: Vrin, 1974.

Conzen, Kathleen Neils, David A. Gerber, Ewa Morawska, George E. Pozzetta, and Rudolf J. Vecoli. "The Invention of Ethnicity: A Perspective from the USA." *AltreItalie,* April 1990, 37–62.

Corbin, Alain. *Women for Hire: Prostitution and Sexuality in France after 1850,* trans. Alan Sheridan. Cambridge: Harvard University Press, 1990.

Cott, Nancy F. "Marriage and Women's Citizenship in the United States, 1830–1934." *American Historical Review* 103, no. 5 (December 1998), 1440–74.

———. *Public Vows: A History of Marriage and the Nation.* Cambridge: Harvard University Press, 2000.

Couder, Laurent. "Les immigrés italiens dans la région parisienne pendant les années vingt." Thesis, Institut d'Études Politiques, 1987.

Cross, Gary. *Immigrant Workers in Industrial France: The Making of a New Laboring Class*. Philadelphia: Temple University Press, 1983.

Crotty, Patricia McGee. *Women and Family Law: Connecting the Public and the Private*. New York: Peter Lang, 1997.

Davin, Anna. "Imperialism and Motherhood." *Tensions of Empire: Colonial Cultures in a Bourgeois World*, ed. Frederick Cooper and Ann Laura Stoler. Berkeley: University of California Press, 1997.

Doezema, Jo. "Forced to Choose: Beyond the Voluntary v. Forced Prostitution Dichotomy." *Global Sex Workers: Rights, Resistance, and Redefinition*, ed. Kamala Kempadoo and Jo Doezema. New York: Routledge, 1998.

————. "Loose Women or Lost Women: The Re-emergence of the Myth of White Slavery in Contemporary Discourses of 'Trafficking in Women.'" *Gender Issues* 18, no. 1 (winter 2000), 23–50.

Domansky, Elisabeth. "Militarization and Reproduction in World War One Germany." *Society, Culture, and the State in Germany, 1870–1930*, ed. Geoff Eley. Ann Arbor: University of Michigan Press, 1996.

Donzelot, Jacques. *The Policing of Families*. New York: Pantheon, 1979.

Dornel, Laurent. "Les usages du racialisme: le cas de la main-d'œuvre coloniale en France pendant la Première Guerre Mondiale." *Génèses* 20 (September 1995), 48–72.

Downs, Laura Lee. *Manufacturing Inequality: Gender Division in the French and British Metalworking Industries, 1914–1939*. Ithaca: Cornell University Press, 1995.

Dubois, Laurent. *A Colony of Citizens: Revolution and Slave Emancipation in the French Caribbean, 1787–1804*. Chapel Hill: University of North Carolina Press, 2004.

Engelstein, Laura. *The Keys to Happiness: Sex and the Search for Modernity in Fin-de-Siècle Russia*. Ithaca: Cornell University Press, 1994.

Estrich, Susan. "Rape." *Feminist Jurisprudence*, ed. Patricia Smith. New York: Oxford University Press, 1993.

Ezra, Elizabeth. *The Colonial Unconscious: Race and Culture in Interwar France*. Ithaca: Cornell University Press, 2000.

Fauré, Christine. *Democracy without Women: Feminism and the Rise of Liberal Individualism in France*. Bloomington: Indiana University Press, 1991.

Ferrer, Ada. "Cuba, 1898: Rethinking Race, Nation, and Empire." *Radical History Review* 73 (winter 1999), 22–46.

Fick, Carolyn E. *The Making of Haiti: The Saint Domingue Revolution from Below*. Knoxville: University of Tennessee Press, 1990.

Fletcher, Yael Simpson. "City, Nation, and Empire in Interwar Marseilles, 1919–1939." PhD diss., Emory University, 1999.

Foucault, Michel. "The Birth of Biopolitics." *Ethics, Subjectivity and Truth*, ed. Paul Rabinow. New York: New Press, 1997.

———. *The History of Sexuality: An Introduction*. New York: Vintage, 1990.

———. "Security, Territory, and Population." *Ethics, Subjectivity and Truth*, ed. Paul Rabinow. New York: New Press, 1997.

Frader, Laura Levine. "From Muscles to Nerves: Gender, 'Race,' and the Body at Work in France 1919–1939." *International Review of Social History* 44 (1999), 123–47.

Frader, Laura Levine, and Sonya O. Rose. "Introduction: Gender and the Reconstruction of European Working-Class History." *Gender and Class in Modern Europe*, ed. Laura L. Frader and Sonya Rose. Ithaca: Cornell University Press, 1996.

Fraisse, Geneviève. *Reason's Muse: Sexual Difference and the Birth of Democracy*, trans. Jane Marie Todd. Chicago: University of Chicago Press, 1994.

Fraser, Nancy. "Beyond the Master/Subject Model: Reflections on Carole Pateman's *Sexual Contract*." *Social Text* 37 (winter 1993), 173–81.

Fraser, Nancy, and Linda Gordon. "Civil Citizenship against Social Citizenship? On the Ideology of Contract-Versus-Charity." *The Condition of Citizenship*, ed. Bart van Steenbergen. London: Sage, 1994.

Fredrickson, George M. "Mulattoes and *Métis*: Attitudes toward Miscegenation in the United States and France since the Seventeenth Century." *International Social Science Journal* 57, no. 1 (2005), 103–12.

Freedman, Jane, and Carrie Tarr, eds. *Women, Immigration and Identities in France*. New York: Berg, 2000.

Gardner, Martha. *The Qualities of a Citizen: Women, Immigration, and Citizenship, 1870–1965*. Princeton: Princeton University Press, 2005.

Garraway, Doris. *The Libertine Colony: Creolization in the Early French Caribbean*. Durham: Duke University Press, 2005.

Gates, Henry Louis, Jr. "Writing Race and the Difference It Makes." *"Race," Writing, and Difference*, ed. Henry Louis Gates Jr. Chicago: University of Chicago Press, 1985.

George, Rosemary M. "Homes in the Empire, Empire in the Home." *Cultural Critique*, winter 1994, 95–127.

Gilfoyle, Timothy J. "Prostitutes in History: From Parables of Pornography to Metaphors of Modernity." *American Historical Review* 104, no. 1 (February 1999), 117–41.

Girard, Alain, and Jean Stoetzel. *Français et immigrés: l'attitude des Français, l'adaptation des Italiens et des Polonais*. Paris: Presses Universitaires de France, 1953.

Glendon, Mary Ann. *The Transformation of Family Law: State, Law, and Family in the United States and Western Europe*. Chicago: University of Chicago Press, 1989.

Goldberg, David Theo. *Racist Culture: Philosophy and the Politics of Meaning*. Cambridge: Blackwell, 1993.

Gouda, Frances, and Julia Clancy-Smith. Introduction. *Domesticating the Empire: Race, Gender, and Family Life in French and Dutch Colonialism*, ed. Julia Clancy-Smith and Frances Gouda. Charlottesville: University Press of Virginia, 1998.

Gould, Stephen J. *The Mismeasure of Man*. New York: W. W. Norton, 1981.

Green, Nancy L. "L'immigration en France et aux États-Unis: historiographie comparée." *Vingtième Siècle* 29 (January–March 1991), 67–82.

———. "The Modern Jewish Diaspora: European Jews in New York, London, and Paris." *European Migrations: Global and Local Perspectives*, ed. Dirk Hoerder and Leslie Page Moch. Boston: Northeastern University Press, 1996.

Grosz, Elizabeth. *Volatile Bodies: Toward a Corporeal Feminism*. Bloomington: Indiana University Press, 1994.

Guglielmo, Jennifer, and Salavatore Salerno, eds. *Are Italians White? How Race Is Made in America*. New York: Routledge, 2003.

Guglielmo, Thomas A. *White on Arrival: Italians, Race, Color, and Power in Chicago, 1890–1945*. Oxford: Oxford University Press, 2003.

Guy, Donna J. *Sex and Danger in Buenos Aires: Prostitution, Family, and Nation in Argentina*. Lincoln: University of Nebraska Press, 1991.

———. *White Slavery and Mothers Alive and Dead: The Troubled Meeting of Sex, Gender, Public Health, and Progress in Latin America*. Lincoln: University of Nebraska Press, 2000.

———. "'White Slavery,' Citizenship, and Nationality in Argentina." *Nationalisms and Sexualities*, ed. Andrew Parker, Mary Russo, Doris Sommer, and Patricia Yaeger. New York: Routledge, 1992.

Habermas, Jürgen. *The Structural Transformation of the Public Sphere: An Inquiry into a Category of Bourgeois Society*, trans. Thomas Burger with Frederick Lawrence. Cambridge: MIT Press, 1989.

Hall, C. Michael, and Chris Ryan. *Sex Tourism: Marginal People and Liminalities*. London: Routledge, 2001.

Hargreaves, Alec G. *Immigration, "Race," and Ethnicity in Contemporary France*. London: Routledge, 1995.

Harris, Ruth. "The 'Child of the Barbarian': Rape, Race, and Nationalism in France during the First World War." *Past and Present* 141 (November 1993), 170–206.

Hause, Steven C., with Anne R. Kenney. *Women's Suffrage and Social Politics in the Third Republic*. Princeton: Princeton University Press, 1984.

Hecht, Jennifer Michael. "The Solvency of Metaphysics: The Debate over Racial Science and Moral Philosophy in France, 1890–1919." *Isis* 90, no. 1 (March 1999), 1–24.

Helg, Aline. "Race in Argentina and Cuba, 1880–1930: Theory, Policies, and Popular Reaction." *The Idea of Race in Latin America, 1870–1940*, ed. Richard Graham. Austin: University of Texas Press, 1990.

Heng, Geraldine, and Janadas Devan. "State Fatherhood: The Politics of Nationalism, Sexuality, and Race in Singapore." *Nationalisms and Sexualities*, ed. Andrew Parker, Mary Russo, Doris Sommer, and Patricia Yaeger. New York: Routledge, 1992.

Henriot, Christian. *Prostitution and Sexuality in Shanghai: A Social History, 1849–1949*, trans. Noel Castelino. Cambridge: Cambridge University Press, 2001.

Hershatter, Gail. *Dangerous Pleasures: Prostitution and Modernity in Twentieth-Century Shanghai*. Berkeley: University of California Press, 1997.

Heuer, Jennifer Ngaire. *The Family and the Nation: Gender and Citizenship in Revolutionary France, 1789–1830*. Ithaca: Cornell University Press, 2005.

———. "The One Drop Rule in Reverse? Interracial Marriages in Napoleonic and Restoration France." Unpublished MS.

Higham, John. *Strangers in the Land: Patterns of American Nativism, 1860–1925*. New Brunswick: Rutgers University Press, 2002.

Hodes, Martha Elizabeth. *White Women, Black Men: Illicit Sex in the Nineteenth-Century South*. New Haven: Yale University Press, 1997.

Holt, Thomas C. "Foreword: The First New Nations." *Race and Nation in Modern Latin America*, ed. Nancy P. Appelbaum, Anne S. MacPherson, and Karin A. Rosemblatt. Chapel Hill: University of North Carolina Press, 2003.

———. *The Problem of Race in the Twenty-First Century*. Cambridge: Harvard University Press, 2002.

Horne, John. "Immigrant Workers in France during World War I." *French Historical Studies* 14, no. 1 (spring 1985), 57–88.

Horowitz, Donald. "Immigration and Group Relation in France and America." *Immigrants in Two Democracies: French and American Experience*, ed. Donald Horowitz and Gérard Noiriel. New York: New York University Press, 1992.

Horowitz, Donald, and Gérard Noiriel, eds. *Immigrants in Two Democracies: French and American Experience*. New York: New York University Press, 1992.

Huber, Michel, Henri Bunle, and Fernand Boverat. *La population de la France: son évolution et ses perspectives*. Paris: Hachette, 1965.

Hunt, Lynn, ed. *Eroticism and the Body Politic*. Baltimore: Johns Hopkins University Press, 1991.

Hyman, Paula E. *The Jews of Modern France*. Berkeley: University of California Press, 1998.

Ignatiev, Noel. *How the Irish Became White*. New York: Routledge, 1995.

Ipsen, Carl. *Dictating Demography: The Power of Population in Fascist Italy*. Cambridge: Cambridge University Press, 1997.

Jacobson, Matthew Frye. *Whiteness of a Different Color: European Immigrants and the Alchemy of Race*. Cambridge: Harvard University Press, 1998.

Kaspi, André, ed. *Le Paris des étrangers*. Paris: Imprimerie Nationale, 1989.

Kempadoo, Kamala, and Jo Doezema, eds. *Global Sex Workers: Rights, Resistance, and Redefinition*. New York: Routledge, 1998.

Kerber, Linda K. "The Meanings of Citizenship." *Journal of American History* 84, no. 3 (December 1997), 833–54.

———. *No Constitutional Right to Be Ladies: Women and the Obligations of Citizenship*. New York: Hill and Wang, 1998.

Kirshner, Julius. "Mulier alibi nupta." *Consilia im späten Mittelalter: Zum historischen Aussagewert einer Quellengattung*, ed. Ingrid Baumgärtner. Sigmaringen: Jan Thorbecke, 1995.

———. "Women Married Elsewhere: Gender and Citizenship in Italy." *Tempi e spazi di vita femminile tra medioevo ed età moderna*, ed. Silvana Seidel Menchi, Anne Jacobson Schutte, and Thomas Kuehn. Bologna: Il Mulino, 1999.

Koos, Cheryl Ann. "Engendering Reaction: The Politics of Pronatalism and the Family in France, 1919–1944." PhD diss., University of Southern California, 1996.

———. "Gender, Anti-individualism, and Nationalism: The Alliance Nationale and the Pronatalist Backlash against the *Femme Moderne*, 1933–1940." *French Historical Studies* 19, no. 3 (spring 1996), 699–723.

Kuhl, Stefan. *The Nazi Connection: Eugenics, American Racism, and German National Socialism*. Oxford: Oxford University Press, 1994.

Kuisel, Richard F. *Capitalism and the State in Modern France: Renovation and Economic Management in the Twentieth Century*. Cambridge: Cambridge University Press, 1981.

Laffey, John. "Racism and Imperialism: French Views of the 'Yellow Peril,' 1894–1914." *Third Republic* 1 (1976), 1–52.

Landes, Joan. *Women and the Public Sphere in the Age of the French Revolution*. Ithaca: Cornell University Press, 1987.

Larbiou, Benoît. "René Martial, 1873–1955: De l'hygiénisme à la raciologie, une trajectoire possible." *Genèses* 60 (2005), 98–120.

Lebovics, Herman. *True France: The Wars over Cultural Identity, 1900–1945*. Ithaca: Cornell University Press, 1992.

Le Bras, Hervé. "The Demographic Argument in France." *Population and Social Policy in France*, ed. Máire Cross and Sheila Perry. London: Pinter, 1997.

———. *Marianne et les lapins: l'obsession démographique*. Paris: Olivier Orban, 1991.

Lequin, Yves, ed. *Histoire des étrangers et de l'immigration en France*. Paris: Larousse, 1992.

———. *La mosaïque France: histoire des étrangers et de l'immigration*. Paris: Larousse, 1988.

Levine, Philippa. *Prostitution, Race, and Politics: Policing Venereal Disease in the British Empire*. New York: Routledge, 2003.

Lewis, H. D. "The Legal Status of Women in Nineteenth-Century France." *Journal of European Studies* 10, no. 39 (1980), 178–88.

Lewis, Martin Dening. "One Hundred Million Frenchmen: The 'Assimilation' Theory in French Colonial Policy." *Comparative Studies in Society and History* 4 (1962), 129–53.

Lewis, Mary Dewhurst. *The Boundaries of the Republic: Migrant Rights and the Limits of Universalism in France, 1918–1940*. Stanford: Stanford University Press, 2007.

———. "Une théorie raciale des valeurs? Démobilisation des travailleurs immigrés et mobilisation des stéréotypes en France à la fin de la Grande Guerre." *L'invention des populations: biologie, idéologie et politique*, ed. Hervé LeBras with the collaboration of Sandrine Bertaux. Paris: Odile Jacob, 2000.

Lloyd, Cathie, and Hazel Waters. "France: One Culture, One People?" *Race and Class* 32, no. 3 (January–March 1991), 49–65.

Lorcin, Patricia M. E. *Imperial Identities: Stereotyping, Prejudice and Race in Colonial Algeria*. London: I. B. Tauris, 1995.

MacMaster, Neil. *Colonial Migrants and Racism: Algerians in France, 1900–1962*. New York: St. Martin's, 1997.

Maier, Charles S. "Between Taylorism and Technocracy: European Ideologies and the Vision of Industrial Productivity in the 1920s." *Journal of Contemporary History* 5, no. 2 (1970), 27–61.

Malik, Kenan. *The Meaning of Race*. New York: New York University Press, 1996.

Marrus, Michael R. *The Politics of Assimilation: The French Jewish Community at the Time of the Dreyfus Affair*. Oxford: Clarendon, 1971.

Marrus, Michael R., and Robert O. Paxton. *Vichy France and the Jews*. New York: Basic Books, 1981.

Massin, Benoît. "Lutte des classes, lutte des races." *Des sciences contre l'homme*, vol. 1, *Classer, hiérarchiser, exclure*, ed. Claude Blanckaert. Paris: Autrement, 1993.

Matsuda, Matt K. *Empire of Love: Histories of France and the Pacific*. New York: Oxford University Press, 2004.

Mayeur, Jean-Marie, and Madeleine Rebérieux. *The Third Republic from Its Origins to the Great War, 1871–1914*. Cambridge: Cambridge University Press, 1984.

Mazower, Mark. *Dark Continent: Europe's Twentieth Century*. New York: Vintage, 1998.

McClelland, Keith. "Masculinity and the 'Representative Artisan' in Britain, 1850–1880." *Manful Assertions: Masculinities in Britain since 1800*, ed. Michael Roper and John Tosh. London: Routledge, 1991.

McClintock, Anne. "Family Feuds: Gender, Nationalism, and the Family." *Feminist Review* 44 (summer 1993), 60–80.

———. *Imperial Leather: Race, Gender, and Sexuality in the Colonial Context*. New York: Routledge, 1995.

McLaren, Angus. *Sexuality and Social Order: The Debate over the Fertility of Women and Workers in France, 1770–1920*. New York: Holmes and Meier, 1983.

McMillan, James F. *Housewife or Harlot: The Place of Women in French Society, 1870–1940*. New York: St. Martin's, 1981.

Miller, Julia Scriven. "The 'Romance of Regulation': The Movement against State-Regulated Prostitution in France, 1871–1946." PhD diss., New York University, 2000.

Mills, Charles W. *The Racial Contract*. Ithaca: Cornell University Press, 1997.

Milza, Pierre. "L'intégration des Italiens en France: 'miracle' ou vertus de la longue durée?" *Pouvoirs* 47 (1988), 103–13.

———. *Les Italiens en France de 1914 à 1940*. Rome: École Française de Rome, 1986.

———. *Voyage en Ritalie*. Paris: Plon, 1993.

Milza, Pierre, and Denis Peschanski, eds. *Exils et migration: Italiens et Espagnols en France, 1938–1946*. Paris: L'Harmattan, 1994.

Moch, Leslie Page. Introduction. *European Migrations: Global and Local Perspectives*, ed. Dirk Hoerder and Leslie Page Moch. Boston: Northeastern University Press, 1996.

Moses, Claire Goldberg. *French Feminism in the Nineteenth Century*. Albany: SUNY Press, 1984.

Mosse, George L. *Nationalism and Sexuality: Middle-Class Morality and Sexual Norms in Modern Europe*. Madison: University of Wisconsin Press, 1985.

———. *Toward the Final Solution: A History of European Racism*. Madison: University of Wisconsin Press, 1978.

Mosset, Paul. *Albert Londres ou l'aventure du grand reportage*. Paris: Bernard Grasset, 1972.

Muñoz-Perez, Francisco, and Michèle Tribalat. "Mariages d'étrangers et mariages mixtes en France: évolution depuis la Première Guerre." *Population* 3 (May–June 1984), 427–62.

Murard, Lion, and Patrick Zylberman. "De l'hygiène comme introduction à la politique expérimentale (1875–1925)." *Revue de synthèse* 115 (July–September 1984), 313–41.

Murray, Alison. "Debt-Bondage and Trafficking: Don't Believe the Hype." *Global Sex*

Workers: Rights, Resistance, and Redefinition, ed. Kamala Kempadoo and Jo Doezema. New York: Routledge, 1998.

Neyrand, Gérard, and Marine M'sili. *Mariages mixtes et nationalité française.* Paris: L'Harmattan, 1995.

Ngai, Mai M. "The Architecture of Race in American Immigration Law: A Reexamination of the Immigration Act of 1924." *Journal of American History* 86, no. 1 (June 1999), 67–92.

Noiriel, Gérard. "Difficulties in French Historical Research on Immigration." *Immigrants in Two Democracies: French and American Experience*, ed. Donald Horowitz and Gérard Noiriel. New York: New York University Press, 1992.

———. *The French Melting Pot: Immigration, Citizenship, and National Identity*, trans. Geoffroy de Laforcade. Minneapolis: University of Minnesota Press, 1996.

———. *Les origines républicaines de Vichy.* Paris: Hachette, 1999.

———. *Population, immigration, et identité nationale en France, 19ᵉ–20ᵉ siècle.* Paris: Hachette, 1992.

———. *La tyrannie du national: le droit d'asile en Europe, 1793–1993.* Paris: Calmann-Lévy, 1991.

———. *Workers in French Society in the Nineteenth and Twentieth Centuries*, trans. Helen McPhail. New York: St. Martin's.

Nye, Robert A. *Crime, Madness, and Politics in Modern France: The Medical Concept of National Decline.* Princeton: Princeton University Press, 1985.

———. *Masculinity and Male Codes of Honor in Modern France.* New York: Oxford University Press, 1993.

Offen, Karen. "Depopulation, Nationalism, and Feminism in Fin-de-siècle France." *American Historical Review* 89 (June 1984), 648–76.

———. "Intrepid Crusader: Ghénia Avril de Sainte-Croix Takes On the Prostitution Issue." *Proceedings of the Western Society for French History* 33 (2005), 357–74.

Ogden, Philip E., and Marie-Monique Huss. "Demography and Pronatalism in France in the 19th and 20th Centuries." *Journal of Historical Demography* 8, no. 3 (1982), 283–98.

Omi, Michael, and Howard Winant. *Racial Formation in the United States from the 1960s to the 1990s.* New York: Routledge, 1994.

Ong, Aihwa. "Making the Biopolitical Subject: Cambodian Immigrants, Refugee Medicine, and Cultural Citizenship in California." *Social Science Medicine* 40, no. 9 (1995), 1243–57.

Pateman, Carole. *The Sexual Contract.* Stanford: Stanford University Press, 1988.

———. "Women and Consent." *The Disorder of Women: Democracy, Feminism, and Critical Theory.* Stanford: Stanford University Press, 1989.

Paxton, Robert O. "Gérard Noiriel's Third Republic." *French Politics, Culture, and Society* 18, no. 2 (summer 2000), 99–103.

Peabody, Sue, and Tyler Stovall, eds. *The Color of Liberty: Histories of Race in France.* Durham: Duke University Press, 2003.

Pedersen, Jean Elisabeth. *Legislating the French Family: Feminism, Theater, and Republican Politics, 1870–1920.* New Brunswick: Rutgers University Press, 2003.

Pederson, Susan. *Family, Dependence, and the Origins of the Welfare State, Britain and France, 1914–1945.* Cambridge: Cambridge University Press, 1994.

Perry, Adele. "The Autocracy of Love and the Legitimacy of Empire: Intimacy, Power, and Scandal in 19th-Century Metlakahtlah." *Gender and History* 16, no. 2 (August 2004), 261–88.

Phillips, Anne. *Engendering Democracy.* University Park: Pennsylvania State University Press, 1991.

———. "Universal Pretensions in Political Thought." *Destabilizing Theory: Contemporary Feminist Debates,* ed. Michèle Barrett and Anne Phillips. Stanford: Stanford University Press, 1992.

Pick, Robert. *Faces of Degeneration: A European Disorder, c. 1848–c.1918.* Cambridge: Cambridge University Press, 1989.

Pierce, Steven, and Anupama Rao, eds. *Discipline and the Other Body: Correction, Corporeality, Colonialism.* Durham: Duke University Press, 2006.

———. "Discipline and the Other Body: Humanitarianism, Violence, and the Colonial Exception." *Discipline and the Other Body: Correction, Corporeality, Colonialism,* ed. Steven Pierce and Anupama Rao. Durham: Duke University Press, 2006.

Pollard, Miranda. *Reign of Virtue: Mobilizing Gender in Vichy France.* Chicago: University of Chicago Press, 1998.

Ponty, Jean. "Les travailleurs polonais en France." Thesis, University of Paris I, 1985.

Rabinbach, Anson. *The Human Motor: Energy, Fatigue, and the Origins of Modernity.* Berkeley: University of California Press, 1992.

Rafael, Vicente L. "Colonial Domesticity: White Women and United States Rule in the Philippines." *American Literature* 67 (December 1995), 639–66.

Reggiani, Andrés Horacio. "Procreating France: The Politics of Demography, 1919–1945." *French Historical Studies* 19 (1996), 725–54.

Reynolds, Siân. *France between the Wars: Gender and Politics.* London: Routledge, 1996.

Rhoades, Michelle. *"No Safe Women": Prostitution, Masculinity, and Disease in France during the Great War.* PhD diss., University of Iowa, 2001.

Roberts, Mary Louise. *Civilization without Sexes: Reconstructing Gender in Postwar France, 1917–1927.* Chicago: University of Chicago Press, 1994.

Roche, Alphonse V. *Provençal Regionalism: A Study of the Movement in the Revue Fé-*

libréene, Le Feu, and Other Reviews of Southern France. Evanston: Northwestern University Press, 1954.

Roediger, David R. *The Wages of Whiteness: Race and the Making of the American Working Class.* London: Verso, 1991.

———. "Whiteness and Ethnicity in the History of 'White Ethnics' in the United States." *Towards the Abolition of Whiteness: Essays on Race, Politics, and Working-Class History.* London: Verso, 1994.

Ronsin, Francis. *La grève des ventres: propagande néo-malthusienne et baisse de la natalité en France, 19ᵉ et 20ᵉ siècles.* Paris: Aubier Montaigne, 1980.

Roper, Michael, and John Tosh. "Historians and the Politics of Masculinity." *Manful Assertions: Masculinities in Britain since 1800,* ed. Michael Roper and John Tosh. London: Routledge, 1991.

Rosanvallon, Pierre. *L'état en France de 1789 à nos jours.* Paris: Le Seuil, 1990.

Rose, Sonya. "Gender at Work: Sex, Class, and Industrial Capitalism." *History Workshop* 21 (spring 1986), 113–31.

———. "Sex, Citizenship, and the Nation in World War Two Great Britain." *American Historical Review* 103, no.4 (October 1998), 1147–76.

Rosemblatt, Karin Alejandra. "Sexuality and Biopower in Chile and Latin America." *Political Power and Social Theory* 15 (2001), 315–72.

Rosenberg, Clifford. "Albert Sarraut and Republican Racial Thought." *French Politics, Culture, and Society* 20, no. 3 (fall 2002), 97–114.

———. *Policing Paris: The Origins of Immigration Control between the Wars.* Ithaca: Cornell University Press, 2006.

Rouch, Monique, ed. *"Comprar un prà": Des paysans italiens disent l'émigration.* Merignac: Sciences de l'Homme de l'Aquitaine, 1989.

Roudinesco, Elisabeth. "Georges Mauco (1899–1988): un psychanalyste au service de Vichy: de l'antisémitisme à la psychopedagogie." *L'Infini* (fall 1995), 73–84.

Saada, Emmanuelle. "Enfants de la colonie: bâtards raciaux, bâtards sociaux." *Discours sur le métissage, identités métisses: En quête d'Ariel,* ed. Sylvie Kandé. Paris: L'Harmattan, 1999.

———. *Les enfants de la colonie: les métis de l'empire français entre sujétion et citoyenneté.* Paris: La Découverte, 2007.

———. "Race and Sociological Reason in the Republic: Inquiries on the *Métis* in the French Empire (1908–37)." *International Sociology* 17, no. 3 (September 2002), 361–91.

Sapiro, Virginia. "Women, Citizenship, and Nationality: Immigration and Naturalization Policies in the United States." *Politics and Society* 13, no. 1 (1984), 1–26.

Schafer, Sylvia. *Children in Moral Danger and the Problem of Government in Third Republic France.* Princeton: Princeton University Press, 1997.

Schneider, William H. "Hérédité, sang, et opposition à l'immigration dans la France des années 30." *Ethnologie française* 24, no. 1 (January–March 1994), 104–17.

———. *Quality and Quantity: The Quest for Biological Regeneration in Twentieth-Century France.* New York: Cambridge University Press, 1990.

Schor, Ralph. *L'immigration en France, 1919–1939: Sources imprimées en langue française et filmographie.* Nice: Centre de la Méditerranée Moderne et Contemporaine, 1986.

———. *L'opinion publique française et les étrangers, 1919–1939.* Paris: La Sorbonne, 1985.

Scott, Joan Wallach. *Only Paradoxes to Offer: French Feminists and the Rights of Man.* Cambridge: Harvard University Press, 1996.

———. *Parité! Sexual Equality and the Crisis of French Universalism.* Chicago: University of Chicago Press, 2005.

———. "Work Identities for Men and Women." *Gender and the Politics of History.* New York: Columbia University Press, 1988.

Silverman, Maxim. *Deconstructing the Nation: Immigration, Racism, and Citizenship in Modern France.* London: Routledge, 1996.

———. "Rights and Difference: Questions of Citizenship in Contemporary France." *Racism, Ethnicity, and Politics in Contemporary Europe,* ed. Alec G. Hargreaves and Jeremy Leaman. Aldershot: Edgar Elgar, 1995.

Skidmore, Thomas E. *Black into White: Race and Nationality in Brazilian Thought.* Durham: Duke University Press, 1993.

———. "Racial Ideas and Social Policy in Brazil, 1870–1940." *The Idea of Race in Latin America, 1870–1940,* ed. Richard Graham. Austin: University of Texas Press, 1990.

Skrobanek, Siriporn, Nattaya Boonpakdi, and Chutima Janthakeero. *The Traffic in Women: Human Realities of the Global Sex Trade.* London: Zed, 1997.

Smith, Paul. *Feminism in the Third Republic: Women's Political and Civil Rights in France, 1918–1945.* Oxford: Clarendon, 1996.

Soloway, Richard A. *Demography and Degeneration: Eugenics and the Declining Birthrate in Twentieth-Century Britain.* Chapel Hill: University of North Carolina Press, 1990.

Sowerwine, Charles. *Sisters or Citizens? Women and Socialism in France since 1876.* Cambridge: Cambridge University Press, 1982.

Spear, Jennifer. "Colonial Intimacies: Legislating Sex in French Lousiana." *William and Mary Quarterly* 60, no. 1 (2003), 75–98.

Spengler, Joseph J. *France Faces Depopulation.* Durham: Duke University Press, 1942; postlude edn 1979.

Stanley, Amy Dru. *From Bondage to Contract: Wage Labor, Marriage, and the Market in the Age of Emancipation*. Cambridge: Cambridge University Press, 1998.

Stepan, Nancy Leys. *"The Hour of Eugenics": Race, Gender, and Nation in Latin America*. Ithaca: Cornell University Press, 1996.

———. "Race, Gender, Science, and Citizenship." *Gender and History* 10, no. 1 (April 1998), 26–52.

Stevens, Jacqueline. *Reproducing the State*. Princeton: Princeton University Press, 1999.

Stocking, George W., Jr. *Race, Culture, and Evolution: Essays in the History of Anthropology*. Chicago: University of Chicago Press, 1982.

Stoler, Ann Laura. *Carnal Knowledge and Imperial Power: Race and the Intimate in Colonial Rule*. Berkeley: University of California Press, 2002.

———. "Intimidations of Empire: Predicaments of the Tactile and Unseen." *Haunted by Empire: Geographies of Intimacy in North American History*, ed. Ann Laura Stoler. Durham: Duke University Press, 2006.

———. *Race and the Education of Desire: Foucault's History of Sexuality and the Colonial Order of Things*. Durham: Duke University Press, 1995.

———. "Rethinking Colonial Categories: European Communities and the Boundaries of Rule." *Contemporary Studies in Society and History* 13 (May 1992), 134–61.

———. "Sexual Affronts and Racial Frontiers: European Identities and the Cultural Politics of Exclusion in Colonial Southeast Asia." *Tensions of Empire: Colonial Cultures in a Bourgeois World*, ed. Frederick Cooper and Ann Laura Stoler. Berkeley: University of California Press, 1997.

———, ed. *Haunted By Empire: Geographies of Intimacy in North American History*. Durham: Duke University Press, 2006.

Stoler, Ann Laura, and Frederick Cooper. "Between Metropole and Colony: Rethinking a Research Agenda." *Tensions of Empire: Colonial Cultures in a Bourgeois World*. Berkeley: University of California Press, 1997.

Stora-Lamarre, Annie. *L'enfer de la IIIe République*. Paris: Imago, 1990.

Stovall, Tyler. "The Color Line behind the Lines: Racial Violence in France during the Great War." *American Historical Review* 103, no. 3 (June 1998), 737–69.

———. "Colour-Blind France? Colonial Workers during the First World War." *Race and Class* 35, no. 2 (1993), 35–55.

———. "Love, Labor, and Race: Colonial Men and White Women in France during the Great War." *French Civilization and its Discontents: Nationalism, Colonialism, Race*, ed. Tyler Stovall and Georges Van den Abbeele. Lanham, Md.: Lexington, 2003.

———. "National Identity and Shifting Imperial Frontiers: Whiteness and the Exclusion of Colonial Labor after World War I." *Representations* 84 (autumn 2003), 52–72.

Streiff-Fenart, Jocelyne. *Les couples franco-maghrébins en France.* Paris: L'Harmattan, 1989.

Studer, Brigitte. "Citizenship as Contingent National Belonging: Married Women and Foreigners in Twentieth-Century Switzerland." *Gender and History* 13, no. 3 (November 2001), 622–65.

Summers, Carol. "Intimate Colonialism: The Imperial Production of Reproduction in Uganda, 1907–1925." *Signs: Journal of Women in Culture and Society* 16, no. 4 (1991), 787–807.

Svanström, Yvonne. *Policing Public Women: The Regulation of Prostitution in Stockholm, 1812–1880.* Stockholm: Atlas Akkademi, 2000.

Taguieff, Pierre-André. "Eugénisme ou décadence? L'exception française." *Ethnologie française* 24, no. 1 (1994), 81–103.

———. *The Force of Prejudice: On Racism and Its Doubles,* ed. and trans. Hassan Melehy. Minneapolis: University of Minnesota Press, 2001.

Takaki, Ronald. *Iron Cages: Race and Culture in Nineteenth-Century America.* Oxford: Oxford University Press, 1979.

Talmy, Robert. *Histoire du mouvement familial en France, 1896–1939.* Paris: UNCAF, 1962.

Taraud, Christelle. *Mauresques: femmes orientales dans la photographie coloniale, 1860–1910.* Paris: Albin Michel, 2003.

———. *La prostitution coloniale: Algérie, Tunisie, Maroc, 1830–1962.* Paris: Payot, 2003.

Teitelbaum, Michael S., and Jay M. Winter. *The Fear of Population Decline.* Orlando, Fla.: Academic, 1985.

Thébaud, Françoise. *La femme au temps de la guerre de 14.* Paris: Stock, 1986.

———. "Le mouvement nataliste dans la France de l'entre-deux-guerres: l'Alliance National pour l'Accroissement de la Population Française." *Revue de l'histoire moderne et contemporaine* 32 (1985), 276–301.

Thompson, E. P. "Time, Work, Discipline, and Industrial Capitalism." *Past and Present* 38 (1967), 56–97.

Todorov, Tzvetan. *On Human Diversity: Nationalism, Racism, and Exoticism in French Thought,* trans. Catherine Potter. Cambridge: Harvard University Press, 1993.

Vaughan, Megan. *Creating the Creole Island: Slavery in Eighteenth-Century Mauritius.* Durham: Duke University Press, 2005.

Vergès, Françoise. *Monsters and Revolutionaries: Colonial Family Romance and Métissage.* Durham: Duke University Press, 1999.

Vidalenc, Jean. "La main-d'œuvre étrangère en France et la Première Guerre Mondiale (1901–1926)." *Francia* 2 (1974), 524–50.

Wade, Peter. *Blackness and Race Mixture: The Dynamics of Racial Integration in Colombia*. Baltimore: Johns Hopkins University Press, 1993.

———. *Race and Ethnicity in Latin America*. London: Pluto, 1997.

Walker, David. *Anxious Nation: Australia and the Rise of Asia, 1850–1939*. Queensland: University of Queensland Press, 1999.

Walkowitz, Judith. *Prostitution and Victorian Society*. Cambridge: Cambridge University Press, 1980.

Wallerstein, Immanuel. "The Ideological Tensions of Capitalism: Universalism versus Racism and Sexism." *Race, Nation, Class: Ambiguous Identities*, ed. Étienne Balibar and Immanuel Wallerstein. London: Verso, 1991.

Warshaw, Dan. *Paul Leroy-Beaulieu and Established Liberalism in France*. De Kalb: Northern Illinois University Press, 1991.

Watson, Molly McGregor. "The Trade in Women: 'White Slavery' and the French Nation, 1899–1939." PhD diss., Stanford University, 1999.

Weber, Eugen. "Nos ancêtres les gaulois." *My France: Politics, Culture, Myth*. Cambridge: Harvard University Press, 1991.

———. *Peasants into Frenchmen: The Modernization of Rural France, 1870–1914*. Stanford: Stanford University Press, 1976.

Weil, Patrick. "Georges Mauco: un itinéraire camouflé." *L'antisémitisme de plume, 1940–1944: études et documents*, ed. Pierre-André Taguieff, Grégoire Kauffmann, and Michaël Lenoire. Paris: Berg International, 1999.

———. *Qu'est-ce qu'un français? Histoire de la nationalité française depuis la Révolution*. Paris: Grasset, 2002.

Weinbaum, Alys Eve. *Wayward Reproductions: Genealogies of Race and Nation in Transatlantic Thought*. Durham: Duke University Press, 2004.

White, Owen. *Children of the French Empire: Miscegenation and Colonial Society in French West Africa, 1895–1960*. Oxford: Clarendon, 1999.

———. "Miscegenation and the Popular Imagination." *Promoting the Colonial Ideal: Propaganda and Visions of Empire in France*, ed. Tony Chafer and Amanda Sackur. London: Palgrave, 2002.

Wildenthal, Lora. *German Women for Empire, 1884–1945*. Durham: Duke University Press, 2001.

Wilder, Gary. *The French Imperial Nation-State: Negritude and Colonial Humanism between the Two World Wars*. Chicago: University of Chicago Press, 2005.

———. "'Impenser' l'histoire de France: les études coloniales hors de la perspective de l'identité nationale." *Cahiers d'histoire: revue d'histoire critique*, 96–97 (October–December 2005), 91–119.

————. "Thinking through Race, Confronting Republican Racism." Unpublished MS.

Winter, J. M. "The Fear of Population Decline in Western Europe, 1870–1940." *Demographic Patterns in Developed Societies*, ed. R. W. Hiorns. London: Taylor and Francis, 1980.

Wright, Gwendolyn. *The Politics of Design in French Colonial Urbanism*. Chicago: University of Chicago Press, 1991.

Yee, Jennifer. "*Métissage* in France: A Postmodern Fantasy and Its Forgotten Precedents." *Modern and Contemporary France* 11, no. 4 (2003), 411–25.

Young, Iris Marion. "Polity and Group Difference: A Critique of the Ideal of Universal Citizenship." *Ethics* 99, no. 2 (January 1989), 255.

Yuval-Davis, Nira, and Floya Anthias, eds. *Women-Nation-State*. London: Macmillan, 1989.

INDEX

morality: gendered notions of, 81–82, 100–102; respectability among French women, 110–12, 123; of sex traffickers, 105–8

Moroccan population, 55, 64, 65, 69, 119. *See also* North African population

motherhood: as mode of citizenship, 5–6, 113, 136–38, 141, 144, 152, 155; social role of, 30–31, 38, 40, 48, 142

national prestige, 18, 117–26

Naudeau, Ludovic, 25, 37–40, 43

neo-Malthusianism, 22–26, 42, 101, 113; critiques of, 26–27, 38–39

Napoleonic Civil Code, 4, 129–35, 138–43, 146, 150–51, 153, 156

New Woman, 8, 31, 40, 99

North African population, 35–36, 55, 60–71, 82, 114–20, 148–49

Oualid, William, 56, 71, 145

Pairault, André, 94–95

particularism, 4, 10–11, 17, 47–48, 52, 57, 76, 89, 92, 146, 157–59

paternalism: feminism as, 18, 103, 111–12, 149–50; regulated prostitution as, 102

Pernot, Georges, 44

Plus Grande Famille, 27, 36

Pluyette, Jean, 15

Polish population, 16, 23, 29, 34–37, 42, 45–48, 52, 71, 95

polygenesis, 79

Pourésy, Emile, 121, 124–125

pronatalism, 16, 22, 23–29, 45–46, 48, 52, 78, 99, 100, 113; as anti-individualism, 33; Code de la Famille of 1939 and, 44; critiques of gender order and,

30–31, 38–40; debates on independent nationality and, 130–31, 137, 140, 144–45, 150–52; eugenicist strand in, 95–96; Republicanism articulated with, 37, 47

prostitutes, 8, 79, 82; colonial women as, 118–19, 124–26; French women as, 17, 104–20; surveillance of, 112–18, 123–25; victimhood of, 111

prostitution, 17; abolitionist campaign against, 99–105, 112–13, 121–22, 125–26; brothels and, 102, 111, 114–19, 123; as enslavement, 100–103, 125; morals police and, 102, 114–16; racial segregation of, 114–20; regulated French system of, 100–104, 109–10, 122–23

race: as culture, 92–95; ethnicity vs., 13–14; scientific discourse on, 76–80, 83–87, 93–96; as transnational whiteness and, 12–13, 38, 75, 121

race mixing. *See* intermarriage; métissage

racial hierarchy, 2–7, 11, 13, 19, 156; labor recruitment and, 52, 55, 60–69; pronatalist arguments for, 24–25, 32, 35, 47; within prostitution, 108–9, 126, 130; reversal of, 26–29, 125; scientific discourse on, 84, 87–88, 91–99

reproduction: gendered citizenship and, 5–6, 113, 136–38, 141, 144, 152, 155; racializing force of, 5, 16–17, 25–32, 41–47, 144–46; labor production and, 7, 8, 32–37, 127. *See also* pronatalism

Republicanism, 8, 10, 77, 85; contractarian, 11, 132, 136–39; ethnocultural, 76, 86, 90, 155–59; hybrid form of, 2–4, 8, 47, 52, 73, 89, 92, 96, 131, 154, 157–

59; racial exclusion from, 35–36, 47–48, 88; sexual difference in, 10, 101–2, 127, 132, 136, 151. *See also* universalism

Richet, Charles, 33

Sainte-Croix, Ghénia Avril, 81, 103, 112

Sauteraud, Marcel, 141–42, 147–50

science du travail, 17, 52, 59–63, 66–67, 70–71

sex trafficking, 18, 99–101; abolition of, 111–13, 121–25; colonial women and, 118–20, 126; exportation of French system of, 108–10; prostitutes' rights in, 110–11, 127–28; racialized metaphors in, 101–7

Simon, Odette, 143, 152

social hygiene, 48, 83, 86, 90

Société Française d'Eugénique (FES), 84–88

Spanish population, 13, 16, 23, 29, 32–37, 42, 45–48, 52, 55, 64, 68, 71, 88, 95

Taine, Hippolyte, 92

Temporary Union against Regulated Prostitution, 107, 109, 112, 116, 122

traite des blanches. *See* sex trafficking

Troullier, Albert, 31–32

Union Française pour le Suffrage des Femmes, 140

universalism, 9, 84–85, 153; as feminist humanism, 133, 144; particularism vs., 4, 10–11, 17, 47–48, 52, 57, 76, 89, 92, 146, 157–59

Vanneufville, Gaston, 36

venereal disease: among immigrant men, 31, 35, 89; prostitution linked to, 100, 102, 116, 124

Vérone, Maria, 110, 142–43, 147–48

Vichy France, 15, 31, 48–49, 77, 84, 86, 90, 158–59

Weil, Lucien, 65–66

whiteness: assimilability and, 28, 37, 64–65, 69, 87–88; French identity and, 11–13, 16, 25, 38, 73, 90–92, 95–96; as racial category, 6–7, 14–15, 75, 121; in work science, 60–63. *See also* race; racial hierarchy

white slavery. *See* sex trafficking

work science, 17, 52, 59–63, 66–67, 70–71

yellow peril, 27–29

Elisa Camiscioli is an associate professor of history and women's studies at the State University of New York, Binghamton.

Library of Congress Cataloging-in-Publication Data
Camiscioli, Elisa, 1967–
Reproducing the French race : immigration, intimacy, and embodiment in the early twentieth century / Elisa Camiscioli.
p. cm.
Includes bibliographical references and index.
ISBN 978-0-8223-4548-0 (cloth : alk. paper)
ISBN 978-0-8223-4565-7 (pbk. : alk. paper)
1. France—Emigration and immigration—History—20th century.
2. Immigrants—Government policy—France—History—20th century.
3. Racism—France—History—20th century. 4. National characteristics, French.
5. France—Ethnic relations—History. I. Title.
JV7925.C28 2009
325.4409'041—dc22   2009006500